Opinion Polls and the Media

Opinion Polls and the Media

Reflecting and Shaping Public Opinion

Edited by

Christina Holtz-Bacha
University of Erlangen-Nürnberg, Germany

and

Jesper Strömbäck
Mid Sweden University, Sweden

First published 2012 by
PALGRAVE MACMILLAN

Palgrave Macmillan in the UK is an imprint of Macmillan Publishers Limited, registered in England, company number 785998, of Houndmills, Basingstoke, Hampshire RG21 6XS.

Palgrave Macmillan in the US is a division of St Martin's Press LLC, 175 Fifth Avenue, New York, NY 10010.

Palgrave Macmillan is the global academic imprint of the above companies and has companies and representatives throughout the world.

Palgrave® and Macmillan® are registered trademarks in the United States, the United Kingdom, Europe and other countries.

ISBN 978–0–230–27889–9

This book is printed on paper suitable for recycling and made from fully managed and sustained forest sources. Logging, pulping and manufacturing processes are expected to conform to the environmental regulations of the country of origin.

A catalogue record for this book is available from the British Library.

A catalog record for this book is available from the Library of Congress.

10 9 8 7 6 5 4 3 2 1
21 20 19 18 17 16 15 14 13 12

Printed and bound in Great Britain by
CPI Antony Rowe, Chippenham and Eastbourne

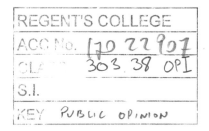

This book is dedicated to the memory of Lynda Lee Kaid, an extraordinary scholar, friend and mentor.

Contents

Tables

Figures

Notes on Contributors

Annette Aw is Associate Professor at the University of Maryland University College, Maryland, USA. She is also an adjunct lecturer for Indiana University in Bloomington, Indiana, USA, and a full-time research consultant focusing on media-related studies for private businesses, trade associations and government agencies. Her current research concentrates on the impact of social media on public relations in Asia. Her most recent book is *Political Communication in Asia* (2009), co-edited with Lars Willnat.

Flávia Biroli is Professor at the Institute for Political Science, University of Brasília, Brazil, and a researcher for the National Council of Scientific and Technological Development in Brazil. Her research focuses on gender and on media and politics. She is the editor, with Luis Felipe Miguel, of *Revista Brasileira de Ciência Política*. Her publications include *Caleidoscópio convexo: mulheres, política e mídia* (2011), co-authored with Luis Felipe Miguel, and *Midia, representação e democracia* (2011), co-edited with Luis Felipe Miguel.

Kathleen A. Frankovic spent more than three decades at CBS News. She retired as Director of Surveys and Producer in 2009 but remains Election and Polling Consultant for CBS and other companies. She is a former academic with a PhD in political science. Most recently she has written chapters about election and opinion polling for the *Market Research Handbook* (2007), *The SAGE Handbook of Public Opinion Research* (2008) and the 'Sample Surveys' volume of the *Handbook of Statistics* (2009). She has also written about women and public opinion polls for *Voting and the Gender Gap* (2008). She has served as President of both the World Association for Public Opinion and the American Association for Public Opinion. Some of her work can be found on her website at www.kathyfrankovic.com.

Christina Holtz-Bacha is Professor of Communication at the School of Economics, University of Erlangen-Nürnberg, Germany. She received her PhD from the University of Münster, Germany, and did her postdoctoral dissertation (habilitation) in Hannover. Prior to her current position, she taught at the universities of Munich, Bochum and Mainz. In 1986 she was a visiting scholar at the University of Minnesota, USA. In 1999 she was a research fellow at the Shorenstein Center, Harvard University, USA, and in 2011 a guest researcher at the University of Gothenburg, Sweden. She has published widely in the area of political communication. Her most recent publications as editor include *Encyclopedia of Political Communication, 1 & 2* (2008), *The Sage Handbook of Political Advertising* (2006), *Medienpolitik für Europa* (*Media Policy for Europe*, 2006) and *Frauen—Medien—Politik* (*Women—Media—Politics*, 2008), and she has written *Medienpolitik für Europa II* (*Media Policy for Europe II*, 2011). She is co-editor of the German journal *Publizistik*, associate editor for the International Communication Association's *Communication Yearbook* and a member of the editorial boards of several international journals. Her main research interests are in political communication and media policy.

Ven-hwei Lo is Professor in the School of Journalism, the Chinese University of Hong Kong. Before joining the Chinese University, he taught at the National Chengchi University in Taipei, Taiwan, for 24 years. His research interests include news media performance and the effects of mass media. He is the author of seven books, and his recent publications have appeared in, for example, *Asian Journal of Communication, Communication Research, Journalism & Mass Communication Quarterly, Journal of Broadcasting & Electronic Media, International Journal of Public Opinion Research, Media Psychology*, the *Chinese Journal of Communication* and the *Harvard International Journal of Press/ Politics*.

Robert Mattes is Professor of Political Studies and Director of the Democracy in Africa Research Unit, in the Centre for Social Science Research, University of Cape Town, South Africa. He is also Senior Adviser to, and a co-founder of, Afrobarometer, a ground-breaking regular survey of public opinion in 20 African countries. He has helped to launch and run other major research projects, such as the South African National Election Study (principal investigator) and the African Legislatures Project (co-principal investigator). He is co-author (with Michael Bratton and E. Gyimah-Boadi) of *Public Opinion, Democracy and Markets in Africa* (2005) and has authored or co-authored articles in journals such as *American Journal of Political Science, British Journal of Political Science, World Development, Journal of Democracy, Democratization* and *Party Politics*. He holds a PhD (1992) in political science from the University of Illinois, Urbana-Champaign, USA.

Luis Felipe Miguel is Professor at the Institute for Political Science, University of Brasília, Brazil, and a researcher at the National Council of Scientific and Technological Development in Brazil. His research focuses on political representation, gender and the political influence of mass media. His publications include *Mito e discurso político* (2000), *Política e mídia no Brasil* (2002) and, with Flávia Biroli, *Caleidoscópioconvexo: mulheres, política e mídia* (2011).

Stephen Mills lectures at the Graduate School of Government at the University of Sydney, Australia. Previously he was a senior political journalist on the personal staff of Prime Minister Bob Hawke and a corporate affairs specialist in the financial services sector, including for the Australian Stock Exchange. He is currently undertaking doctoral research on the development of Australian political parties' head offices and election campaigning. He is the author of the influential book *The New Machine Men: Polls and Persuasion in Australian Politics*.

Fernanda Ferreira Mota is taking her master's degree in political science at the University of Brasília, Brazil. Her research and publications are focused on the connections between gender, media and politics.

Patricia Moy is the Christy Cressey Professor of Communication and Adjunct Professor of Political Science at the University of Washington, Seattle, USA. She is Editor-in-Chief of *Oxford Bibliographies Online: Communication* and Associate Editor of *Public Opinion Quarterly*.

Thomas Petersen is Project Director at the Allensbach Institute für Public Opinion Research, Germany. He is also an associate lecturer at the universities of Dresden and Krems, Past-President of the World Association for Public Opinion Research and Chair of the Visual Communication Division of the German Society for Communication Research (DGPuK). He has published numerous books and articles in journals and handbooks.

Eike Mark Rinke is a doctoral student and research associate in the Department of Media and Communication Studies at the University of Mannheim, Germany.

Slavko Splichal is Professor of Communication and Public Opinion in the Faculty of Social Sciences, University of Ljubljana, Slovenia; Fellow of the Slovenian Academy of Sciences and Arts; and Director of the European Institute for Communication and Culture, as well as Editor of its journal, *Javnost–The Public*. His primary areas of research include communication theory, public opinion and the public sphere, political communication and communication research methods. His most recent publication is *Transnationalization of the Public Sphere and the Fate of the Public* (2011).

Jesper Strömbäck is Professor of Media and Communication and Ludvig Nordström Professor and Chair in Journalism, Mid Sweden University, Sweden. He is also Research Director at the Center for Political Communication Research, Mid Sweden University. He has published numerous articles in journals such as *Journal of Communication, International Journal of Press/Politics* and *Political Communication*. His most recent books include *Political Public Relations: Principles and Applications*, co-edited with Spiro Kiousis (2011), and *Political Communication in European Parliamentary Elections*, co-edited with Lynda Lee Kaid and Michaela Maier (2011).

Rodney Tiffen is Emeritus Professor in Government and International Relations at the University of Sydney, Australia. He is the author or co-author of seven books and editor of three books as well as of more than 60 academic articles and book chapters. Many of these have been on Australian media and politics, including *News and Power* (1989) and *Scandals: Media, Politics and Corruption in Contemporary Australia* (1999).

Michael Traugott is Professor of Communication Studies and Political Science and Senior Research Scientist at the Center for Political Studies, University of Michigan, Ann Arbor, Michigan, USA. He is the author or editor of 12 books and of more than 90 journal articles. His most recent books are *The Voter's Guide to Election Polls*, co-authored with Paul Lavrakas, and the *Handbook of Public Opinion Research*, co-edited with Wolfgang Donsbach.

Lars Willnat is Professor in the School of Journalism at Indiana University in Bloomington, Indiana, USA. Before joining Indiana University in 2009, he taught at the George Washington University, Washington, DC, USA, and at the Chinese University of Hong Kong. His research interests include media effects on political attitudes, theoretical aspects of public opinion formation and international communication. He has published articles in journals such as *Journalism & Mass Communication Quarterly, International Journal of Public Opinion Research, Political Communication* and *Journalism*. His most recent book is *The Global Journalist in the 21st Century* (2011), co-edited with David Weaver.

1
The Media and Their Use of Opinion Polls: Reflecting and Shaping Public Opinion

Jesper Strömbäck

Introduction

The histories of mass media, public opinion and opinion polling have always been closely intertwined. Before the invention of scientific opinion polling, both political leaders and lay people used media coverage as a proxy for public opinion, while in addition and after the invention of opinion polling, the media's use of opinion polls has become an important part of their coverage of politics in general and of election campaigns in particular.

But do the media mainly reflect or shape public opinion, in particular with respect to their use of opinion polls? This question is ultimately at the heart of this volume.

While straightforward, it is, however, not an easy question to answer. There are at least six reasons for this. First, public opinion 'continues to be one of the fuzziest terms in the social sciences' (Donsbach & Traugott 2008, p. 1). As noted by Key (1964, p. 8), 'To speak with precision of public opinion is a task not unlike coming to grips with the Holy Ghost.' If the core concept of public opinion is contested and fuzzy, it is consequently complicated to measure and to disentangle the media's role in reflecting or shaping it. Second, for many 'the phenomena of public opinion and mass media are largely conflated' (Herbst 1998, p. 5), making it difficult to pull them apart and differentiate from each other. Third, while opinion polling is the best methodology yet invented to investigate public opinion, it is fraught with difficulties related to, for example, sampling and question ambiguity, wording and context (Weisberg 2008). It is also a methodology that can be used as well as misused (Traugott 2008). Hence, it cannot be taken for granted that responses in an opinion poll represent true public opinion, if a true public opinion even exists on a particular matter (Bishop 2005; Moore 2008). Fourth, the processes of shaping media content are complex and involve influences from many sets of actors, making it difficult to determine the precise influence of the public or even the media's audiences (Shoemaker & Reese 1996). Fifth, while research on agenda setting, priming and framing has shown that the media can exert considerable influence over the public, all such processes are highly contingent upon, for example, the media, the message, audience characteristics and contextual factors (Nabi & Oliver 2009). Hence, while it can be assumed that the media, at least to some extent, take public opinion into consideration when covering politics and current affairs, and that the public, at least to some extent, are influenced by the media's coverage of politics and current affairs, this does not provide a satisfactory answer as to whether the media mainly reflect or shape public opinion. Sixth, and finally, there is not yet enough research on factors influencing the media's use of opinion polls and the effects of published opinion polls.

There is, however, no doubt that public opinion is a crucial concept in democracies, and that opinion polls are ubiquitous in the media's coverage of politics in general and of election campaigns in particular. This combination makes it highly important to further investigate the media's use of opinion polls as well as their antecedents and consequences, and is why we decided to edit this volume.

This chapter will proceed as follows. In the next section we will analyze the importance of public opinion in representative democracies, and discuss the linkage between public opinion and opinion polling. In the following section we will review research on the media's use of opinion polls. As will be detailed, research suggests that polls are ubiquitous in the media's coverage of politics and current affairs, particularly during election campaigns. Based on this review, the section thereafter will outline a framework for understanding why the media show such great interest in opinion polls. We will then summarize the main results of this review, before introducing the chapters in this volume.

Public opinion: The main currency in representative democracies

To understand the role of public opinion in representative democracies, it may be helpful to return to the origins of democracy. The term itself was coined in Ancient Greece from the words *demos*, the people, and *kratos*, to rule. Literally speaking, democracy thus means rule by the people. In Ancient Greece, all male citizens were also entitled – and expected – to participate in the ruling of the city, with the main method for selecting people for public duties being lotteries (Dahl 1998; Manin 1997). Those who were selected carried out their duties for one year only, and they were not allowed to occupy the same position more than once. This was done to ensure that as many people as possible over a lifetime served both as governor and governed; to ensure that everyone had an equal chance of being selected for office; and to avoid political power becoming centralized with a permanent class of rulers. The procedures were intended to ensure that democracy indeed was rule by the people – although 'the people' were narrowly defined and excluded those under 30 years, women and slaves (Manin 1997).

All the early systems of democratic rule in Greece and other places were, however, confined to smaller city-states or communities. As highlighted by Dahl (1998, p. 17; original emphasis), they also lacked what is today considered 'basic political institutions: *a national parliament* composed of *elected representatives*, and *popularly chosen local governments* that were ultimately subordinate to the national government. A system combining democracy at local levels with a popularly elected parliament at the top level had yet to be invented.'

Size matters, however, and as nation-states replaced city-states and societies increased in size, direct democracy was no longer an option. The ideal of direct democracy had to face and conform to Dahl's *'law of time and numbers: The more citizens a democratic unit contains, the less that citizens can participate directly in government decisions and the more that they must delegate authority to others'* (1998, p. 109). The representative form of democracy, where the people elect representatives and transfer to them the authority and legitimacy to take binding decisions, was the answer to this democratic dilemma.

Whether representative democracy represents a necessary evil when direct democracy is not possible, or whether it represents a form of democracy that is actually superior to direct democracy, is, however, a matter of contention. There are in addition several different normative models of democracy, positioning the role of the people versus representatives of the people and the role of public opinion differently. While different theorists use different terminologies, the three most prominent models of democracy are *elite* or *competitive democracy* (Schumpeter 1975), *participatory democracy* (Pateman 1970) and *deliberative democracy* (Elster 1998). Although an exhaustive discussion about these and other

Table 1.1   Normative models of democracy and their central mechanisms for securing the common good

	Competitive democracy	Participatory democracy	Deliberative democracy
Central mechanism for securing the primacy of the common good	Competition between political elites in effective competitive elections	Citizen participation in political and civic life, both outside and within parties	Deliberative discussions among all sections of the public and their representatives

models of democracy is beyond the scope of this chapter (for overviews, see Clawson & Oxley 2008; Held 2006; Strömbäck 2005), the central mechanisms for securing the primacy of the public good according to each model are summarized in Table 1.1.

Normative differences notwithstanding, most theorists agree that direct democracy is not feasible in large-scale democracies. Modern democracies are – save for referendums – largely representative democracies. In these, Sartori (1987, p. 108) reminds us, 'elections do not enact policies; elections establish, rather, who will enact them. Elections do not decide issues; they decide, rather, who will decide issues.' The original understanding of democracy as rule by the people is, however, still present, as those who are elected are expected to represent the people and take public opinion into consideration when making decisions. Their legitimacy hinges on the perception that they are responsive to, and act as representatives of, the public and public opinion.

In other words, the importance of public opinion in representative democracy has its origins in the understanding of political leaders as representatives for the public that ideally should enact policies and decide issues for themselves. In Splichal's (2001, p. 24) words, 'Whereas premodern states legitimized their origin and development with the divine will, in modern democracies this function is largely assumed by public opinion. It is indispensable to the legitimacy of governments that claim their power is based on the consent of the governed.' From this perspective, disregarding public opinion equals disregarding the public.

The problem of representation

If political leaders in representative democracies are supposed to represent the people and public opinion, this raises two crucial questions. First, what does 'the public' refer to, and second, what does 'representation' refer to? To begin with the first question, and broadly following Sartori (1987, p. 22), at least six conceptualizations of 'the public' in the context of democratic representation can be distinguished:

1. the public as including literally everybody;
2. the public as an undetermined large part, a great many;
3. the public as organized interests in non-governmental organizations and interest groups;
4. the public as including a qualified majority of the people;
5. the public as including a simple majority of the people;
6. the public as a party's or elected official's constituency.

The problem for political leaders with the ambition to represent public opinion, then, is not only to find out what public opinion thinks – a major challenge in itself – but also to navigate through different conceptualizations of the public and hence of public opinion. Different publics may furthermore hold opposing views. Hence, even if political leaders could have perfect information about the opinion of different publics, they would not necessarily be able to represent the opinion of all publics.

With the invention of scientific opinion polls, the predominant conceptualization of public opinion has, however, become the view held by the majority or plurality of people responding in opinion polls. If an opinion poll shows that the majority or plurality approves or disapproves of the president, or prefers policy A to policy B, or thinks that X and Y are the most important issues facing the country, then this is taken to represent public opinion, and political leaders are expected to follow or at least seriously consider public opinion in this specific sense (Geer 1996).

The problem here is not only that opinion polls do not necessarily show what the public think (Bishop 2005; Clawson & Oxley 2008; Moore 2008) but also that it is not clear what it really means to represent public opinion. This leads us to the second question, that is, what 'representation' refers to.

According to Pitkin's classic account (1967), several different views of representation can be identified. The first is the formalistic view, according to which 'a representative is someone who has been authorized to act' (p. 38). This view of representation is relevant insofar as it legitimizes the taking of authoritative decisions by popularly elected politicians. The second view of representation is descriptive representation or 'standing for', which 'depends on the representative's characteristics, on what he *is* or is *like*, on being something rather than doing something' (p. 61). In the context of representing public opinion, this view implies that representatives should share and follow the views of public opinion. The third view of representation is symbolic representation, where different objects 'stand for' something else. Examples might be a flag, standing for a country, or a party leader, standing for a party. The fourth view is representation as 'acting for', described by Pitkin (1967, p. 113) as 'an activity in behalf of, in the interest of, as the agent of, someone else'. According to this view, what matters is not whether representatives mirror those represented, but whether the actions of representatives are taken in the interest of those who are represented.

In the context of representing public opinion, these different views of representation form a classic controversy: Should representatives always follow and be bound by public opinion, or should representatives be free to act as seems best to them in the pursuit of the public and the public's interest? Considering that public opinion is most often perceived as aggregate responses in opinion polls, should political leaders always follow opinion polls regardless of whether public opinion is informed or uninformed, consistent or inconsistent, democratically enlightened or not enlightened? Or should political leaders – while taking the results of opinion polls into account – be free to pursue other policies or activities if other information suggests that this may be a better approach to act on behalf of the public?

While there may not be a universal answer to these questions, they highlight the complexities of the relationships between the public, public opinion, opinion polls, political representation and political leadership. The premise in most public discussion following the presentation of results of opinion polls is that political leaders should follow the polls, as disregarding them explicitly or implicitly is considered as disregarding the public that political leaders are supposed to represent. 'Followership', as summarized by Geer (1996, p. 7), has become 'the order of the day'. Such views are, however, too narrow and simplified. First, there are several different notions of what the public is. Second, responses in opinion polls cannot *a priori* be assumed to accurately reflect true public opinion, if a true public opinion even exists. Third, even if there were to be no contradictions between different notions of the public, there was such a thing as a public opinion and the polls accurately reflected this public opinion, it is not self-evident that political leaders should always follow the polls. If political leaders have more knowledge and information than the public, then not following opinion polls may in fact be a better way to act on behalf of the public interest. This is not to say that political leaders always should, or should not, follow opinion polls. It is only to say that to presume that political leaders should *always* follow the results of opinion polls may not *necessarily* lead to better political representation.

The media's use of opinion polls

The many complexities involved in the relationships between the public, public opinion, opinion polls and political representation notwithstanding, opinion polls have become a staple of both politics and the media coverage of politics (Frankovic 1998). Focusing on the media, the history of media covering or doing polling can be traced as far back as 1820 (Atkin & Gaudino 1984; Brettschneider 2008; Gallup & Rae 1940). It was, however, not until the invention of scientific polling in the 1930s that poll coverage began to take its present shape.

Before the 1936 election, the media and others relied on straw polls. The 1936 US presidential election changed this. Before that, the magazine *Literary Digest* was the most prominent medium in terms of doing straw polls and predicting the election outcome. It sent out millions of ballots, asking people to send in their votes. In all elections between 1916 and 1932, the magazine accurately predicted the winner based on this methodology.

In the 1936 election, *Literary Digest* failed miserably, however, predicting that the Republican candidate Alfred A. Landon would get 57 per cent of the major party vote over the Democratic candidate Franklin D. Roosevelt. Instead, Roosevelt won the election with 62 per cent of the major party vote (Gallup & Rae 1940, pp. 40–43). The election result was, however, accurately predicted by a young pioneer in opinion polling, George Gallup, who was one of the first to employ scientific sampling. He showed that a sample of just a few thousand respondents, scientifically sampled to represent the overall population, was superior to a straw poll, despite the fact that about 2.3 million respondents participated in the straw poll.

Since the beginning, newspapers were among the subscribers of the opinion polls conducted by Gallup's *American Institute of Public Opinion*. When polling organizations were subsequently formed in other countries, the same pattern often followed (Petersson 2008). During the 1940s and 1950s, the news media usually subscribed to results from polling institutes, but since the 1960s it has become more common for the media to sponsor or conduct their own polls (Brettschneider 2008). Thus, 'from the very beginning, there has been a symbiotic relationship between pollsters and journalists' (Traugott 2009, p. 4).

Reviewing research on the media's use of opinion polls, there is no doubt that polls are frequently covered in the news. The lack of longitudinal and comparative research makes it difficult to draw firm conclusions about changes over time and similarities or differences across countries, but research from a wide set of countries confirms that polls are frequently covered by the media, particularly during election campaigns. In Germany, the number of poll reports in a sample of news-papers before each federal election increased from 65 in 1980 to 651 in 1994 (Brettschneider 1997, 2008). In Sweden, the number of poll reports in the most important national TV news programs and newspapers went from 98 in 1998 to 117 in 2006 (Strömbäck 2009), while in Israel the number of poll reports in a sample of 15 newspapers increased from just 16 in 1969 to 409 in 1988 (Weimann 1990; see also Sheafer, Weimann & Tsfati 2008). In the USA, the number of publicly released trial heat polls during the general election campaign increased from 27 in 1984 to 245 in 2000 (Traugott 2005), while the number of media-sponsored election polls almost tripled between 1976 and 1988 (Ladd & Benson 1992). Research in other countries such as Canada (Ferguson & de Clercy 2005; Gidengil 2008), Australia (Tiffen 2008), South Africa (Gouws & de Beer 2008) and Italy (Roncarolo 2008) confirms that polls have become more common, or that they are common, in election news. In addition, research suggests that it has become even more common for journalists to just refer to 'polls', without actually presenting any new poll results (Frankovic 2005). Thus, in one form or another, opinion polls are ubiq-uitous, leading Patterson (2005, p. 722) to argue that the media's use of opinion polls 'extend beyond reason', while Weimann (1990) writes about an 'obsession to forecast'.

A matter of both quantity and quality

The question of the media's coverage of opinion polls is however a mat-ter not only of quantity but also of quality. Since opinion polling is a method for investigating people's opinions, the quality of an opinion poll cannot be taken for granted. Neither can it be evaluated without some basic information about the poll. This is why organizations such as *World Association for Public Opinion Research* (WAPOR), *European Society for Opinion and Marketing Research* (ESOMAR) and *American Association for Public Opinion Research* (AAPOR) have guidelines pertaining to what kind of information should be included when the media cover opinion polls. As stated in the ESOMAR/WAPOR *International Code for Practice for the Publication of Public Opinion Poll Results*:

> The validity and value of public opinion polls depend on three main considerations: (i) the nature of the research techniques used and the efficiency with which they are applied, (ii) the honesty and objectivity of the research organization carrying out the study, (iii) the way in which the findings are presented and the uses to which they are put.
> (ESOMAR/WAPOR 2010, p. 12)

Consequently, in this code for practice ESOMAR/WAPOR writes that any time public opinion polls are published in print media, 'these should always be accompanied by a clear statement of: (a) the name of the research organization carrying out the survey; (b) the universe effectively represented (i.e., who was interviewed); (c) the achieved sample size and its geographical coverage; (d) the dates of fieldwork; (e) the sampling method used [...]; (f) the method by which the information was collected [...]; and (g) the relevant questions asked' (p. 14). The requirements for broadcast media are more liberal, but they are also required to cover points (a) through (d). Similar guidelines are included in the AAPOR *Code of Professional Ethics & Practice*, with the important addition that the media should also disclose information about 'the precision of the findings, including estimates of sampling error' (p. 4).

Despite these codes of conduct, research on the extent to which the media include the necessary information shows that the media often fail at this (Brettschneider 2008; Ferguson & de Clercy 2005; Smith & Verrall 1985; Strömbäck 2009; Welch 2002). It is also common for journalists, when covering polls, to discuss changes that are within the margin of error as if they were substantial (Traugott 2008) and that they make unsupported causal attributions when they try to explain results in opinion polls (Bauman & Lavrakas 2000). What journalists or pundits in the media may present as factual explanations for changes in or for the state of public opinion, as measured by polls, are oftentimes nothing more than speculations.

Most of this research focuses on so-called trial heat or horse race polls, that is, polls about people's party preferences or voting intentions. While important, particularly during election campaigns, there are other kinds of polls as well. Among those are polls focused on issues or policies, candidate traits, and performances in debates or other mediated appearances. In many cases the media sponsor the polls, but in other cases polls are used as tools for political actors in their attempts to manage the news. In either case, the major media focus on opinion polls calls for an explanation. Why do the media devote so much attention to opinion polls?

Towards a framework for understanding the media's interest in opinion polls

To understand the news media's use of opinion polls – both those they have commissioned themselves and those presented by various interest groups and political actors – it is imperative to understand the impact of news values on news selection processes and the logic of news production in commercial news media. While it normatively may be true that the most important function of news journalism in democracies is to 'provide people with the information they need to be free and self-governing' (Kovach & Rosenstiel 2001, p. 12; see also McQuail 2003; Strömbäck 2005), the fact is that most news journalism is produced by journalists working for commercial media companies, and for commercial media companies the ultimate goal is not primarily the public good. It is rather to generate profits.

In order to do so, they have to be successful when competing on each of the four markets where commercial media are present. These are the *market for investors*, where investors offer capital and direction in exchange for future profits; the *market for advertisers*, where advertisers offer advertising revenue in exchange for audience attention; the *market for news*, where news sources offer information that can be transformed into news in exchange for audience attention; and the *market for audiences*, where audiences offer their attention in exchange for news and other media content (McManus 1994, p. 60).

The most important of these markets is the audience market, not because commercial media value news audiences higher than advertisers or investors, but rather because success in the battle for audience attention is a prerequisite for success in the battles for investor capital, information that can be transformed into news and for advertising revenue. Hence, to be successful, news journalism produced within commercial news media has to attract as many as possible in the audience segments that advertisers are interested in reaching. In the words of McManus (1994, p. 85), commercial and rational news departments 'should compete with each other to offer the least expensive mix of content that protects the interests of sponsors and investors while garnering the largest audience advertisers will pay to reach' (see also Baker 2002; Hamilton 2004; Picard, 2005).

The tougher the competition between different news media, the more important it becomes for them to attract as large audiences as possible while keeping down the costs and controlling the return on investments. Hence, while the democratic logic dictates that the news media should focus on information that people need in order to be free and self-governing and making sure the information is accurate, commercial logic dictates that the news media should focus on information that attracts as many as possible within the segments that advertisers are interested in while keeping down the costs.

This tension is important both with respect to *what* news the media cover and *how* they cover it. Ultimately, all news journalism is selective, as the number of events or occurrences are too many for any media to cover. One of the most important tasks of news journalism is thus that of gatekeeping, defined as 'the process of selecting, writing, editing, positioning, scheduling, repeating and otherwise massaging information to become news' (Shoemaker, Vos & Reese 2009, p. 73). To guide in this process, there are a number of news values and news selection criteria that journalists apply. Among traditional news values and news selection criteria are, for example, drama, visual attractiveness, entertainment value, importance, proximity, negativity, recency, involvement of elites and power, unexpectedness, unambiguity, continuity, and size or the number of people affected by the news (O'Neill & Harcup 2009; see also Campbell 2004; Gans 1980). To these traditional news values, Allern (2002, p. 145) has added four 'commercial news criteria': (1) the more resources it costs to cover an event, the less likely it is that it will become a news story; (2) the more news sources subsidize the news by journalistically preparing a story for publication, the more likely it will become news; (3) the more selectively a story is distributed and the more exclusive it is to a particular news medium, the more likely it will become news; and (4) 'The more a news medium's strategy is based on arousing sensations to catch public attention, the greater the likelihood of a "media twist", where entertaining elements count more than criteria like relevance, truth and accuracy.'

On the one hand, commercial news media need news stories that deal with important events and topics such as politics and current affairs that are relevant to people in their role as citizens. This is important for their legitimacy as news providers contributing positively to democracy. On the other hand, commercial news media need news stories that are inexpensive to cover and that are filled with attention-grabbing drama and that are interesting to people in their role as consumers. News focusing on opinion polls and the horse race may fulfill both criteria. This is, however, only one side of the story. The other is related to the relationship between news journalism and politics.

Among the criteria of newsworthiness is that the news should focus on events that are important, relevant, affect a great number of people, and that involve individuals or institutions with power. Consequently, much news is focused on politics, where political actors offer information that can be transformed into news in exchange for visibility in the news and potential audience attention. While much research has shown that official and elite actors outnumber other news sources (Bennett 1990; Dimitrova & Strömbäck 2009; Manning 2001; Reich 2009; Shehata 2010), the relationship between journalists and their political news sources is oftentimes uneasy and filled with tension. In this relationship and 'negotiation of newsworthiness' (Cook 2005, p. 102), both sides command resources on their own, but both sides also want to control the other. Not least important, journalists oftentimes do not want to be reduced to mouthpieces for or carriers of the messages of their political sources. As much as they 'rely heavily on institutionally positioned officials for the raw materials of news' (Lawrence 2000, p. 5), journalists want to have and mark their independence (Shehata 2010; Wolfsfeld & Sheafer 2006; Zaller 2001).

The more skilled in and focused on news management and pseudo-events mainly created to attract the attention of the news media that political actors have become (Kumar, 2007; Maltese 1994; Zoch & Molleda 2006), the more problematic it has become for journalists to guard their independence from political actors. When deciding what to cover and how to cover it, journalists can follow the traditional five 'Ws' when writing their stories: Who, What, Where, When and Why. In the minds of many journalists, doing so would, however, give political actors too much influence over the news, encouraging them first to focus more on the Why than the Who, What, Where and When (Patterson 1993), second to cover politics with a critical or negative tone (Farnsworth & Lichter 2011; Zaller 2001) and third to focus on news stories where journalists have greater control over what the news is about and how it should be framed. To capture this phenomenon, Zaller (2001, p. 255) has suggested his 'rule of product substitution', according to which 'the more strenuously politicians challenge journalists for control of a news jurisdiction, the more journalists will seek to develop substitute information that the mass audience is willing to accept as news and that gives expression to journalistic voice'. In such a context, opinion polls – particularly when done or sponsored by the news media – offer a close to perfect substitution for news provided by political actors.

The media's use of opinion polls may consequently be understood as an example of the mediatization of politics, where the media successively have increased their autonomy from political institutions and actors, and where media content – according to the theory – is increasingly shaped by media logic rather than political or partisan logic (Asp 1986; Hjarvard 2008; Mazzoleni & Schulz 1999; Strömbäck 2008; Strömbäck & Dimitrova 2011; Strömbäck & Esser 2009).

Why news media sponsor and cover opinion polls

Based on the above, several although overlapping explanations can be offered for why contemporary news media find opinion polls so attractive when covering politics and why they decide to sponsor and cover their own opinion polls.

First, sponsoring and covering their own opinion polls gives the news media access to exclusive news. This is attractive partly because polls function as a newsgathering tool (Ismach 1984) and partly because it helps in the marketing of the news organization. As noted by Rosenstiel (2005, p. 699): 'In an age when an expanding number of news outlets has put added pressure on all of them to produce audience, indeed, marketing has become a bigger part of news generally and has intensified as a motive in political polling in particular.'

Second, sponsoring and covering their own opinion polls gives the news media full control over the news. The news media commission the opinion polls, cover the results, and interpret the results and their antecedents and potential consequences (Frankovic 1998; Petersson et al. 2006). In essence, by sponsoring and covering their own opinion polls, the news media are making their own news (Hoffman 1980).

Third, the news media need stories that offer drama and that can appeal to audiences that otherwise may not be very interested in politics. In this context, opinion polls are attractive as they offer drama and change, are assumed to be attention-grabbing (Iyengar, Norpoth & Hahn 2004) and do not require that their audiences have too much knowledge about politics. Covering the polls becomes the functional equivalent to covering sports results, a genre with which many are familiar and comfortable.

Fourth, opinion polls fit perfectly with, while simultaneously driving, the framing of politics as a strategic game or a horse race rather than as substance or issues (Cappella & Jamieson 1997; Patterson

1993). Framing politics as a strategic game has become an increasingly common feature of election news coverage in a wide range of countries around the world (Strömbäck & Kaid 2008), driven not least by media commercialism and the need to attract audience attention (Strömbäck & van Aelst 2010). In this framing of politics, opinion polls are indispensable.

Fifth and related, sponsoring and covering their own opinion polls serves as a perfect substitute for news provided by and pseudo-events created by political actors. Zaller (2001, p. 155) consequently notes that 'like a detergent company that wants to get consumers to buy liquid gel instead of soap bars, journalists must offer something that is the functional equivalent of the product they replace, that is, something that provides information about the campaign'. Much of the horse race and poll coverage meets this requirement of the rule of product substitution.

Sixth, and again related, most journalists are generalists and not policy experts. They oftentimes have a hard time following, explaining and analyzing the substance of different policy problems or proposals. Covering politics through the lens of the 'game they play' (Fallows 1996) does not require as much knowledge on the part of journalists and is thus easier. It may also be the case that for many journalists, politics is a game. It is not just a frame they apply, but also the major part of their cognitive schemas of politics. If journalists believe that the game is what ultimately matters, then it is natural to frame politics as a game, and to use opinion polls to find indicators of how the game is going.

Seventh, when polls are presented by external source organizations, such as businesses, interest groups, political parties and campaigns, these polls function as close-to-perfect news subsidies (Gandy 1982). Not only are the results in the polls new, and thus qualify as news. Oftentimes the source organizations present them in a journalistic format, and even if they do not there are ready templates for how to write news stories focusing on new opinion polls. In both cases, covering opinion polls commissioned and presented by source organizations offers an efficient and economic way to gather and present news.

Eighth, covering opinion polls allows journalists a 'quasi-objective, *proactive* role in the news making process' (Lavrakas & Traugott 2000, p. 4). As the numbers produced by opinion polls appear as objective, journalists feel that they can cover opinion polls without running the risk of being accused of being biased. They can base their criticism of political parties, candidates and campaigns in the poll results. At the same time, seldom or never do the numbers speak for themselves, and the kind of polls commissioned by the news media seldom or never include enough questions to investigate what might have caused the results of a particular opinion poll. Hence, when discussing antecedents or possible consequences of opinion poll results, journalists have to interpret or speculate. Still, these interpretations and speculations tend to appear as anchored in the opinion poll results and as being factual. Taken together, covering opinion polls thus allows journalists to be interpretive and proactive while still appearing as objective.

Ninth, by covering opinion polls, the news media are sending 'the symbolic message' (Lavrakas & Traugott 2000, p. 4) that the will and preferences of the public matters and, explicitly or implicitly, that the news media are watching out for the interests of the public. Between politicians and news journalists there is an implicit battle with respect to whether politicians or news journalists are the true guardians of the public will and the public opinion. Both sets of actors claim to be working for the common good, and both sets of actors claim to reflect and represent public opinion. While elected politicians have the upper hand according to the formalistic view of representation, by covering opinion polls and how elected officials do not follow public opinion news journalists seek to demonstrate that they too function as representatives for the public in the sense of 'acting for' public opinion. This becomes part of their role as the 'Fourth Estate'. Hence, it is a means to legitimize the news media's role as representatives of the public, and to mark independence from elected officials.

Tenth, and more generally, opinion polls fit the criteria of newsworthiness commonly applied when deciding what is news, for example drama, entertainment value, importance, proximity, negativity, recency, involvement of elites and power, and unexpectedness (O'Neill & Harcup 2009; see also Campbell 2004; Gans 1980).

There are consequently at least ten reasons for why the media find opinion polls attractive, and which may help explain why the media – and political news journalism in particular – sponsor and cover opinion polls so frequently. In short, 'News polls function as information source, as attention-getters, and as a source of journalistic power' (Frankovic 1998, p. 162). Whether it is a good or a bad thing is, however, another matter. Partly it depends on normative views related to democracy and the role of the media and political news journalism in democracies. Partly it is a matter of proportions. Most observers would agree that politics and election campaigns are about both policies and substance on the one hand, and a strategic game on the other, but the question is how much the media focus on the political substance and the game, including the opinion polls, respectively. Partly it also depends on the quality of the poll coverage and the polls themselves. As already noted, opinion polling is the best methodology yet invented to investigate public opinion, but it is far from perfect, and polls can be both used and misused. The same holds for the media's coverage of opinion polls. This is relevant also in the context of whether the media mainly reflect or shape public opinion through their use of opinion polls. To the extent that the media cover opinion polls that are well executed and that focus on issues where people are informed and have thought through their opinions, the media may reflect rather than shape public opinion. To the extent that the media cover opinion polls that are not well executed or that focus on issues where significant parts of the population are not well informed, have not thought through their opinions or where opinions are fluid, the media may instead shape rather than reflect public opinion. In addition, it depends on whether the media provide their audiences with enough information to assess the results of the polls that are presented in the media. Thus, it is a matter both of the polls themselves and about the media's coverage of them.

Outline of the book

This chapter has reviewed theory and research on the role of public opinion in democracies, the problem of representation in general and with respect to representing public opinion in particular, and the quantity and quality of the media's coverage of opinion polls; and it has outlined a framework for understanding the media's interest in opinion polls. In subsequent chapters, many of the same themes that have been touched upon in this chapter will be addressed in much greater depth.

The book is divided into three parts. Part I – 'Theoretical and Methodological Approaches' – includes three chapters. In Chapter 2 – 'Public Opinion and Opinion Polling: A Complex Relationship' – Slavko Splichal analyzes different conceptualizations of public opinion, how they have changed over time, enduring controversies in conceptualizations of public opinion, and how the emergence and predominance of opinion polls have changed our understanding of public opinion as a concept and phenomena.

While the freedom to conduct opinion polls and publish the results can be derived from legal provisions granting people freedom of expression, the controversies surrounding opinion polling as a methodology, and fear that the publication of opinion results may affect public opinion as much as reflect it, have created incentives for countries to regulate the execution of opinion polls and the publishing of their results.

Different countries have, however, taken different approaches to the regulation of opinion polling. In Chapter 3 – 'Regulations of Opinion Polls: A Comparative Perspective' – Thomas Petersen reviews and analyzes discourses surrounding the regulation of opinion as well as the regulations of opinion polls in a comparative, cross-national perspective.

As mentioned in this introductory chapter, opinion polling is a methodology for surveying people's opinions, and as such it has both strengths and weaknesses. For example, there are different modes through which people's responses can be collected, and numerous controversies related to the survey methodology. However, opinion polling is also evolving, partly to address the methodological problems and challenges involved. Against this background, Chapter 4 – 'Methodological Trends and Controversies in the Media's Use of Opinion Polls' – by Michael Traugott reviews and analyzes opinion polling as a methodology and methodological trends in opinion polling.

Part II of the book focuses on 'The Media's Publication of Opinion Polls' from an international perspective. Although there may be many similarities across countries, the media's publication of opinion polls is always situated in the contexts in which the media operate, and this context is in turn shaped by the political as well as the media systems in respective countries as well as by contextual factors. In essence, the media and political systems as well as the contexts matter, which makes it important to investigate the media's publication of opinion polls in different countries. Hence, for this book we selected six countries, guided by the ambition to include a diverse set of democratic countries covering all five continents. Consequently, Part II of this book includes six chapters, each focused on one particular country, and the purpose of these is to review and analyze research within each country with respect to the media's publications of opinion polls. The chapters are Chapter 5 – 'Opinion Polls and the Media in Germany: A Productive but Critical Relationship' – by Christina Holtz-Bacha, Chapter 6 – 'Opinion Polls and the Media in the United States' – by Kathleen Frankovic, Chapter 7 – 'Opinion Polls and the Media in Brazil' – by Flávia Biroli, Luis Felipe Miguel and Fernanda Ferreira Mota, Chapter 8 – 'Opinion Polls and the Media in Australia' – by Stephen Mills and Rodney Tiffen, Chapter 9 – 'Opinion Polls and the Media in South Africa' – by Robert Mattes and Chapter 10 – The Good, the Bad, and the Ugly: Opinion in Taiwan – by Lars Willnat, Ven-hwei Lo and Annette Aw. Taken together, the chapters in Part II provide an extensive review of how the media use and cover opinion polls worldwide.

Part III of the book is devoted to the 'Effects and Consequences of Published Opinion Polls' and includes three chapters. The first of these,

Chapter 11 – 'Attitudinal and Behavioral Consequences of Published Opinion Polls' – is written by Patricia Moy and Eike Mark Rinke. It consequently deals with the extent to which the media's use of opinion polls shapes, rather than reflects, public opinion. Briefly, the chapter shows that research suggests that people's attitudes, opinions and behaviors are affected by polls published by the media. For example, research has shown that the publication of opinion polls by the media can produce bandwagon as well as underdog effects. These are discussed in Chapter 11, along with theories such as spiral of silence and the theory of impersonal influence that deals with the effects of published opinion polls on the public.

Published opinion polls do not just have effects on the public: they may also have effects on and consequences for political parties and their leaders, who may simultaneously attempt to strategically use opinion polls in their efforts to manage the news. How published opinion polls may affect political parties and their leaders, and how political parties and leaders use opinion polls in news management processes, is the focus of Chapter 12 – 'Published Opinion Polls, Strategic Party Behavior, and News Management' – by Jesper Strömbäck.

Part III of the book concludes with Chapter 13 – 'Opinion Polls, Media and the Political System' – by Christina Holtz-Bacha. In this chapter the author discusses the issue of whether opinion polls in general – and as used by the media and political actors in particular – reflect or shape public opinion; the role of opinion polls in contemporary democracies; how they are used by and influence both the media and political actors; and the implications for the political system and democracy.

Taken together, it is hoped that the chapters in this volume will shed new light and serve as a springboard for further research on the relationships between the media, opinion polls, public opinion, politics and democracy. Do opinion polls, as covered by the media, mainly serve as *Vox Populi* – the voice of the people – or as *Vox Media* – the voice of the media? And what are the democratic consequences?

References

Allern, S. (2002) 'Journalistic and Commercial News Values: News Organizations as Patrons of an Institution and Market Actors', *Nordicom Review*, 23(1/2), 137–152.

American Association for Public Opinion Research (AAPOR) (2010) *Code of Professional Ethics & Practice*, retrieved from http://www.aapor.org/Standards_andamp_Ethics/2410.htm, 20 October 2010.

Asp, K. (1986) *Mäktiga massmedier. Studier i politisk opinionsbildning* (Stockholm: Akademilitteratur).

Atkin, C. K. and J. Gaudino (1984) 'The Impact of Polling on the Mass Media', *The Annals of the American Academy*, 472, 119–128.

Baker, C. E. (2002) *Media, Markets, and Democracy* (New York: Cambridge University Press).

Bauman, S. L. and P. J. Lavrakas (2000) 'Reporter's Use of Causal Explanation in Interpreting Election Polls', in P. J. Lavrakas and M. W. Traugott (eds), *Election Polls, the News Media, and Democracy* (New York: Chatham House).

Bennett, W. L. (1990) 'Toward a Theory of Press-State Relations', *Journal of Communication*, 40(2), 103–125.

Bishop, G. F. (2005) *The Illusion of Public Opinion: Fact and Artifact in American Public Opinion Polls* (Lanham: Rowman & Littlefield).

Brettschneider, F. (1997) 'The Press and the Polls in Germany, 1980–1994', *International Journal of Public Opinion Research*, 9(3), 248–264.

Brettschneider, F. (2008) 'The News Media's Use of Opinion Polls', in W. Donsbach and M. W. Traugott (eds), *The SAGE Handbook of Public Opinion Research* (London: Sage).

Campbell, V. (2004) *Information Age Journalism: Journalism in an International Context* (London: Arnold).

Cappella, J. N. and K. H. Jamieson (1997) *Spiral of Cynicism: The Press and the Public Good* (New York: University of Chicago Press).

Clawson, R. A. and Z. M. Oxley (2008) *Public Opinion: Democratic Ideals, Democratic Practice* (Washington, DC: CQ Press).

Cook, T. E. (2005) *Governing with the News: The News Media as a Political Institution*, 2nd edn (Chicago, IL: University of Chicago Press).

Dahl, R. A. (1998) *On Democracy* (New Haven, CT: Yale University Press).

Donsbach, W. and M. W. Traugott (2008) 'Introduction', in W. Donsbach and M. W. Traugott (eds), *The Sage Handbook of Public Opinion Research* (London: Sage).

Elster, J. (ed.) (1998) *Deliberative Democracy* (New York: Cambridge University Press).

European Society for Opinion and Marketing Research (ESOMAR) and World Association for Public Opinion Research (WAPOR) (2010). *ESOMAR/WAPOR Guide to Opinion Polls including the ESOMAR International Code of Practice for the Publication of Public Opinion Poll Results*, retrieved from http://www.esomar.org/knowledge-and-standards/codes-and-guidelines.php, 3 November 2011.

Fallows, J. (1996) *Breaking the News: How the Media Undermine American Democracy* (New York: Pantheon).

Farnsworth, S. J. and S. R. Lichter (2011) *The Nightly News Nightmare: Media Coverage of U.S. Presidential Elections, 1988–2008* (Lanham: Rowman & Littlefield).

Ferguson, P. A. and C. de Clercy (2005) 'Regulatory Compliance in Opinion Poll Reporting During the 2004 Canadian Election', *Canadian Public Policy*, 31(3), 243–257.

Frankovic, K. A. (1998) 'Public Opinion and Polling', in D. Graber, D. McQuail and P. Norris (eds), *The Politics of News – The News of Politics* (Washington, DC: CQ Press).

Frankovic, K. A. (2005) 'Reporting "the Polls" in 2004', *Public Opinion Quarterly*, 69(5), 682–697.

Gallup, G. and S. F. Rae (1940) *The Pulse of Democracy: The Public-Opinion Poll and How It Works* (New York: Simon & Schuster).

Gandy, O. H., Jr. (1982) *Beyond Agenda Setting: Information Subsidies and Public Policy* (Norwood, NJ: Ablex).

Gans, H. J. (1980) *Deciding What's News: A Study of CBS Evening News, NBC Nightly News, Newsweek and Time* (New York: Vintage).

Geer, J. G. (1996) *From Tea Leaves to Opinion Polls: A Theory of Democratic Leadership* (New York: Columbia University Press).

Gidengil, E. (2008) 'Media Matter: Election Coverage in Canada', in J. Strömbäck and L. L. Kaid (eds), *The Handbook of Election News Coverage Around the World* (New York: Routledge).

Gouws, A. and A. S. de Beer (2008) 'Media and Elections in South Africa: Finding a Foothold on the Democratic Path', in J. Strömbäck and L. L. Kaid (eds), *The Handbook of Election News Coverage Around the World* (New York: Routledge).

Hamilton, J. T. (2004) *All the News That's Fit to Sell: How the Market Transforms Information Into News* (New Haven, CT: Yale University Press).

Held, D. (2006) *Models of Democracy*, 3rd edn (Malden, MA: Polity Press).

Herbst, S. (1998) *Reading Public Opinion: How Political Actors View the Democratic Process* (Chicago, IL: University of Chicago Press).

Hjarvard, S. (2008) 'The Mediatization of Society: A Theory of the Media as Agents of Social and Cultural Change', *Nordicom Review*, 29(2), 105–134.

Hoffman, N. von (1980) 'Public Opinion Polls: Newspapers Making Their Own News?', *Public Opinion Quarterly*, 44(4), 572–573.

Ismach, A. H. (1984) 'Polling as a News-Gathering Tool', *Annals of the American Academy of Political and Social Science*, 472, 106–118.

Iyengar, S., H. Norpoth and K. S. Hahn (2004) 'Consumer Demand for Election News: The Horserace Sells', *Journal of Politics*, 66(1), 157–175.

Key, V. O., Jr. (1964) *Public Opinion and American Democracy* (New York: Alfred A. Knopf).

Kovach, B. and T. Rosenstiel (2001) *The Elements of Journalism: What Newspeople Should Know and the Public Should Expect* (New York: Crown).

Kumar, M. J. (2007) *Managing the President's Message: The White House Communications Operation* (Baltimore, MD: John Hopkins University Press).

Ladd, E. C. and J. Benson (1992) 'The Growth of News Polls in American Politics', in T. E. Mann and G. R. Orren (eds), Media Polls in American Politics (Washington, DC: Brookings).

Lavrakas, P. J. and M. W. Traugott (2000) 'Why Election Polls are Important to a Democracy: An American Perspective', in P. J. Lavrakas and M. W. Traugott (eds), *Election Polls, the News Media, and Democracy* (New York: Chatham House).

Lawrence, R. (2000) 'Game-Framing the Issues: Tracking the Strategy Frame in Public Policy News', *Political Communication*, 17(2), 93–114.

Maltese, J. A. (1994) *Spin Control: The White House Office of Communications and the Management of Presidential News*, 2nd edn (Chapel Hill, NC: University of North Carolina Press).

Manin, B. (1997) *The Principles of Representative Government* (New York: Cambridge University Press).

Manning, P. (2001) *News and News Sources: A Critical Introduction* (London: Sage).

Mazzoleni, G. and W. Schulz (1999) 'Mediatization of Politics: A Challenge for Democracy?', *Political Communication*, 16(3), 247–261.

McManus, J. H. (1994) *Market-Driven Journalism: Let the Citizen Beware?* (Thousand Oaks, CA: Sage).

McQuail, D. (2003) *Media Accountability and Freedom of Publication* (New York: Oxford University Press).

Moore, D. W. (2008) *The Opinion Makers: An Insider Exposes the Truth Behind the Polls* (Boston, MA: Beacon Press).

Nabi, R. L. and M. B. Oliver (eds) (2009) *The Sage Handbook of Media Processes and Effects* (Thousand Oaks, CA: Sage).

O'Neill, D. and T. Harcup (2009) 'News Values and Selectivity', in K. Wahl-Jorgensen and T. Hanitzsch (eds), *Handbook of Journalism Studies* (New York: Routledge).

Pateman, C. (1970) *Participation and Democratic Theory* (New York: Cambridge University Press).

Patterson, T. E. (1993) *Out of Order* (New York: Vintage).

Patterson, T. E. (2005) 'Of Polls, Mountains', *Public Opinion Quarterly*, 69(5), 716–724.

Petersson, O. (2008) 'Ofrånkomliga, men problematiska', in O. Petersson (ed.), *Medierna: folkets röst?* (Stockholm: SNS Förlag).

Petersson, O., M. Djerf-Pierre, S. Holmberg, J. Strömbäck and L. Weibull (2006) *Media and Elections in Sweden* (Stockholm: SNS Förlag).

Picard, R. G. (2005) 'Money, Media, and the Public Interest', in G. Overholser and K. H. Jamieson (eds), *The Press* (New York: Oxford University Press).

Pitkin, H. A. (1967) *The Concept of Representation* (Berkeley, CA: University of California Press).

Reich, Z. (2009) *Sourcing the News: Key Issues in Journalism* (Cresskill, NJ: Hampton Press).

Roncarolo, F. (2008) 'News Coverage of Elections in the Long Transition of Italian Democracy', in J. Strömbäck and L. L. Kaid (eds), *The Handbook of Election News Coverage Around the World* (New York: Routledge).

Rosenstiel, T. (2005) 'Political Polling and the New Media Culture: A Case of More Being Less', *Public Opinion Quarterly*, 69(5), 698–715.

Sartori, G. (1987) *The Theory of Democracy Revisited. Part One: The Contemporary Debate* (Chatham: Chatham House).

Schumpeter, J. A. (1975) *Capitalism, Socialism and Democracy* (New York: Harper Perennial).

Sheafer, T., G. Weimann and Y. Tsfati (2008) 'Campaigns in the Holy Land: The Content and Effects of Election News Coverage in Israel', in J. Strömbäck and L. L. Kaid (eds), *The Handbook of Election News Coverage Around the World* (New York: Routledge).

Shehata, A. (2010) 'Marking Journalistic Independence: Official Dominance and the Rule of Product Substitution in Swedish Press Coverage', *European Journal of Communication*, 25(2), 123–137.

Shoemaker, P. J. and S. D. Reese (1996) *Mediating the Message: Theories of Influences on Mass Media Content*, 2nd edn (White Plains: Longman).

Shoemaker, P. J., T. P. Vos and S. D. Reese (2009) 'Journalists as Gatekeepers', in K. Wahl-Jorgensen and T. Hanitzsch (eds), *The Handbook of Journalism Studies* (New York: Routledge).

Smith, T. J. and D. O. Verall (1985) 'A Critical Analysis of Australian Television Coverage of Election Opinion Polls', *Public Opinion Quarterly*, 49(1), 58–79.
Splichal, S. (2001) 'Publicity, Democracy, and Public Opinion', in S. Splichal (ed.), *Public Opinion & Democracy: Vox Populi – Vox Dei?* (Cresskill, NJ: Hampton Press).
Strömbäck, J. (2005) 'In Search of a Standard: Four Models of Democracy and Their Normative Implications for Journalism', *Journalism Studies*, 6(3), 331–345.
Strömbäck, J. (2008) 'Four Phases of Mediatization: An Analysis of the Mediatization of Politics', *International Journal of Press/Politics*, 13(3), 228–246.
Strömbäck, J. (2009) 'Vox Populi or Vox Media? Opinion Polls and the Swedish Media, 1998–2006', *Javnost – The Public*, 16(3), 55–70.
Strömbäck, J. and D. V. Dimitrova (2011) 'Mediatization and Media Interventionism: A Comparative Analysis of Sweden and the United States', *International Journal of Press/Politics*, 16(1), 30–49.
Strömbäck, J. and F. Esser (2009) 'Shaping Politics: Mediatization and Media Interventionism', in K. Lundby (ed.), *Mediatization: Concept, Changes, Consequences* (New York: Peter Lang).
Strömbäck, J. and L. L. Kaid (eds) (2008) *The Handbook of Election News Coverage Around the World* (New York: Routledge).
Strömbäck, J. and P. van Aelst (2010) 'Exploring Some Antecedents of the Media's Framing of Election News: A Comparison of Swedish and Belgian Election News', *International Journal of Press/Politics*, 15(1), 41–59.
Tiffen, R. (2008) 'Australia: Gladiatorial Parties and Volatile Media in a Stable Polity', in J. Strömbäck and L. L. Kaid (eds), *The Handbook of Election News Coverage Around the World* (New York: Routledge).
Traugott, M. W. (2005) 'The Accuracy of the National Preelection Polls in the 2004 Presidential Election', *Public Opinion Quarterly*, 69(5), 642–654.
Traugott, M. W. (2008) 'The Uses and Misuses of Polls', in W. Donsbach and M. W. Traugott (eds), *The SAGE Handbook of Public Opinion Research* (London: Sage).
Traugott, M. W. (2009) *Changes in Media Polling in Recent Presidential Campaigns: Moving from Good to 'Average' at CNN*, Discussion paper #R-33 (Cambridge, MA: Joan Shorenstein Center on the Press, Politics and Public Policy).
Weimann, G. (1990) 'The Obsession to Forecast: Pre-Election Polls in the Israeli Press', *Public Opinion Quarterly*, 54(3), 396–408.
Weisberg, H. F. (2008) 'The Methodological Strengths and Weaknesses of Survey Research', in W. Donsbach and M. W. Traugott (eds), *The Sage Handbook of Public Opinion Research* (London: Sage).
Welch, R. L. (2002) 'Polls, Polls, and More Polls: An Evaluation of How Public Opinion Polls are Reported in Newspapers', *Harvard International Journal of Press/Politics*, 7(1), 102–114.
Wolfsfeld, G. and T. Sheafer (2006) 'Competing Actors and the Construction of Political News: The Contest over Waves in Israel', *Political Communication*, 23(3), 333–354.
Zaller, J. R. (2001) 'The Rule of Product Substitution in Presidential Campaign News', in E. Katz and Y. Warshel (eds), *Election Studies: What's Their Use?* (Boulder, CO: Westview Press).
Zoch, L. M. and J. C. Molleda (2006) 'Building a Theoretical Model of Media Relations Using Framing, Information Subsidies, and Agenda-Building', in C. H. Botan and V. Hazleton (eds), *Public Relations Theory II* (New York: Lawrence Erlbaum).

Part I
Theoretical and Methodological Approaches

2
Public Opinion and Opinion Polling: Contradictions and Controversies

Slavko Splichal

Many philosophers have discussed the nature of human opinions at least since Ancient Greece, but the concept of 'public opinion' was not in use until the eighteenth century. It was missing despite the fact that the processes and phenomena that are at least related to, if not constitutive of, public opinion – judging by the historical records – clearly existed, such as narratives about the rulers who have, disguised as ordinary people, mingled with the crowd to hear what people think about their government.

A great social and political significance of opinion processes was perhaps first grasped by Thomas Hobbes, who wrote in *Behemoth* (1668/1999, p. 16) that 'the power of the mighty hath no foundation but in the opinion and belief of the people'. In fact, half a century earlier, Machiavelli advised his Prince to never forget to think of people's opinion, and thus create the reputation, popularity and 'impression that he is a great man' among his subjects, and ensure their affection to him (Machiavelli 1513/1992, p. 63). Hobbes' 'opinion theorem' was widely promoted by Locke, Hume and many others in the century to follow.

The concept of 'public opinion' first appeared in the eighteenth-century English and French political philosophy of the Enlightenment that gave rise to the development of the liberal bourgeois public. With Jean-Jacques Rousseau and particularly Jeremy Bentham, the idea of the public as a sort of popular tribunal expressing opinions and representing the general will gained prominence in political-philosophical discourses. The notion of public opinion was always associated with the debates of democracy and the rule of law, people's sovereignty, majority rule, political representation and formal, constitutionally established ways of participation in the political decision-making processes. Legitimate government in modern liberal democracies is believed to ideally represent, reflect and respond to public opinion.

Bentham's and Kant's ideas of publicness

Early normative theories considered publicness to be one of the fundamental principles of democratic governance, and emphasized the principal role of the public as the fourth power or watchdog maintaining surveillance over the government. The principle of *publicness* referring to *discursive visibility* is central to the concept of public opinion since its very first conceptualizations (Splichal 2011). It is normatively 'enacted' in an ethical *principle* or universally acknowledged *norm*. It tends to develop into a universal *human right* of the public use of reason and personal right to communicate, which includes two complementary rights – to speak and to be heard. In contemporary (deliberative) democracies, the idea of publicness primarily refers to the public sphere, where the 'public use of reason' or 'public discussion' of free and equal citizens can – or ought to – take place, and where public opinion is formed and expressed.

Jeremy Bentham and Immanuel Kant founded two main intellectual currents of conceptualizing 'publicness' in the centuries to follow. Kant (1784) advocated free public discussion as a means for the development and public use of reason, in contrast to the existing censorship in the public domain of the time. His conceptualization derives from the transformation of the natural personal right of free expression into a civil right to communicate, as a realization of the generic human freedom, embedded in the press as the common means of individuals to communicate their spiritual existence and participate in a collective (and particularly political) life. Bentham (1791/1994) conceived of publicness as a universal remedy against any misuse of power. His conceptualization rests on functions performed by the public and its immediate instrument, the press, to ensure the surveillance of the 'public opinion tribunal' over those in (political) power.

In his treatise, *To Perpetual Peace*, Kant (1795/1983) suggested that the principle of publicness is the fundamental and universal principle of human public agency. In defense of the *public use of reason*, Kant insisted that – since the sovereign power is legitimized by the general will – the sovereign would lose the basis of his legitimacy if alienated from the only source of knowledge, which he needs to make right decisions – *the critical voices expressed by citizens*. Yet in fact, it was Bentham who should be credited for the first in-depth discussion of the relationship between public opinion and the principle of publicness, including the definition of the latter as the foundation of public opinion and people's sovereignty.

Whereas Kant emphasized the importance of free public discussion as an instrument for the development and expression of autonomous rationality, Bentham favored a free press as an instrument for public surveillance of government, in the interest of general happiness. He was the first to conceptualize the rule of publicity as the foundation of the doctrine of the sovereignty of public opinion. His views on public opinion as 'the only force from which the force of government when operating in a sinister direction can experience any the least impediment to its course' (Bentham 1822/1990, p. 121) provide an intellectual foundation for the later 'watchdog' concept of the press as an essential part of the control over government.

Bentham differentiated between three segments of the public: (1) the most numerous class, consisting of those who cannot occupy themselves with public affairs at all because they 'have not time to read, nor leisure for reasoning'; (2) those whose political judgments are borrowed from others, because they are not able to form opinions on their own; and (3) those who are able to judge for themselves. The last group constitutes the 'Committee of the Public Opinion Tribunal'. Those who agree with the Committee's publicly expressed opinions form 'the body of public opinion at large', which may consist of any number of members up to the total number of members of society.

Important publications on public opinion have appeared continuously since Bentham and Kant. Many influential works were published before the twentieth century by G. W. F. Hegel (1821/1971), Albert Venn Dicey (1905/1981), Gabriel Tarde (1901) and Gustave LeBon (1895/2001), to name just the most inspiring authors, followed in the beginning of the twentieth century by the Chicago School sociologists in the USA, and Wilhelm Bauer (1914) and Ferdinand Tönnies (1922) in Germany (Splichal 1999). Nevertheless, after almost a 300-year history of conceptual debates, a consensus on the definition of public opinion is far from being reached.

The rise and fall of the public

From the earliest theorizations in the eighteenth century to contemporary times, conceptualizations of public opinion have undergone many radical transformations and revisions. The concept of the rule of public opinion and its surveillance over political authorities would soon become the object of severe criticism. The period of confidence in public opinion, based on the belief in the moral judgment of the 'common man' proclaimed in the age of Enlightenment, would be followed by a period of distrust in his capabilities and competence.

Doubts about the judgment of public opinion were first expressed by Hegel. His favorable accounts of the sphere of public opinion as a field 'open to everyone where he can express his purely personal political opinions and make them count' (1821/1971, p. 248), and publicity as an 'antidote to the self-conceit of individuals singly and *en mass*' and the chief means of popular education (ibid., pp. 203–204), were contrasted by severe criticism. Hegel compared public opinion with an ignorant vulgar person who reproves everyone and talks most of what he understands least. As Hegel suggested, in public opinion one can find as much truth as error; it deserves to be respected when the truth is found in it, and despised when it is expressed in gossip.

Hegel's critique was followed by Tocqueville's libertarian political-philosophical critique of the tyranny of the majority in the 1840s, and his followers J. S. Mill (1859/1985), James Bryce (1888/1995) and Walter Lippmann (1922/1998). This stream of thought continued to dominate until the advent of socio-psychological positivism and empiricism in the early 1900s.

By the beginning of the twentieth century, two dominant public opinion paradigms had been established. The *normative-democratic paradigm* represented by Tarde, Tönnies and Dewey, among others, links public opinion as *opinion of the public*(s) to political participation and democracy. The *authoritarian paradigm*, which emphasizes the repressive role of public opinion that hinders individuals' freedom of expression (e.g. Bryce, Ross and Lippmann), has 'lost' public opinion's subject, the public, yet publicness of public opinion is not reduced to an aggregate of individuals' opinions made public. Both paradigms nearly crumbled in the 1930s in the face of the polling industry, which challenged both paradigms and was the deciding factor of the rise of a new *social-psychological* paradigm, which focuses on processes of individual opinion formation and expression.

In the late nineteenth and early twentieth centuries, the term 'the public' retained its constitutive status in the public opinion theories of American pragmatists Park and Dewey, and European sociologists Tarde and Tönnies. Tönnies and Dewey were the last vigorous defenders of the normative concept of 'opinion of *the public*' in the sense of a common judgment formed and expressed by those who constitute the public. Dewey, for example, defined public opinion as 'judgment which is formed and entertained by *those who constitute the public* and is about public affairs' (Dewey 1927/1991, p. 177; emphasis added). Even when – with Park (1904/1972) and Blumer (1948) – the public had lost its strictly political and rational character, it remained an 'elementary and spontaneous *collective grouping*'.

Later on, plurality and diversity of *opinions* typical of democratic societies preponderated over the unity of *the public* in conceptualizations of public opinion. The scholarly attention was redirected from the final *state* and *normative goal* (consensus) to the everyday *processes* of opinion formation and expression. In this perspective, *the* public opinion should be understood in the sense of V. O. Key's *consensus on fundamentals* (which must exist in any human collectivity) that *permits* or *limits* rather than *directs* certain governmental actions (Key 1961/1967). In other words, the ('solid', according to Tönnies) public opinion or 'opinion of *the public*' is not an organized, active opinion directly entangled in (political) discussions, but a judgment – formed and entertained by those who constitute the public, and about public affairs – which may be activated if organized by a specific (political) actor, such as an interest group, political party or the media. A further step away from the traditional normative concept of public opinion is represented by blurring out the difference between public and private opinions brought about by Lippmann's concept of 'public opinions' as individuals' perceptions of the outside world, 'the picture inside people's heads' (Lippmann 1922/1960, p. 31).

Since the mid-1800s, control over the ruling authorities by the public as the main social function of public opinion has been increasingly substituted (critically) by that of control over individuals' behavior. It was Tocqueville who first realized that public opinion was not only a safeguard against the misrule of those in power but also a means of coercion in the hands of the majority against any minority of those who would not share the majority opinion. In contrast to Bentham, who believed the primary task of the public was in its surveillance of political representatives who could otherwise fail to advance the public interest, the re-conceptualization of public opinion in psychological and sociological theories emphasized the impelling power of public opinion to discipline the people liberated of their critical function as an active part in forming public opinion. Consequently, the 'authoritarian paradigm' disentangled itself completely from the public in its conceptualization of public opinion.

With the supremacy of empirical sociological and social-psychological research over political-philosophical critique, the social foundation of public opinion expanded from intellectual elites to the masses or even the whole population of a state – not as the subject of public opinion but rather as the object to be influenced. Edward Ross, one of the proponents of the new dominant stream, believed that public opinion was merely a 'primitive technique' that became 'simply one coercive agent alongside of others' (1901/1969: 98). Similarly, Tarde recognized that 'the need to agree with the public of which one is a part, to think and act in agreement with [public] opinion, becomes all the more strong and irresistible as the public becomes more numerous, the opinion more imposing, and the need itself more often satisfied' (Tarde 1969, p. 318). This stream of thought was later followed by Tom Harrisson (1940), who emphasized 'a tendency for most ordinary people to follow what they believe to be the majority' (p. 370), and Elisabeth Noelle-Neumann, who conceptualized public opinion as 'opinions that one can express in public without isolating oneself' (1984/1993, p. 62).

The increase in the number of discussions on public opinion in the twentieth century also enhanced controversies on what exactly constitutes the object of discussion. In the 1920s, American political scientists still managed to reach a consensus on the meaning of 'opinion', which has already then been in strong opposition to Tönnies' understanding of *Meinung*. While American political scientists agreed that 'opinion needs not be result of rational process' (Binkley 1928, p. 389), Tönnies (1922, p. 19) emphasized 'believing pertains to the heart, and opining to the head'. At that time, the relationships between 'public' and 'opinion' and between 'the public' and 'public opinion' had already become matters of dispute among American political scientists.[1] In the following decades, the list of controversial questions was greatly expanded. This led Childs (1965) to the conclusion that the best way out of the growing perplexities would be to substitute the term 'mass opinion' for 'public opinion'. Many others followed him, including V. O. Key (1967), Benjamin Ginsberg (1989), James Beniger (1987) and John Zaller (1992), who contributed to the advance of the critical empirical tradition in the conceptualization of public opinion. With the constitutive elements of public opinion becoming increasingly *transnational*, the unresolved issues of efficacy and legitimacy of (transnational) public opinion made the concept even more tangled (Fraser 2007).

After centuries of debates about whom or what constitutes public opinion, it would be curious to say that 'public opinion does not even exist', as provocatively suggested by Bourdieu (1972/1979). Should we consider three centuries of debates and reflections on opinion processes in society, largely initiated by the Enlightenment, a simple (scientific) error? This is unlikely, indeed. One can problematize the appropriateness of the phrase 'public opinion' (as it did the American Political Science Association almost a century ago), but not the social processes that are studied under the common denominator of 'public opinion'. It would surely make more sense to speak of the process as 'public opining',[2] to stress the dynamics of mass processes of (trans)formation of opinions in contrast to the relatively static condition of an individual opinion. In the popular jargon, 'opinion' can easily create an erroneous impression of its singularity, conclusiveness and direct visibility. The ambiguity of the phrase 'public opinion' is further aggravated by difficulties in defining its constitutive concepts 'opinion' (e.g. in contrast to 'attitude') and 'publicness' (in contrast to privacy), and linguistic differences (e.g. between German *Meinung* and French *l'opinion*, which has also been adopted in English).

Public opining is not intended for the search of truth or increase in knowledge – and almost never has been understood this way – but for formation and expression of general will. The Ancient Greeks already made a clear distinction between the concepts of *doxa* (δόξα) and *episteme* (επιστήμη): the former refers to opinion and the latter to knowledge (and its specific form, *technê*, to practical or applied knowledge). Kant distinguished between opining, believing and knowing as three fundamental kinds of 'holding for true', which Tönnies used – similarly to the concepts of the general and social will – as one of the foundations of his theory of public opinion. In Tönnies' work, opining is no more conceptualized in opposition to knowing (as it was in Ancient Greece), but rather in opposition to believing. According to Tönnies, opining always includes elements of knowledge and is based on them, which does not apply to believing. Lippmann's chief argument in his indirect polemic with Dewey that 'public opinions' (as opposed to expert judgments) are uninformed, held and/or expressed by outsiders and biased – which made the public nothing but a 'phantom' (as he entitled his second book on public opinion published in 1925) – completely ignores the important distinction between knowing and opining, and distinctive relevance of each of them to social relations.

If we do not want to relinquish the idea of public opinion, we have to reconcile ourselves to the fact that *universal* definitions of the public and public opinion cannot be attained. As we have seen, the reason for that is not simply in the fact that too numerous and mutually exclusive definitions exist (which renders it impossible to formulate a 'standard definition'), but derives instead from the contradictions inherent in the very concept of 'public opinion', and perspectives pursued by different theoretical paradigms.

Invention of polling

The early twentieth century not only saw the most important neo-classical theoretical works on public opinion but also created the most important scientific 'product' in the field – opinion polling. This period is marked by the most prominent representatives of the democratic political-philosophical and sociological theories of public opinion, such as Tarde, Tönnies, Park and Dewey. The distinctiveness of their ideas did not completely overshadow the critiques of more 'empirically minded' political scientists and sociologists, such as Lippmann, Ross and later Blumer, who criticized the 'classics' from very different, even opposing perspectives. When in the 1930s most of these intellectual debates abated already, opinion polls were born in the USA. In Europe (e.g. France and Germany), this 'scientific invention' was first treated with ridicule, but after the Second World War polls experienced great popularity and helped to revise classical conceptualizations of public opinion. Polling has radically marked conceptualizations of 'the public' and 'public opinion', and brought in a differentiation between formerly inseparable concepts. The breakthrough of polling was so rapid and all-embracing that Berelson and Janowitz felt compelled to emphasize that 'Contrary to popular notions and even to the ideas of some practitioners, the study of public opinion did not spring full-panoplied from the brow of George Gallup in the 1930s' (1959, p. 1).

Nevertheless, polling has significantly influenced 'conceptions of public opinion, and public opinion's role in modern economies, polities and societies' (Beniger 1992, p. 218). It typically divided the academic community into those admiring polling as a tool of making democratic life more efficacious and legitimate, and critics arguing that it undermined it fatally. Table 2.1 indicates some momentous controversies between the arguments of advocates ('pros') and opponents ('cons') of polling in the (re-)conceptualizations of critical dimensions of public opinion as defined in the 'traditional' normative-critical stream of thought.

Polling is not unique in this. Newspapers as a new means of expressing opinions, made possible by developments in economics, technology and politics, brought about Bentham's 'Public Opinion Tribunal'.

Table 2.1 (Re)conceptualizations of key dimensions in public opinion and opinion polls

Conceptual dimensions	Normative-critical conceptualizations of public opinion	Polls	
		Pros	Cons
Public opinion	Complex form of social will created in an autonomous dynamic discursive process	Uniformities observed in opinions; opinions held by private persons which 'clients' find it prudent to heed (Allport); the aggregate of the views on matters that affect or interest the community (Bryce, Gallup)	Static cross-section of responses of a representative sample of citizens at a given point of time
Subject	The public – all potentially affected by political decisions involved in public deliberation	Majority of population; the public 'superfluous for the purpose of research' (Allport)	Arbitrarily defined population, mass; 'loss of generic subject' (Blumer)
Opinion	Publicly expressed spontaneous assertion constitutive of communicative action	Internal dispositions (to be measured) Reactions of individuals	Non-opinion
Content of opining	Autonomous selection of issues relevant for the public	Checking interest claims (Albig)	Externally subsidized and constrained response
Form of expression	Public deliberation on controversial issues	Interview response; Private approval or disapproval	Interview response; Prevents and/or substitutes public discussion (Ginsberg)

Table 2.1   (Continued)

Conceptual dimensions	Normative-critical conceptualizations of public opinion	Polls	
		Pros	Cons
Course of action	Surveillance of power	Leaders take account of accurate appraisal of public opinion in reaching their decisions (Gallup) and countering claims of pressure groups (Albig)	Control of citizens and pacification of public opinion (Ginsberg)
Democratic legitimacy	All potentially affected (may) participate in deliberations	'A continuous monitoring of the elusive pulse of democracy' (Moore)	None (undemocratic)
Social function	Holding political powers accountable; Regulation of consequences of transactions	'Ascertaining the will of the majority of citizens at all times' (Gallup)	Legitimization of the dominant political order and hindering democratic formation and expression of public opinion (Dryzek 1990)
Defining principle	Publicness	Anonymity	

Similarly, computer-mediated communication and the Internet are likely to affect the formation of public opinion and its nature. What was unique with polling was that it tended to implode the concept of public opinion into that of polling.

In the discussion of the nature of public opinion in *The American Commonwealth* (1888), Bryce distinguished three stages in the evolution of public opinion from its unconscious and passive state into the conscious and active state. According to his scheme, the most elementary level comprises public opinion accepting the will of the monarch whom it was accustomed to obey. In the next stage, conflicts appear between the ruling elites and the 'more independent or progressive spirits' (i.e. the bourgeois class) which were eventually decided in revolutions. In the third stage, in (until then) the most developed phase, the sovereign multitude expresses its will in certain intervals – in elections – and it is supposed that the general will expressed in that way would be taken into account by the legislative and executive branches of power. In principle, a higher stage of development should be possible, provided that 'the will of the majority of the citizens were to become ascertainable at all times, and without the need of its passing through a body of representatives, possibly even without the need of voting machinery at all'. Yet Bryce considered such development quite utopian mainly due to 'technical' problems, as 'the machinery for weighing or measuring the popular will from week to week or month to month has not been, and is not likely to be, invented' (Bryce 1888/1995, p. 919).

Bryce clearly underestimated the power of changes and innovations. A 'machinery' that seemed utopian in Bryce's time has been invented only a few decades later in the form of public opinion polls, almost in the very form predicted a few years earlier by Carl Schmitt who in a cynical way, and alluding to the American 'voting machines', anticipated that some day, 'without leaving his apartment, every man could continuously express his opinions on political questions through an apparatus, and all these opinions will be automatically recorded in the head office' (Schmitt 1928/1954, p. 245). What has been considered a complete nonsense to an advocate of public opinion to appear in the form of mass rallies, such as Schmitt, definitely materialized barely a decade later – in opinion polls.

With reference to what Bryce identified as the next and final stage of democracy, Gallup proudly announced, 'With the development of the science of measuring public opinion, it can be stated with but few qualifications, that this stage in our democracy is rapidly being reached' (Gallup 1938, p. 9). The founding father of polling seemed to be greatly inspired by Bryce, to whom he referred in most of his short articles on 'testing public opinion', to solve both conceptual and methodological problems related to 'public opinion'. Following Bryce, Gallup defended an ostensive definition of 'public opinion':

> Those of us who launched this effort to measure public opinion by sampling methods did not regard public opinion as a mysterious force which manifested itself in unknown ways. To us, as to James Bryce, public opinion was 'the aggregate of the views men hold regarding matters that affect or interest the community'.
>
> (Gallup 1957, p. 23)

While having reduced public opinion to 'the uniformities observed in opinions', Hyman believed that 'we stand close to a sound theory of opinion formation, and only because of the riches and variety of empirical research' (Hyman 1957, p. 59). Converse was convinced that 'the firm establishment of a public opinion polling industry [...] homogenized the definition [of public opinion] and stabilized it for foreseeable future' (Converse 1987, p. S13).

Gallup also referred to Bryce when arguing for specific methodological solutions. Thirty-five years after the first polling experiment, his institute presented a new procedure for 'measuring public opinion on issues of the day' – the 'public opinion referendum technique' – as a materialization of an old Bryce's idea:

> James Bryce regarded the referendum [...] as the logical resource, 'but it is troublesome and costly to take the votes of millions of people over an area so large as that of one of the greater states; much more, then, is this difficult to apply in federal matters'. The plan worked out here and tested in the 1970 election meets most of Bryce's objections as to cost and trouble. The way is open to the wide employment of this procedure to shed light on the public's views on local issues and to illuminate, for the benefit of the representatives of the people, the state of public opinion on the major issues confronting the nation.
>
> (Gallup 1971, p. 227)[3]

The main advantage of the new procedure was, according to Gallup, its *close resemblance of the election process*, which ought to make it also more easily understandable to citizens. The new procedure differed from the traditional surveys in that counties rather than individuals were used as sampling units, within which each household ought to be polled by self-administered ballots, rather than interviewers. Gallup (1971, p. 220) believed that 'this approach can reveal more dramatically the relationship between the way people live and the way they vote'. Another methodological issue, which should have convinced even the most enthusiastic doubters of polling, was its reliability and predictive validity: 'Time has permitted polling methods to be tested in the cruelest of all possible ways–by election returns. Not once, but 15 times in as many national elections, polls have come under the scrutiny of critics, many of them hopeful that forecasts would be on the wrong side' (Gallup 1965/1966, p. 544).

The issues of empirical verifiability and reliability of polling dominated scholarly debates on public opinion to such a degree that in the 1930s polling reached the position of the dominant public opinion paradigm, thus shoving aside the traditional normative conceptualizations of public opinion. 'The advent of so-called "scientific polls" during the 1930s has gone far toward solving the problem of ascertaining quickly, economically, and accurately the states and trends of public opinion on a large scale,' wrote Childs (1965, p. 45). Polls provided information about individuals' attitudes relevant for the political process and predictions of their voting behavior, but also commercially relevant information on the purchasing habits and power of consumers, and relationships between advertisements, consumer preferences and buying decisions, which became a key area in market research.

The invention of opinion polling influenced the development of theories of public opinion in the twentieth century in two directions. Opinion polls certainly play an important role in the political process, particularly in democratic societies. Modern, especially popular perceptions of public opinion are apparently closely associated with it Polling was often considered not only a research technique (a scientific instrument) to 'measure popular will' but also a political artifact – a new institution of (political) democracy. Before the advent of polling, social sciences made rather unsuccessful attempts at scientific operationalization of the normative concept of public opinion. With polling, however, it seemed that a satisfactory degree of empirical validity had been achieved, as its prophets and pollsters believed. The new empirical paradigm in the conceptualization of public opinion was strongly influenced by new methodological procedures: sampling, attitude measurement and scaling. However, while pollsters hailed polling as part of a solution for the growing democratic deficit, its opponents saw a serious threat to democracy in it.

One particular issue raised by polling was privatization and anonymization of public opinion. How can *public* opinion emerge out of individuals' 'opinion' *anonymously* expressed in the *private* sphere? Anonymous communication may occasionally relate with public reasoning, but it is unlikely that it would become the site of social criticism because it lacks 'the self-referential features that first emerged in the reading public and given normative and institutional structure in the inclusive citizenship of democratic publicity' (Bohman 1999, p. 195). In terms of Dewey's conceptualization of the public, anonymity fails to create access to public discussion of transactions that significantly affect members of a public. As Albig (1939, p. 171) argued, anonymity does not even change individuals' tendency to give a socially desirable or conventional answer, which may be more typically the case in 'public' expression of attitudes or in public actions.

'Polls create public opinion'

Polls conceptually replaced the public as the subject of public opinion (e.g. in Bentham's 'tribunal of public opinion', composed of politically reasoning individuals, or Tönnies' 'opinion of the public') with a dispersed mass or even any group composed of two or more individuals. Allport eliminated the public from the definition of public opinion as 'superfluous for the purpose of research' (Allport 1937, p. 9) and reduced public opinion to a multi-individual situation, as earlier suggested by Bryce (1888/1995). Individuals do not produce (public) opinion because opinions are only 'reactions of individuals'. According to Childs (1965, p. 13), 'Theoretically, the number of possible publics is the number of groups of two or more individuals that may be selected. The word "public" and the word "group" are for all practical purposes interchangeable.' Helmut Bauer (1965, p. 121) radicalized this understanding of public opinion by suggesting that 'if the concept of public opinion is meaningful at all', it should be conceived of as 'the sum of all relevant individual opinions, as a cut through the peoples' opinions. It is thus nothing but summing of equal or at least similar opinion expressions of citizens inquired by ballot or opinion polls.' Public opinion was thus reduced to an aggregate of individual opinions. In contrast to neo-classical paradigms, the new conceptualization of public opinion was liberated from any historical determination or normative assumption.

In that perspective, the emergence of the polling industry seems to be a major scientific achievement. It is suggested that the phenomenon of public opinion is created by social sciences: 'the term "public opinion" conjures up, as its necessary technical part, the public opinion poll' (Osborne & Rose 1999, p. 371). In their criticism of the critical theory (e.g. Habermas 1962/1995; Bourdieu 1972/1979), Osborne and Rose argue that 'public opinion is created by the procedures that are established to "discover" it. The phenomenon of opinion is an artifact of the technical procedures that are designed to capture it' (ibid., p. 382).

In opposition to Bourdieu, who argues that public opinion may (or does) exist elsewhere but it does not exist 'in the form which some people, whose existence depends on this illusion, would have us believe' (Bourdieu 1972/1979, p. 129), i.e. in polls, Osborne and Rose (1999, p. 387) claim that 'clearly *without* surveys and forms of measurement we would not know of public opinion at all; we would have no knowledge of what there is to measure without procedures of measurement'. They suggest that 'public opinion does not exist in so far as there are technologies – and respondents attuned to the technologies – to ensure that it does so' (ibid.). On the other hand, however, they claim that 'the existence of questionnaires and surveys themselves promote the idea that there is a public opinion "out there" to be had and measured' (ibid.). In other words, these procedures ought to suggest that public opinion exists 'out there' independently of the procedures. However, if a procedure is aimed at 'capturing' a phenomenon, it is implied that the phenomenon exists prior to and independently of measurement.

The suggestion that there could be no knowledge of public opinion without interview response data gathering is based on two invalid assumptions. Firstly, it implies that the presentation of interview response data *is* public opinion, but the description of an empirical procedure is at best its *operational definition*. Secondly, it suggests that there was no observable manifestation of public opinion at all (and thus public opinion was non-existent in empirical terms, or at least nobody was able to comprehend it) prior to the invention of polling, which is obviously historically incorrect. That would further imply that, for three strange centuries, public opinion theorists have acted as if public opinion existed, when in fact it did not exist; all 'public opinion organs', discussed since Bentham, ought to be mere illusions. Were all dissertations on public opinion before the advent of polling – discussing (1) 'In what form should political institutions recognize public opinion?' (2) 'What characteristics should public opinion possess?' and (3) 'What kind of political power should it be given?' (Althaus 2006, p. 98) – discussions on what empirically did not exist? Whereas Althaus argues that 'empirical research, from the early twentieth century to the present, eagerly ran with the second question but punted the others to philosophers' (ibid.), Osborne and Rose deny that philosophers can say anything about the first question and made the other two irrelevant: there is only one form in which public opinion exists (polls), and the question of its characteristics and power is purely empirical rather than normative.

Even Bryce, to whom Gallup frequently referred in order to vindicate his judgments, would disagree on that. In the discussion of the nature of public opinion, he discussed the USA of the late nineteenth century as an example of the inexpedient 'government by public opinion' in which, according to Bryce, 'the wishes and views of the people prevail, even before they have been conveyed through the regular law-appointed organs, and without the need of their being so conveyed'

(Bryce 1888/1995, p. 925). According to Bryce, public opinion was expressed through four main organs: (1) the press; (2) public meetings, primarily during election campaigns; (3) elections; and (4) citizen associations. The idea of 'organs' of public opinion goes back at least to Bentham, and was further elaborated by authors such as Tarde, Tönnies, and many others. They believed that although none of these diverse instruments or organs can provide a constant, instant and reliable estimation of public opinion, elites act as if such instruments existed: they 'look incessantly for manifestations of current popular opinion, and [...] shape their course in accordance with their reading of those manifestations' (Bryce 1888/1995, p. 920). 'Monitoring' of public opinion would later, particularly with V. O. Key's definition, become the critical point in conceptualization of public opinion.

We may consider polling a great (scientific) invention, but we should not leave out other public opinion 'technologies' invented earlier in history, and take the polls as 'the proper *discipline* necessary for public opinion to exist' (Osborne & Rose 1999, p. 382). The idea that 'the notion of opinion is the product of the particular procedure by which opinion is elicited' omits the fact that opining – as a specific form of 'holding for true' which differs from believing and knowing – exists independently of any external 'elicitation', and so are created personal opinions. People 'know how to create that phenomenon called opinion' and they validate their opinions in communication even if pollsters do not ask them questions. They have known it for thousands of years, and they invented other 'technologies to ensure that public opinion exists', most notably the newspaper.

In other words, it is not the measuring instrument that 'establishes the objective field called public opinion', but the process of communication (including asking and responding to questions in polling) in which individuals express and validate their opinions. Arguing that public opinion can only exist with the technology of polling also implies that public opinion is merely a sum of individual opinions expressed privately to pollsters.[4] Such a privatized conception of public opinion makes political relations, institutions, processes and outcomes of democratic systems irrelevant to public opinion; what counts is only the ways that individual citizens (pretend to) make sense of them. Yet such a conception is methodologically very convenient, which is probably the main reason that the privatized conception of public opinion became so popular among many researchers.

In a counter-factual way, Osborne and Rose are right about 'the procedure by which opinion is elicited'. Rather than 'eliciting opinions' from respondents, polls often do bring out 'non-opinions' or 'non-attitudes' (i.e. opinions that *appear* to be individual opinions because they were recorded by pollsters, although they did not exist prior to the polling procedure). According to Converse's empirically tested non-attitude thesis, people's opinions may be 'extremely labile for individuals over time' (Converse 1964, p. 241); 'large portions of an electorate do not have meaningful beliefs, even on issues that have formed the basis for intense political controversy among elites for substantial periods of time' (ibid., p. 245). Only for the non-attitudes, it is true that they are largely, if not exclusively, the product of a particular procedure – which inspired Bourdieu to conclude that 'public opinion' as elicited in polls does not exist in reality.

The concept of non-attitude suggests that people's opinions as identified in polls – in contrast to their true opinions – may change easily. To a large extent, changes emerge (1) randomly because non-attitudes are simply too vague and instantaneously formed, but also (2) as a consequence of measurement errors caused by vague wording, order of questions, interviewer bias, scaling error, context in which the questions are asked, and (3) because of the lack of individuals' awareness of how other people think and feel or false social knowledge of other people (Splichal 1999). The critique blames the tool of opinion polls rather than the public, and the experiments with 'deliberative polls' created by James Fishkin (1997) and his colleagues at the University of Texas provide strong empirical support to this criticism. Deliberative polls clearly suggest that when (additional) information is available to 'respondents' participating in an open discussion, they are likely to form a more consistent opinion often different from the one instantaneously formed as a reaction to the question asked by an interviewer.

Political institutionalization of polling

Deliberative polling experiments suggest that polling could be considered intrinsically similar and functionally equivalent to some other institutionalized political processes, such as elections and referenda. 'Participating in a survey, either as investigator, interviewer, or respondent, is no less natural than voting, meeting in a town hall, serving on a jury, or any other political practice' (Sanders 1999, p. 256). Public opinion *polls* were created in a similar way as political institutions. The technologies of general (or, indeed, any) political elections and referenda on important social issues differ from polling on party preferences and/or political attitudes in only two respects: (1) polling has no direct political/legal consequences, in contrast to elections and referenda, which have significant immediate consequences for the competing parties and candidates; and (2) polling is based on random sampling, in contrast to self-selection in elections. Yet both elections and polling are based on the same normative idea of representation: the results of parliamentary elections and the results of polling are assumed to represent fairly the general will of the constituency. As Gallup (1971) suggested, the main advantage of polling was exactly its similarity to the election process.

Elections define the composition of parliaments and other (political) institutions; results of legislative referenda have direct legislative effects (enacting or suppressing a law). In contrast, consequences of polls in society are indirect, mediated by political institutions or other institutions participating in the governance. In polls, preferences are *measured* in a random sample of the electorate (with corrections related to the expressed intention of respondents to vote or not to vote); random sampling 'demonstrates' their scientific character. In a genuine election, 'respondents' (i.e. voters) are self-selected (and thus less valid or even invalid in scientific terms because they are not necessarily representative of the entire population), their preferences are *decisive*, and this process is considered political participation.

Nevertheless, the idea that polls are epistemologically and ontologically comparable to elections and referenda rather than substantiating public opinion is hardly getting any support in the scholarly (and even less in professional) literature. Elections and referenda are commonly considered *parts of the political process* rather than a form of research whereas polls are considered a *form of 'research'* rather than a form of political institutionalization of public opinion. Yet should the division between commonly accepted forms of political process and a (declared) form of research be taken up as a matter of course? In a dissenting perspective, general (or, indeed, any) political elections and referenda on important (controversial) social issues may be conceived of as a kind of poll on party preferences and/or political attitudes with direct political/legal consequences.

The most obvious argument for the thesis that *polls are part of the political process* is the case of pre-election and exit polls. They measure exactly the same as elections (i.e. citizens' preferences for political parties and individual candidates for political positions) with exactly the same instrument (secret ballot), but with slightly different procedures and degrees of reliability and, for sure, different (but still always political) consequences.

In practice, the general utility of polls for political democracy and their efficacy in influencing behavior of politicians seem to be widely recognized despite a good many dissenting opinions, whereas much more skepticism is expressed regarding the genuineness of representation of public opinion by polls. This leaves us with a rather frustrating dilemma: The founding fathers of polling as a means of 'monitoring of the elusive pulse of democracy' (Moore) persistently grounded the efficacy of polls in 'accurate appraisal of public opinion' (Gallup). How can polls be 'good for democracy' if they do not 'represent the true public opinion'? Who actually affects politicians' decisions if polls are believed to misrepresent public opinion?

Conversely, these controversies indicate that opinion polls are a political rather than a scientific phenomenon, and they should be clearly distinguished from scientific methods of gathering interview response data and public opinion *research*. The fact that polls were invented as a *form of research* rather than a form of political institutionalization of public opinion, whereas elections and referenda were invented as *parts of the institutionalized political process* and clearly not as a kind of research, is quite irrelevant. Specific functions of polls are not their intrinsic characteristics but depend on, and are defined by, users and observers; they do not exist in a phenomenon as 'natural facts' irrespective of the human context, but are always relative to observer and context. In short, functions in the sense of the performance of a social phenomenon to attain an effect congruent with the defined goal are social constructs and thus culturally specific. It may well be that polls had been designed by Gallup and others with the goal to develop a research procedure to 'measure public opinion'. However, the embeddedness of polls in the political system results in specific *political* functions assigned to polls irrespective of their *scientific* functions (e.g. 'illuminating the state of public opinion for the benefit of the representatives of the people', according to Gallup). The conceptualizations of 'public opinion' as 'a tool of collective system control' (Allport 1940, p. 253) makes polls hardly compatible with any – let alone critical – scientific endeavor.

Notes

1. Binkley (1928, p. 389) reported: 'The main points of disagreement were as follows: 1. whether there is and must of necessity be a single public opinion, or whether there may be a number of public opinions upon a given question; 2. whether opinion is public because of the subject matter to which it relates or the kind of persons who hold it; 3. what part of the public must concur in

an opinion to make it public; 4. and must there be acquiescence by those who do not concur.'

2. The word *die Meinung* in the German term *die öffentliche Meinung* denotes both a process of opining as well as a single unit of opinion. In many other languages, including English (opinion), French (*l'opinion*), or Slovenian (*mnenje*), 'opinion' only denotes an entity or a state rather than the entire process of opining.

3. Bryce argued that the absence of a reliable means of ascertaining public opinion was less of a problem than the danger of suppression of minorities by the majority in all spheres of public life. He was the first to identify, in addition to the 'tyranny of the majority' discussed by Tocqueville, the phenomena of a passive 'silent majority' and the 'fatalism of the multitude', which make the idea of the decisive role of public opinion problematic.

4. Interview response data collected by pollsters are often limited to a very particular type of 'opinion'. As Allport (1940, p. 252) argued, 'public opinion' was popularly regarded 'not as something graded or measurable, like all scientific variables upon a continuum, but as an "all or none" affair. It is either for a thing or against it.' This dichotomous view of public opinion, as Allport believed, was responsible for most of the distortions of polling methods, which made polls hardly compatible with scientific research.

References

Albig, W. (1939) *Public Opinion* (New York: McGraw Hill).

Allport, F. H. (1937) 'Toward a Science of Public Opinion', *Public Opinion Quarterly*, 1(1), 7–23.

Allport, F. H. (1940) 'Polls and the Science of Public Opinion', *Public Opinion Quarterly*, 4(2), 249–257.

Althaus, S. L. (2006) 'False Starts, Dead Ends, and New Opportunities in Public Opinion Research', *Critical Review*, 18(1–3), 75–106.

Bauer, H. (1965) *Die Presse und die öffentliche Meinung* (München: Günter Olzog).

Bauer, W. (1914) *Die öffentliche Meinung und ihre geschichtlichen Grundlagen* (Tübingen: J. C. B. Mohr).

Beniger, J. R. (1992) 'The Impact of Polling on Public Opinion: Reconciling Foucault, Habermas, and Bourdieu', *International Journal of Public Opinion Research*, 4(3), 204–219.

Bentham, J. (1791/1994) 'Of Publicity', *Public Culture*, 6(3), 581595.

Bentham, J. (1822/1990) *Securities Against Misrule and Other Constitutional Writings for Tripoli and Greece* (Oxford: Clarendon Press).

Berelson, B. and M. Janowitz (eds) (1959) *Reader in Public Opinion and Mass Communication* (New York: Free Press).

Binkley, R. C. (1928) 'The Concept of Public Opinion in the Social Sciences', *Social Forces*, 6(3), 389–396.

Blumer, H. (1948) 'Public Opinion and Public Opinion Polling', *American Sociological Review*, 13(4), 542–554.

Bohman, J. (1999) 'Citizenship and Norms of Publicity: Wide Public Reason in Cosmopolitan Societies', *Political Theory*, 27(2), 176–222.

Bourdieu, P. (1972/1979) 'Public Opinion Does Not Exist', in A. Mattelart and S. Siegelaub (eds), *Communication and Class Struggle*, Vol. 1 (New York: International General), pp. 124–130.

Bryce, J. (1888/1995) *The American Commonwealth* (Indianapolis, IN: Liberty Fund).

Childs, H. L. (1965) *Public Opinion: Nature, Formation, and Role* (Princeton, NJ: D. van Nostrand).

Converse, P. E. (1964) 'The Nature of Belief Systems in Mass Publics', in D. E. Apter (ed.), *Ideology and Discontent* (New York: Free Press), pp. 206–261.

Converse, P. E. (1987) 'Changing Conceptions of Public Opinion in the Political Process', *Public Opinion Quarterly*, 51(4), 12–24.

Dewey, J. (1927/1991) *The Public and Its Problems* (Athens: Swallow).

Dicey, A. V. (1905/1981) *Lectures on the Relation Between Law and Public Opinion in England During the Nineteenth Century* (New Brunswick, NJ: Transaction Books).

Dryzek, J. S. (1990) *Discursive Democracy* (New York: Cambridge University Press).

Fishkin, J. S. (1997) *The Voice of the People: Public Opinion and Democracy* (New Haven, CT: Yale University Press).

Fraser, N. (2007) 'Transnationalizing the Public Sphere: On the Legitimacy and Efficacy of Public Opinion in a Post-Westphalian World', *Theory, Culture & Society*, 24(4), 7–30.

Gallup, G. (1938) 'Testing Public Opinion', *Public Opinion Quarterly*, 2(1), 8–14.

Gallup, G. (1957) 'The Changing Climate for Public Opinion Research', *Public Opinion Quarterly*, 21(1), 23–27.

Gallup, G. (1965/1966) 'Polls and the Political Process – Past, Present, and Future', *Public Opinion Quarterly*, 29(4), 544–549.

Gallup, G. (1971) 'The Public Opinion Referendum', *Public Opinion Quarterly*, 35(2), 220–227.

Ginsberg, B. (1989) 'How Polling Transforms Public Opinion', in M. Margolis and G. A. Mauser (eds), *Manipulating Public Opinion* (Pacific Grove, CA: Brooks/Cole), pp. 271–293.

Habermas, J. (1962/1995) *The Structural Transformation of the Public Sphere* (Cambridge, MA: MIT Press).

Harrisson, T. (1940) 'What is Public Opinion?', *Political Quarterly*, 11(4), 368–383.

Hegel, G. W. F. (1821/1971) *Philosophy of Right* (London: Oxford University Press).

Hobbes, T. (1668/1999) *Behemoth or the Long Parliament* (Chicago, IL: University of Chicago Press).

Hyman, H. H. (1957) 'Toward a Theory of Public Opinion', *Public Opinion Quarterly*, 21(1), 54–59.

Kant, I. (1784) *An Answer to the Question: What is Enlightenment?*, viewed 20 October 2010, http://www.totalb.com/~ mikeg/phil/kant/enlightenment.html#1.

Kant, I. (1795/1983) *To Perpetual Peace*, in I. Kant, *Perpetual Peace and Other Essays* (Cambridge: Hackett), pp. 107–144.

Key, V. O. Jr. (1961/1967) *Public Opinion and American Democracy* (New York: Knopf).

LeBon, G. (1895/2001) *The Crowd: A Study of Popular Mind* (Kitchener: Batoche Books).

Lippmann, W. (1922/1998) *Public Opinion* (New Brunswick, NJ: Transaction Publishers).

Lippmann, W. (1925) *The Phantom Public* (New York: Harcourt, Brace and Co).

Machiavelli, N. (1513/1992) *The Prince* (New York: W.W. Norton).

Mill, J. S. (1859/1985) *On Liberty* (London: Penguin).

Moore, D. W. (1995) *The Superpollsters* (New York: Four Walls Eight Windows).

Noelle-Neumann, E. (1984/1993) *The Spiral of Silence: Public Opinion – Our Social Skin* (Chicago, IL: University of Chicago Press).

Osborne, T. and N. Rose (1999) 'Do the Social Sciences Create Phenomena? The Example of Public Opinion Research', *British Journal of Sociology*, 50(3), 367–396.

Park, R. E. (1904/1972) *The Crowd and the Public*, H. Elsner Jr. (ed.) (Chicago, IL: University of Chicago Press).

Ross, E. A. (1901/1969) *Social Control: A Survey of the Foundations of Order* (Cleveland, OH: The Press of Case Western Reserve University).

Sanders, L. M. (1999) 'Democratic Politics and Survey Research', *Philosophy of the Social Sciences*, 29(2), 248–280.

Schmitt, C. (1928/1954) *Verfassungslehre* (Berlin: Duncker and Humblot).

Splichal, S. (1999) *Public Opinion: Developments and Controversies in the 20th Century* (Lanham, MD: Rowman & Littlefield).

Splichal, S. (2011) *Transnationalization of the Public Sphere and the Fate of the Public* (Cresskill, NJ: Hampton Press).

Tarde, G. (1901) *L'opinion et la foule* (Paris: Les Presses Universitaires de France).

Tarde, G. (1969) *On Communication and Social Influence*, T. N. Clark (ed.) (Chicago, IL: University of Chicago Press).

Tönnies, F. (1922) *Kritik der öffentlichen Meinung* (Berlin: Julius Springer).

Zaller, J. R. (1992) *The Nature and Origins of Mass Opinion* (Cambridge: Cambridge University Press).

3
Regulation of Opinion Polls: A Comparative Perspective

Thomas Petersen

Introduction

If we want to understand the complicated relationship between public opinion research and government authorities, we should start by considering the relationship between survey researchers and journalists. The state, the media and survey research all find themselves in a tense three-way relationship, where each is dependent on the others and each views the other two as a potential threat. The great German publisher Rudolf Augstein once referred to survey research as journalism's 'ravenous baby brother', in that it attempts to break the media's monopoly on interpreting the current social conditions, thereby devouring a piece of the media's right to tell the public how the world allegedly looks. 'We opinion journalists', he remarked, 'had gotten used to speaking for entire groups and segments of the population, even for our readership as a whole, and we were certainly prepared – albeit somewhat begrudgingly – to be contradicted every four years when the federal elections came around, but not every month or even every week' (Augstein 1973, XVIII; cf. Noelle-Neumann 1993a, p. 111). Nevertheless, the media use survey research continuously and with increasing intensity: in fact, the media need survey results as they offer information that their users expect but that cannot be obtained reliably from any other sources.

Conversely, complaints are rife among survey researchers about the misuse of their data by the media and the media's inability to understand or, respectively, their tendency to distort survey findings. A prime example here is the powerful, and in the meantime renowned, speech given by the American survey scholar Daniel Yankelovich on accepting the Helen Dinerman Award, which is the highest award for scientific achievements in the field of survey research. At the awards ceremony,

Yankelovich took the opportunity to decry the media's handling of surveys, stating:

> Sad to say, the media who sponsor opinion polls on policy issues have little or no stake in the quality of the poll findings they report [...] as the mass media have taken control over the polling profession, Gresham's law applies in full force. The quickie poll becomes the standard. Fewer resources are available for the kinds of searching studies conducted [in earlier years, T. P.], and when such studies are done, they are lumped together with all the others. The prevailing attitude is, 'a poll is a poll is a poll.' Poor quality drives out good quality.
>
> (Yankelovich 1996, pp. 3–4)

Thanks to this speech, the World Association for Public Opinion Research (WAPOR) was jolted into action, deciding to hold a special seminar every two years focusing on the question of how to define scientifically valid quality criteria for survey research – criteria that go beyond the superficial standards we are all familiar with – and how to communicate these quality criteria to the public and, especially, to journalists. Fourteen years later, when the seventh conference on this issue was held in 2008, the organizers were forced to admit that the situation had actually gotten worse since the time when Yankelovich gave his speech (Petersen 2008a). Nevertheless, survey researchers – even those who do not succumb to the rule described by Yankelovich – also need the media, for only the media can communicate their findings to the public.

By the same token, both the media and survey research have an especially problematic and in many respects similarly tense relationship with politicians and, by extension, with government authorities. In this case too, politicians simultaneously both need and fear journalists and survey researchers, which is why the authorities have repeatedly tried to gain control over journalists and survey researchers practically right from the beginning. The only difference is that journalists, with their exclusive access to the public and their avenues for influencing public opinion, ultimately wield much more power than survey researchers do. Whereas journalists have been able to use this power – in western democracies, at least – to resist state interference and, conversely, to force politicians to accept their rules in a broad range of areas (Kepplinger 1998; Patterson 1993), survey researchers have no comparable means of whipping up popular outrage and mobilizing the public on their behalf. Hence, they are subject to pressure from the state even in many countries that otherwise adhere to the ideals of freedom and democracy.

Four different strategies to exert pressure on survey research

Based on my observations, such pressure is generally exerted by means of four distinct strategies, each of which plays a more or less major role depending on the political circumstances in the country in question.

1. There are only a few known instances in which government authorities have tried to influence or even falsify survey results retroactively. This does not mean that such cases occur only rarely, but that they are, as a rule, very difficult to prove. Still, we can assume that attempts to directly manipulate survey findings are fairly rare. Although laypersons may commonly imagine that clients can just call up a polling institute and order the desired findings if they are willing to pay enough, this notion is in most cases misguided – even if one does occasionally hear rumors about such goings-on. One example here, reported by the Russian sociologist Vladimir Shlapentokh, is a whispered joke that was making rounds among Russian social scientists in the 1990s: An advisor comes to Boris Yeltsin and tells him he has good news and bad news. The bad news is that 60 per cent of the Russians intend to vote for Yeltsin's opponent, Gennadi Sjuganov. The good news is that 80 per cent intend to vote for Yeltsin.

Rather than direct manipulations, attempts to influence survey results are more commonly made during the stage of questionnaire design. Survey researchers often find that politicians display a great interest in question wordings. Often, this interest reflects what are essentially unconscious strategic motivations, rather than explicit intentions to manipulate the results: since they sense that question wordings can have a significant influence on survey findings, politicians understandably attempt to prevent the 'wrong' questions from being asked, in other words questions that would obtain results which would cast them in an unfavorable light.

Nevertheless, attempts to directly influence surveys are less of a problem in conjunction with political survey research than they are in some areas of market and media research, where clients commissioning surveys do occasionally put survey institutes under massive pressure to pose questions that are to their liking, occasionally even going as far as to blatantly demand that they include leading questions in their surveys. The attempts to influence individual studies cannot, however, be systematically organized, or at best only with very great effort. Some dictatorships, of course, do endeavor to do so. In China, for example, every questionnaire must be submitted to the State Security Bureau for approval before it can go into the field. The results also must be approved by the state before they can be passed on to the client (Spangenberg 2003, p. 13). In such cases, we are dealing with far-reaching before-and-after censorship, similar to the early forms of censorship of the press in the seventeenth and eighteenth centuries (Wilke 2009). Since no reliable information is available to the outside world on the concrete processes used to control survey research in such countries, we can only speculate on the extent to which the questionnaires and survey findings are changed. As a rule, we can, however, assume that these efforts are primarily aimed at preventing unwelcome information from being collected in the first place, rather than altering it once it has been obtained.

In most cases and most countries, the question of whether survey institutes give in to attempts to influence their surveys or whether they resist such efforts is ultimately a matter of moral resilience (and financial independence) and, consequently, a question of ethics and self-regulation by survey researchers themselves. Bernd-Jürgen Martini, a German journalist who specialized in the field, once remarked briefly and succinctly that he distinguishes between *insight-oriented* and *result-oriented* survey research (Noelle-Neumann 1993a, p. 112).

2.   In practice, efforts to directly influence individual studies are of far less importance than administrative measures that are employed in hopes of controlling – or at least channeling or even preventing – the publication of socio-political survey findings. This is widespread also in democratically governed countries. In many cases, the reason for such attempts is that people must be protected from the ostensibly harmful influence of survey results. Such measures range from officially obliging survey researchers to document certain survey data, or requiring them to use only 'recognized' survey methods, all the way up to prohibiting the publication of survey results, generally in a certain time span leading up to an election. The issues involved here are especially important, since they touch upon the fundamental issue of the social significance of survey research. Although there is generally a consensus in free countries that it is necessary to have a free press that acts as a watchdog over the government and its actions, it is not widely recognized that a free society also needs unfettered survey research that can correct

inaccurate representations of public opinion in the press. These issues will be discussed in greater detail in the following sections.

3. Another tactic that is also not uncommon is attempts by government authorities to hamper or obstruct survey research as a whole. In dictatorships, this can mean simply banning survey research, or at least surveys on certain subjects. In China, for example, researchers are not permitted to conduct surveys on overtly political topics (Spangenberg 2003, p. 13). Researchers have also been subjected to direct physical threats. For example, in 2003 two Iranian researchers were sentenced to jail for publishing polling results (EFAMRO/ESOMAR/WAPOR 2003). Yet there are also more subtle methods: When the author of this chapter asked a researcher from a Middle Eastern country to tell him whether the state ever attempted to obstruct political survey research in his country, he was unable to understand the question, replying that since there are no elections in his country there are no election surveys. The notion that there could also be other kinds of political surveys apparently did not occur to him – not even when he was expressly asked again. Obviously, even the thought of independent survey research bordered on being a kind of social or political taboo.

Government authorities have obstructed survey research ever since the early days of the field – and such attempts are not limited to authoritarian regimes (Institut für Demoskopie Allensbach 1955). Here it is also important to consider instances in which government authorities obstruct survey research without actually intending to do so. This is the case, for example, when it comes to the current efforts by the European Union and many of its member states to protect people from aggressive telemarketing. A legislation that would require that people give their written consent before they can be contacted by telephone would have potentially massive consequences for survey research, if the legislation does not explicitly distinguish between the fundamentally different nature of telemarketing and survey research. In Italy, for example, a law was passed a few years ago to combat the misuse of personal data obtained by telephone. This law would have made it impossible for researchers to conduct telephone surveys, an inadvertent side effect that was only prevented via follow-up negotiations between Italian legislators and survey researchers (Befani 2005).

4. Finally, there are cases in which government institutions, finding themselves unable to block survey research as a whole, try to gain complete administrative control over survey institutes. In some dictatorships, survey research has no alternative but to find a niche where

it can exist as a state-run organization. The research conducted by such institutions can certainly be quite valuable. One example here is the Polish CBOS institute, which was established in 1982 when Poland was still under communist rule. The institute survived the fall of the Iron Curtain and is now a scientifically oriented survey research institute that is highly respected around the world. The East German Zentralinstitut für Jugendforschung (Central Institute for Youth Research) in Leipzig also conducted a number of illuminating studies, within the framework of what the East German regime would allow. Although these studies were thematically quite limited and ideologically tinged, they still provide us with the only insights into the thoughts and feelings of the young generation in East Germany at the time (Friedrich & Hennig 1976). Of course, the work completed by organizations of this kind cannot be compared with that of free survey research organizations. One of the most important social functions of public opinion research is to document public opinion independently of any interpretations via third parties, a task that state-run institutes can fulfill only to a very limited extent.

Self-regulation by survey research organizations

For readers with knowledge of politics, it will seem obvious that authoritarian rulers view unfettered survey research as a potential threat to their hold on power and thus do whatever they can to combat it. The fact that many democratic governments also have qualms about survey research – and occasionally even view such research as a threat to democracy – is not so readily apparent and needs some explaining.

The main line of reasoning used by many governments attempting to impede survey research, and particularly election polling, is that publishing polling data on the strength of the candidates or the political parties during the course of an election campaign allegedly influences the citizens' voting behavior. This accusation has been levied ever since the early days of survey research and has repeatedly given rise to heated debates and intensive investigations over the past decades. In this respect, there is a remarkably large array of assumptions as to how publishing polling results ostensibly influences voting behavior.

The most widespread theory is that of bandwagon effects, which posits that the party leading in the polls profits from the publication of the results, since this draws undecided voters over to their side (Donsbach 1984, p. 393; 2001; Hardmeier 2008). Scholars have also argued, however, for the exact opposite effect, that is, the so-called underdog effect (Faas & Schmitt-Beck 2007, p. 262), along with other possible effects, for example, on the behavior of strategic voters (Cain 1978; Reumann 1983).

This chapter does not intend to discuss these theories in depth (see Chapter 11). For the moment, suffice it to say that it is widely assumed that publishing election survey results has a strong impact on voting behavior. For example, in a survey conducted by communication scholar Frank Brettschneider among German journalists in 2002, 83 per cent of the journalists interviewed said they believed that publishing survey data does have such an effect (Brettschneider 2005). This is the case, even though most studies on this issue have detected either weak effects or no effects at all (Donsbach 1984, pp. 394–395; Hardmeier 2008, p. 506). And when all significant results are taken together, they may even cancel each other out (Lang & Lang 1984; Lavrakas 1991) or only apply under specific circumstances (Jandura & Petersen 2009). Today, it is therefore fair to say that the notion that publishing survey findings generally has an influence on voter behavior has been largely refuted (Donsbach 1984, p. 296; Petersen 2008b, p. 1488).

Apart from the assumption that opinion polls have a concrete impact on individual voting behavior, survey research is also occasionally accused of undermining the entire democratic system in the long run, since it ostensibly removes the opinion formation process from the elected authorities' sphere of influence, thus ultimately relieving them of their decision-making responsibility and, for example, making referendums and elections superfluous (see, e.g., Pomper 1977; Sontheimer 1964). There are, however, no empirical findings to support such contentions.

Even in the early days of modern survey research, the newly established survey organizations began addressing the concerns voiced by large swaths of the political and social elites regarding the presumed impact of survey research on politics. One of the means used in attempting to allay these fears was far-reaching voluntary commitments to adhere to various professional codes and standards. In addition, in response to the regularly raised demands that the research process be as transparent as possible, researchers pledged to publish various technical details relating to the polls – commitments which were often not fulfilled in practice and which were also unrealistic at times (Petersen 2008a).

There are also cases in which survey institutes gave in to the public's demands and abstained from publishing survey results in the final weeks before Election Day, even if not forced to do so by law. For example, in the West German parliamentary elections of 1965, Germany's two leading survey institutes – the EMNID Institute in Bielefeld and the Allensbach Institute – entrusted the findings of their last election surveys prior to the election to a notary public, who did not open the envelopes until after the polling stations had closed. In response to accusations that it was trying to manipulate the election, the Allensbach Institute had ceased reporting its findings a month before Election Day – only to find itself faced with this very same accusation on Election Night, since the strength of the parties had changed substantially in the month that had passed. Now, the Allensbach Institute was accused of having tried to manipulate the election by withholding its findings (Noelle-Neumann 1993b, pp. 13–16). As a result, most institutes quickly abandoned this practice.

The most important tools for self-regulation are the detailed 'codes of ethics' and lists of 'best practices' which have been compiled by numerous associations and organizations in the field of survey research. The members of these organizations – be they institutes that belong to national associations, as is often the case, or individual researchers who belong to the most important international organizations – pledge to abide by these rules and standards. The three most important codes of this kind, which were compiled by the three most important and oldest international survey research associations, are the *Code on Market and Social Research* by the European Society for Opinion and Marketing Research (ESOMAR) (ICC/ESOMAR 2008), the *Standard Definitions* of the American Association for Public Opinion Research (AAPOR) (AAPOR 2009) and the *WAPOR Code of Professional Ethics and Practices* by the World Association for Public Opinion Research (WAPOR 2010a). All of these documents are continuously updated. They are supplemented by a number of guidelines developed for specific types of surveys, for example, guidelines for customer satisfaction studies (ESOMAR 2003), surveys of children and young people (ESOMAR 1999) or exit polls (WAPOR 2010b). In contrast, certifying institutes according to the ISO 9000 standard is of lesser importance. Repeated attempts over the past decades to establish this standard for survey research have been unsuccessful. Ultimately, attempts to gauge survey institutes according to such industrial standards or even to impose standardized norms throughout the field will have to be recognized as a misapprehension of the research process.

One problem with voluntary commitments or pledges is that they are generally the result of complicated discussions within the survey research associations, whose members are, of course, keen to ensure that the methods which they themselves prefer are not called into question by the association's rules and standards. The corresponding codes are, therefore, inevitably compromises that are often worded in a very generalized way. Even more problematic, however, is the fact that it is practically impossible to verify whether the rules are actually adhered to. In most countries, survey institutes have not established any kind of enforcement body that could impose sanctions on polling organizations that fail to adhere to the rules. One exception here is the German 'Rat der deutschen Markt- und Sozialforschung', a supervisory body modeled along the lines of the various self-enforcement institutions in the field of journalism. The organization's by-laws state:

> Any person is entitled to approach the board of arbitration if he feels his rights as a respondent, client, or competitor are being infringed upon by an action of a market or social researcher, a market or social research agency, or a corporate division or other institution working in the field of market and social research in that this action violates the principles and rules of professional conduct for German market and social research.
>
> (Niedermann 2008; Rat der deutschen Markt- und Sozialforschung e.V. 2006)

Yet similar to the bodies responsible for enforcing journalistic standards, the Rat der deutschen Markt- und Sozialforschung exerts only limited direct influence, since the censures it issues obtain only minimal public attention.

Another problem in this context is the fact that the documents issued by the various survey research associations for purposes of self-regulation need to be continuously examined and updated, which presents an ideal opportunity for various parties to attempt to influence the revisions in line with their own interests. For example, when the ESOMAR Code was being revised in 2007, serious efforts were made to weaken the rule stipulating that survey researchers strictly protect respondents' anonymity. Had this attempt been successful, the new rule would have offered respondents hardly any protection at all. The reason for this attempt, apparently, was that some parties were hoping to use the personal data obtained from respondents for more lucrative purposes than just research. Via a concerted effort by other survey organizations, particularly scientifically oriented associations of survey researchers, the rule change was ultimately prevented (Petersen 2007).

Despite all of these problems, the various codes governing self-regulation in the field of survey research are by no means insignificant.

They represent a minimum quality standard that is taken as a point of orientation not only by survey research organizations themselves but also by external entities and clients, thus putting those institutes that do not follow the rules under pressure to justify themselves.

At the same time, it should be noted that all of these codes concentrate on technical and practical aspects of survey research, along with basic ethical issues, yet not on the fundamental political issue of the role of survey research in society, as described above. Of course, this issue ultimately cannot be clarified in the context of self-regulation, but only within the framework of the political debate.

The regulation of survey research around the world

In 2003, Frits Spangenberg, a survey researcher from the Netherlands, conducted an extensive survey among survey researchers around the world in order to determine which countries were attempting to impede survey research via administrative measures, with a special focus on the obstruction of election research (Spangenberg 2003). The study followed up on a similarly designed investigation completed by WAPOR in 1996. For this article, the author has updated Spangenberg's findings for some countries. The findings definitely corroborate Spangenberg's results from 2003. Since we can assume that his findings still largely apply today, they serve as the basis for the following discussion.

Spangenberg's survey was completed in 68 different countries on all continents around the globe. One country (Qatar) was added during the update in 2010. Almost half of these countries impose restrictions on the publication of election surveys prior to elections – including substantial restrictions of seven days or more in one out of two cases (Table 3.1 and Figure 3.1).

When it comes to the question of which regions of the world have an especially great share of countries that impose considerable restrictions on survey research, we find that Europe and North America take the lead. One out of three countries in these regions have legal regulations that seriously restrict the freedom of survey research – and primarily of election research. In Asia, the same applies to only 20 per cent of the countries involved in the study and to only one out of six countries in Latin America and Africa (Figure 3.2).

This result is surprising at first glance, since it would seem to suggest that the greatest obstacles to survey research are posed in precisely those parts of the world in which practically all countries are free democracies.

Table 3.1 Legal restrictions on the publication of pre-election polls in 69 countries

Countries with substantial restrictions (seven days embargo or more and/or other restrictions)	Countries with minor restrictions (embargo of six days or less, no other restrictions)	Countries with no legal restrictions on the publication of pre-election polls
Europe		
Bulgaria	Croatia*	Austria*
Czech Republic*	Macedonia	Belgium
Cyprus	Poland	Bosnia and Herzegovina
France	Portugal	Denmark
Greece*	Romania	Estonia
Italy*	Spain*	Finland
Luxembourg		Germany*
Slovakia		Iceland
Slovenia		Ireland
Switzerland		Kazakhstan
Turkey		Latvia
Ukraine*,†		Netherlands
		Norway
		Russian Federation
		Sweden
		UK
North America	Canada	USA
Latin America		
Mexico*	Argentina	Brazil
Peru*	Bolivia	Honduras
	Colombia	Puerto Rico
	Costa Rica	
	Panama	
	Uruguay*,‡	
	Venezuela	
Asia/Pacific		
China	Nepal	Australia
Rep. of Korea		Bangladesh
Singapore		India
		Indonesia
		Japan*
		Malaysia
		New Zealand*
		Pakistan
		Philippines*
		Taiwan
		Thailand
Africa/Middle East		
Egypt	Israel	Nigeria
		Qatar
		South Africa
		United Arab Emirates

Notes: * Update 2010. All other data: Spangenberg 2003.
† Change for the worse since 2003.
‡ Improvement since 2003.

58

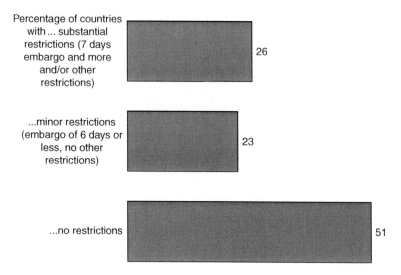

Figure 3.1 Restrictions on the publication of pre-election polls
Source: Spangenberg 2003, updated by the author.

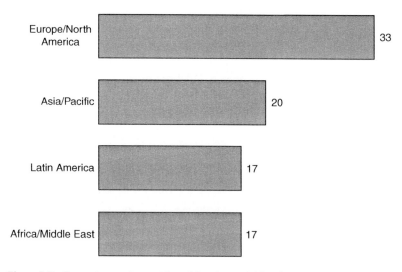

Figure 3.2 Percentages of countries with substantial legal restrictions in different regions
Source: Spangenberg 2003, updated by the author.

This finding must, however, be viewed in light of the fact that the study was not completed in all countries around the world, but rather only in those countries in which survey research is a well-developed field and in which survey researchers felt free enough to report on their activities and methods, and thus also on any restrictions they may face. In other words, the study was completed almost exclusively in democracies or in countries with less rigid authoritarian regimes. There were only a few cases in which it was possible to obtain reliable responses from dictatorships. This fact greatly relativizes the ostensibly low shares of countries in Africa and Asia in which the state interferes with survey research. If the study findings had included the numerous dictatorships in these regions, the share of countries that impose restrictions in these parts of the world would invariably be a great deal higher.

Nevertheless, it is still remarkable that efforts by government authorities to obstruct survey research are commonplace also in the western world. In precisely that region of the world that views itself as the guardian of democracy, one out of three countries place restrictions on research or, respectively, the publication of research findings – thus also curtailing the freedom of the press in this area. This clearly suggests that the notion that there is a need for free and independent survey research is hardly firmly rooted in western societies.

It is also quite telling that in most cases, restricting the freedom of survey research is justified as a way of protecting the democratic process. The classic argument used by authoritarian regimes – that is, banning survey research in the interest of protecting national security – is found in only a few cases (Figure 3.3). In other words, curtailing the basic democratic rights of freedom of research, freedom of the press and freedom of information is intended to protect democracy. A line of reasoning of this kind could probably not be upheld in any other field (although we should perhaps make an exception here for extraordinary political situations in which extremists abuse these basic democratic principles in making their grab for power). We must assume that the parties defending the restrictions imposed on survey research are generally unaware of how contradictory their reasoning is. There are also no signs that any new thought is being given to the issue in any significant number of countries. Compared with 1996, the share of countries that ban the publication of election survey results prior to elections increased from 39 to 46 per cent.

A special role in this context is played by exit polls, in other words, post-election surveys in which survey organizations interview people about their voting decision just as they are leaving the polling stations.

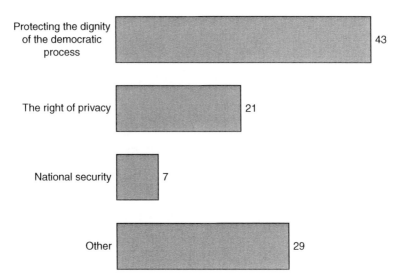

Figure 3.3 Reasons for legal restrictions
Source: Spangenberg 2003.

Exit polls are extremely precise, since they do not have to contend with many of the factors that can interfere with the precision of forecasts based on pre-election surveys; that is, only actual voters are interviewed, there is no need to assign undecided voters to the various parties or candidates running for election, and there is no chance that some surprising events will occur that abruptly change the political situation and thus the citizens' voting behavior after the survey has already been completed.

In many countries, exit polls are therefore perceived as especially credible. In cases where exit poll results deviate from the actual election outcome, this is sometimes taken as a sign that an election has been tampered with. For example, in Venezuela in 2004, a referendum was held to decide whether President Hugo Chavez should be removed from office (Barone 2004). Although exit polls indicated that Chavez had been clearly defeated, he nevertheless won the vote by 58–42 per cent according to the official vote count. Subsequently, the Carter Center, which had monitored the election, commissioned AAPOR and WAPOR to examine the exit poll methods employed. At first glance, the data would seem to indicate that the discrepancy was due to methodological flaws in the exit polls, rather than election fraud (Rosnick 2004). Nevertheless, the AAPOR and WAPOR representatives investigating the

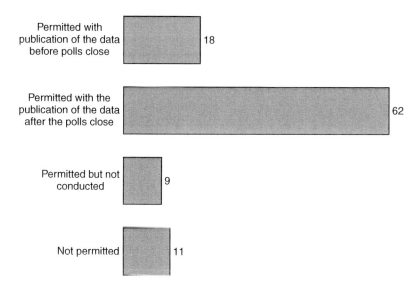

Figure 3.4 Legal restrictions on the publication of exit polls
Source: Spangenberg 2003.

discrepancy were so strongly impeded that they were ultimately unable to complete their examination of the polls' methodology. Until today, the question of whether the exit polls or the vote count were skewed remains unresolved.

The special authority that is often ascribed to exit polls is probably the reason why they are often viewed with particularly great distrust – and not just in countries with authoritarian governments. Thus, only 27 per cent of the countries included in Spangenberg's study permit the unrestricted publication of exit polls. True, most countries do allow researchers to conduct these kinds of surveys, yet the results generally may not be published until after the polling stations have closed (Figure 3.4), even though numerous studies have shown that publishing partial election results before the polling stations have closed has little or no influence on voting behavior (Fuchs 1966; Hartenstein 1967; Jandura & Donsbach 2007; Mendelsohn & Crespi 1970).

Defending the freedom of research

The question of how the international community of social scientists should counter the tendencies to regulate survey research is the subject of heated debate among survey experts. One approach often advocated would be to impart as much knowledge about the survey method as possible to government institutions and authorities, so that they are in a better position to assess the methods used. Here, special emphasis is placed on more formal quality criteria in survey research (i.e. sample size, margins of error, etc.).

Yet there are reasons to doubt whether such an approach would be of any use. In fact, it could also be counterproductive: imparting methodological knowledge to government institutions does not necessarily lessen the authorities' fear of the ostensible power of surveys and, conversely, may actually even lead to the passage of even more elaborate restrictions on survey research than would have been implemented otherwise. A law passed in Greece in August 2007, which, among other things, contains the following provisions, illustrates this:

- The samples drawn for election surveys may only be based on methods and basic data that have been officially approved by the Greek Office of Statistics.
- Samples must comprise more than 1000 respondents.
- Subgroups that comprise fewer than 100 respondents may not be interpreted in terms of contents.
- It is not permitted to analyze subgroups that include fewer than 60 respondents.
- The findings of different surveys may not be compared unless the differences between the surveys – for example, the methods used – are also pointed out simultaneously.
- The survey results may not be passed on to third parties before they have been published in the media.
- No election poll results may be published in the final 15 days before an election.

Along with these conditions, the law also contains a number of regulations that ultimately amount to strict state surveillance of survey research and reporting on survey research findings in Greece (Law No. 3603).

What is interesting here are not so much the political intentions that might be behind the law, but rather how the concrete regulations are crafted. In their present form, they are only comprehensible if we assume that they are the result of the kind of superficial knowledge that is created when the public are given to believe that adhering to certain technical and formal criteria is the most important quality criterion in survey research. For example, survey researchers generally agree that election polls can only provide reliable information if the survey samples are drawn based on certain methodological principles; that is, random or quota samples that are based on reliable data, which usually means official statistics. Obviously, the authors of the Greek law have heard of the need for representative samples and the approach they describe is certainly correct in principle. However, the attempt to limit researchers to one certain methodological approach essentially squelches all creativity and thus also precludes any innovations in the field. If there had been a law like this in the USA in the 1930s, George Gallup would never have had his breakthrough, since the 'recognized' method at the time was that used by the *Literary Digest*, which is now viewed as unsuitable.

Likewise, it is also undisputed that election surveys ideally should be based on a sample of 1000 respondents or more, since this, as a rule, is the only way to arrive at a reliable election forecast, especially when it comes to elections in European countries with multiparty systems and proportional representation. We can also assume that the authors of the Greek law have heard of the connection between sample sizes and margins of error. Yet they obviously have no understanding of the various investigative aims that can be fulfilled via election surveys. Even surveys with only a few hundred respondents can provide important insights for election analyses. Ultimately, the sample size tells us nothing about the fundamental quality of a survey. The upshot of a law of this kind is that larger, well-financed institutes are able to fulfill the requirements quite easily – even if their performance is methodologically weak in other respects – whereas potentially innovative studies conducted by smaller institutes operating on smaller budgets – for example, in an academic environment – will fall through the cracks when such a law is in effect. The most revolutionary and renowned election study until today – Paul Lazarsfeld and colleagues' investigation of the 1940 US presidential election (1944) – would have been prohibited under the Greek law.

One particularly remarkable aspect here is the Greek lawmakers' attempt to dictate which analytical steps researchers may or may not complete. The authors of the law appear to realize that it generally makes no sense to interpret the findings obtained for subgroups that comprise fewer than 100 respondents, and that it is almost irresponsible to draw conclusions based on fewer than 60 respondents. What the lawmakers do not understand, however, is when these rules apply and when they do not. Enforcing such a rule would, for example, in many cases make it impossible to analyze people's reasons for voting for small, extremist parties. The same applies to a large share of studies focusing on swing voters.

As this example shows, simply educating the public and lawmakers about the possibilities and methodological limitations of survey research is hardly enough to stem attempts to place survey research under state control and supervision. Ultimately, this is not a methodological issue but a political one, which essentially boils down to the question of whether the freedom of research is respected in a particular country or not. Thus, there is probably no way of getting around the fundamental political debate on the role of survey research in society, as discussed above.

In this connection, exerting international pressure and encouraging survey researchers to offer assistance to other researchers beyond their own national borders can also play an important role. On a few occasions over the past years, the international scientific community has successfully blocked plans by national governments to restrict the freedom of survey research. For example, it was based on information provided by WAPOR and other organizations that the Supreme Court of the Philippines declared on 5 May 2001 that the bans on publishing election polls prior to elections that had been in effect until that time were unconstitutional (Mangahas 2001). In contrast, attempts to convince the Greek government to revise the law mentioned above were less successful. Letters sent to the government by the international scientific community only persuaded officials to postpone enacting the law. A similar case is currently hanging in the balance in Peru.

In the long run, survey researchers will probably become more adept at resisting attempts to impose government regulations on their work. Ever since the early years of survey research, the field has been characterized by strong international links among researchers, and these links have grown even stronger over the past few decades. At the same time, modern communication technologies make it easier to circumvent bans on publishing results. In 2002, for example, when government authorities prohibited the French branch of the British MORI institute from publishing the results of its surveys on the upcoming French presidential election, the mother organization in London responded by promptly posting the results online – written in French and, of course, accessible throughout all of France.

Conclusion

The conflict between survey research institutes and government officials will remain as long as there is no common understanding about the political function of public opinion research in democratic societies.

One remarkable aspect in this context is that in the debate on how publishing election polls allegedly affects the citizens' voting behavior, it is always assumed that this effect is illegitimate and necessarily harmful to the democratic process. The mere assumption that there is an effect is offered as sufficient reason to justify banning the publication of survey results. Yet this line of reasoning calls for closer scrutiny. After all, going by the same line of reasoning, it would also be necessary – if we want to be consistent – to ban the publication of newspapers and magazines prior to an election. In fact, following the same logic, banning the publication of newspapers and magazines prior to an election would be even more justified than banning election surveys, since there are – in contrast to investigations focusing on election polls – a variety of empirical findings that clearly point to the effect of press reports on voting behavior. Nevertheless, no one would think of making such a demand – at least not in the western world – since it is generally recognized that citizens have the right to inform themselves about the political situation via a free press.

Obviously, the debate on the role of survey research in the political process has a basic legal dimension that ties in with the fundamental principles underlying the concept of the democratic state. In Germany, for example, commensurate calls for the restriction of election polling consistently fail to get off the ground, since they run contrary to the right to freedom of information that is anchored in the German constitution. In the public debate on the issue, however, it is seldom recognized that this right also applies to survey findings.

Moreover, from the perspective of democratic theory, calls for prohibiting the publication of election polling results also appear dubious. In western societies, it is generally assumed that people's political opinions and voting decisions should ideally be based solely on factual information and a rational decision-making process. Even if empirical research has repeatedly shown that the ideal of the 'rational voter' is generally not in keeping with reality (Kepplinger & Maurer 2005), the ideal as such is not contested. Of course, it is precisely for such rational voters that information on the expected strength of the candidates or parties running for office is important, for example, when they are considering casting their vote strategically in order to support a certain coalition of parties.

Hence, it is inconsistent to demand, on the one hand, that voters make their decision as rationally as possible, based on factual information, but then, on the other hand, to forbid the publication of such factual information.

Survey findings are the only source of information on this issue that is obtained by scientific means, and thus they are by far the most reliable information of this kind (even if they may be misleading in rare cases). Banning election surveys means leaving the field wide upon for non-verifiable, biased statements based on personal impressions, political calculation or hearsay – and, at the same time, making it impossible to refute such statements if need be.

It is at this point that survey research's important watchdog function becomes apparent: survey research can be used to keep an eye on the media and to verify journalistic claims, and as such is an important part of the democratic process. In most countries, however, this watchdog function is not yet a recognized aspect of the public debate on the issue of election research.

References

AAPOR (ed.) (2009) *Standard Definitions. Final Dispositions of Case Codes and Outcome Rates for Surveys* (No place of publication: AAPOR).

Augstein, R. (1973) 'Demoskopie und Politik', in E. Noelle and E. P. Neumann (eds), *Jahrbuch der öffentlichen Meinung 1968–1973* (Allensbach/Bonn: Verlag für Demoskopie), pp. xv–xxii.

Barone, M. (2004, October 8) 'Exit Polls in Venezuela', *U.S. News.* http://www.usnews.com/usnews/opinion/baroneweb/mb_040820.htm

Befani, S. (2005) 'Italy: Are Telephone Surveys Endangered?', *WAPOR Newsletter* (2), 3.

Brettschneider, F. (2005, September 8) 'Wahlumfragen. Was Journalisten über sie denken und wie sie auf die Wähler wirken', *Informationsdienst Wissenschaft.* Press release.

Cain, B. E. (1978) 'Strategic Voting in Britain', *American Journal of Political Science*, 22, 639–655.

Donsbach, W. (1984) 'Die Rolle der Demoskopie in der Wahlkampf-Kommunikation. Empirische und normative Aspekte der Hypothese über den Einfluß der Meinungsforschung auf die Wählermeinung', *Zeitschrift für Politik*, 31, 388–407.

Donsbach, W. (2001) *Who's Afraid of Election Polls? Normative and Empirical Arguments for the Freedom of Pre-Election Surveys* (Amsterdam: ESOMAR).

EFAMRO, ESOMAR, WAPOR (eds) (2003) 'Support for Releasing Iranian Pollsters', *WAPOR Newsletter* (1), 2.

ESOMAR (ed.) (1999) *Interviewing Children and Young People* (Amsterdam: ESOMAR).

ESOMAR (ed.) (2003) *Customer Satisfaction Studies* (Amsterdam: ESOMAR).

Faas, T. and R. Schmitt-Beck (2007) 'Wahrnehmung und Wirkung politischer Meinungsumfragen. Eine Exploration zur Bundestagswahl 2005', in F. Brettschneider, O. Niedermayer and B. Wessels (eds), *Die Bundestagswahl 2005. Analysen des Wahlkampfes und der Wahlergebnisse* (Wiesbaden: Verlag für Sozialwissenschaften), pp. 233–267.

Friedrich, W. and W. Hennig (eds) (1976) *Jugendforschung – Methodologische Grundlagen, Methoden und Techniken* (Ost-Berlin: VEB Deutscher Verlag der Wissenschaften).

Fuchs, D. A. (1966) 'Election-Day Radio-Television and Western Voting', *Public Opinion Quarterly*, 30, 226–236.

Hardmeier, S. (2008) 'The Effect of Published Polls on Citizens', in W. Donsbach and M. W. Traugott (eds), *The Sage Handbook of Public Opinion Research* (Thousand Oaks, CA: Sage), pp. 504–513.

Hartenstein, W. (1967) 'Mit Prognosen leben: Der Einfluß von Wahlvoraussagen auf das Wählerverhalten', in C. Böhret and D. Grosser (eds), *Interdependenzen von Politik und Wirtschaft. Festschrift für Gert von Eynern* (Berlin: Westdeutscher Verlag), pp. 285–306.

ICC/ESOMAR (ed.) (2008) *ICC/ESOMAR International Code on Market and Social Research* (Amsterdam: ESOMAR).

Institut für Demoskopie Allensbach (ed.) (1955) 'Die Stimmung im Saargebiet. Ergebnisse einer Bevölkerungsumfrage', *Allensbach Archives*, IfD Report No. 416.

Jandura, O. and W. Donsbach (2007) 'I Know What You Did Last Summer. How the Knowledge of Possible Election Outcomes Determines Voting Decisions', paper presented at the WAPOR Regional Seminar, 'Public Opinion, Communication and Elections', Jerusalem and Haifa, June 26–29.

Jandura, O. and T. Petersen (2009) 'Gibt es eine indirekte Wirkung von Wahlumfragen? Eine Untersuchung über den Zusammenhang zwischen der auf Umfragen gestützten und sonstigen politischen Berichterstattung im Bundestagswahlkampf 2002', *Publizistik*, 54, 485–497.

Kepplinger, H. M. (1998) *Die Demontage der Politik in der Informationsgesellschaft* (Freiburg: Verlag Karl Alber).

Kepplinger, H. M. and M. Maurer (2005) *Abschied vom rationalen Wähler. Warum Wahlen im Fernsehen entschieden werden* (Freiburg: Alber).

Lang, K. and G. E. Lang (1984) 'The Impact of Polls on Public Opinion', *The Annals of the American Academy of Political and Social Science*, 472(1), 129–142.

Lavrakas, P. J. and J. K. Holley (eds) (1991) *Polling and Presidential Election Coverage* (Newbury Park, CA: Sage).

Law No 3603 Regulation of Gallup Issues (2007) *Government Gazette of the Hellenic Republic*, Sheet No. 188. August 8, 2007.

Lazarsfeld, P. F., B. Berelson and H. Gaudet (1944) *The People's Choice: How the Voter Makes Up His Mind in a Presidential Campaign* (New York: Columbia University Press).

Mangahas, M. (2001) 'Address to the WAPOR 2001 Conference, September 21, 2001: Victory for Survey Freedom in the Philippines', *Social Weather Stations Media Release*, September 24.

Mendelsohn, H. and I. Crespi (1970) *Polls, Television and the New Politics* (Scranton, PA: Chandler).

Niedermann, A. (2008) 'Enforcing Quality Standards and Rules of Professional Conduct of German Market and Social Research by a Board of Arbitration: "Rat der deutschen Markt- und Sozialforschung e.V.", paper presented at the WAPOR Thematical Seminar, 'Quality Criteria in Survey Research VII.' Cadenabbia, Italy. July 10–12.

Noelle-Neumann, E. (1993a) 'Brüderchen verbrennt man nicht', *Spiegel Spezial*, 6, 111–113.

Noelle-Neumann, E. (1993b) *The Spiral of Silence: Public Opinion – Our Social Skin* (Chicago, IL: University of Chicago Press).

Patterson, T. E. (1993) *Out of Order* (New York: Alfred A. Knopf).

Petersen, T. (2007) 'National Representative Report: Germany', *WAPOR Newsletter* (1), 5–6.

Petersen, T. (2008a) 'Why Our Efforts to Establish Quality Criteria May Be Leading Us in the Wrong Direction', paper presented at the WAPOR Thematical Seminar, "Quality Criteria in Survey Research VII", Cadenabbia, Italy, July 10–12, 2008.

Petersen, T. (2008b) 'Election Polls and Forecasts', in W. Donsbach (ed.), *The International Encyclopedia of Communication*, vol. 4 (Malden, MA: Blackwell), pp. 1487–1489.

Pomper, G. M. (1977) 'The Decline of the Party in American Elections', *Political Science Quarterly*, 92, 21–42.

Rat der deutschen Markt- und Sozialforschung e.V. (ed.) (2006) *Beschwerdeordnung*. Frankfurt. http://rat-marktforschung.de/beschwerdeordnung, retrieved October 18, 2010.

Reumann, K. (1983, March 9) 'Gibt es einen Fallbeil-Effekt für die kleinen Parteien?', *Frankfurter Allgemeine Zeitung*, p. 4.

Rosnick, D. (2004, August 19) 'Polling and the Ballot: The Venezuelan Referendum', *cepr Issue Brief*.

Sontheimer, K. (1964) 'Meinungsforschung und Politik. Eine kritische Auseinandersetzung mit den Ansprüchen der "Demoskopie" ', *Der Monat*, (187), 41–46.

Spangenberg, F. (2003) *The Freedom to Publish Opinion Poll Results. Report on a Worldwide Update* (Amsterdam: Foundation for Information).

WAPOR (ed.) (2010a) *WAPOR Code of Professional Ethics and Practices*, http://wapor.unl.edu/ethics, retrieved October 18, 2010.

WAPOR (ed.) (2010b) *Guideline for Exit Polls*, http://wapor.unl.edu/exit-poll-guidelines, retrieved October 18, 2010.

Wilke, J. (2009) 'Pressegeschichte', in E. Noelle-Neumann, W. Schulz and J. Wilke (eds), *Fischer Lexikon Publizistik Massenkommunikation* (Frankfurt: Fischer), pp. 501–535.

Yankelovich, D. (1996) 'A New Direction for Survey Research', *International Journal of Public Opinion Research*, 8, 1–9.

4
Methodological Trends and Controversies in the Media's Use of Opinion Polls

Michael Traugott

Polls have been an integral part of news coverage for more than 200 years, although scientific polls have been in use for only the last eight decades. Pollsters and news organizations have enjoyed a symbiotic relationship over this time period because of the interest of the pollsters in promoting their commercial business and the interest of news organizations in enhancing their coverage. Over time, polling itself has undergone a number of methodological advances that produced distinctive shifts in how polls are conducted, analyzed and presented. But this marriage of convenience has not been without its problems, often producing controversies in the conduct of the polls and how the media report them.

This chapter focuses on the trends in the conduct of the polls, with an emphasis on the USA, especially as technological innovation has affected the way surveys are conducted. Often, these shifts have been coupled with a reduction in the costs of conducting polls, a virtue that has coincided with growing cost pressures on news organizations. This in turn has often raised questions about data quality, as well as issues of data presentation. These lowered costs have also meant that many individuals can start polling businesses without any formal training in survey methods, which also has had important consequences for the field.

The technological shifts in polling methods

The modern polling period started during the 1930s in the USA, ignoring the straw polls of various forms that had been conducted in the preceding century. The early mode of interviewing involved face-to-face encounters in people's homes. These interviewers were primarily female, and they had a number of responsibilities besides interviewing – most notably respondent selection through quota methods. They typically worked under a regional supervisor who received the study materials from the central office, distributed them to the interviewers, and then collected the completed interviews and returned them to a location in New York, Princeton or Denver. In this setting, it could take up to one month to prepare a questionnaire, distribute them in numbers across the country, get them back for tabulation and then prepare a series of syndicated newspaper columns from the results. There were many time-consuming steps involved, and the newspaper columns began with the most time-sensitive content from the survey, typically having to do with current events in a political campaign. The later stories could deal with 'evergreen' topics involving popular culture or typical patterns of daily life.

The problems associated with estimation of candidate preference in the 1948 'Dewey beats Truman' election were linked to a number of methodological issues including the use of quota samples and the termination of interviewing too early (Converse 1987; Squire 1988). Given the crystallized support for Franklin D. Roosevelt in four election campaigns during the Depression as well as the difficulties of fielding each survey, it is not surprising that the public pollsters stopped interviewing late into October. After Truman won the election, the Social Science Research Council organized a review of the polls with which the main polling organizations were glad to cooperate in order to restore public confidence in the nascent industry (Mosteller et al. 1949). It was clear that the image of the entire industry depended upon the performance of the public pollsters in election campaigns because of the unusual nature of the direct validation of their final pre-election estimates in the actual election results. The pollsters could claim that they were only taking 'snapshots' of the public's preferences during the campaign, but they nevertheless trumpeted the accuracy of their estimates in their post-election assessments of their own performance.

Technological and methodological trends in polling in the twentieth century

A number of technological trends have occurred in the last half century that have had an impact on the polling industry. Each can be linked to an associated drop in the costs of interviewing, while at the same time introducing new potential sources of error in estimation because of the differential penetration of the new technology into society. At each turn, pollsters were faced with the problem of estimating the potential errors due to the new technology, their impacts on measuring public opinion, and the development of methodological adjustments where necessary and possible while waiting for greater adoption of the new technology.

Although the telephone was invented in the late nineteenth century, there were only 1.3 million subscribers in 1900. The penetration of landline phones into US households was exponential, and by 1950 there were more than 50 million phones in use, one for every three people in the population; the number hit 144 million by the mid-1970s. By that time, the personal computer (PC) had been developed and reduced in size to the point where it could fit on a desktop (Bellis 2010). These dual inventions and adoptions made interviewing on the telephone possible, based upon a questionnaire that was stored in a computer in which each response could be recorded. As a result of administrative controls and efficiencies that reduced the cost of polling, the standard mode of interviewing switched from face-to-face to the telephone. The appeal was overwhelming because surveys could be put into the field more quickly, including as a follow up to breaking news events; and a full dataset was ready for analysis as soon as the last interview was completed. A telephone interviewing facility provided better opportunities for quality control through central monitoring of the interviewing process. And data could be analyzed with statistical software available on the same PCs, eliminating the possibility of the data's loss of value due to intervening events in the real world.

An initial problem with telephone interviewing was the lack of access to unlisted numbers. Furthermore, a growing number of households had multiple phone lines coming into them to support fax machines and dial-up access to the Internet. In addition, new technologies were available to identify the caller trying to make contact or to take a voice message if the phone were not answered, and many individuals refused to answer their phone when the call came from an unknown or unfamiliar number. This increased the number of calls needed – and hence the cost – to make contact with a potential respondent. Eventually, telemarketers adopted techniques that simulated interviews, and response rates suffered as a result until a 'Do Not Call' list was adopted that exempted legitimate polling.

While telephone polls presented new opportunities for rapid data collection at reduced cost, they also presented methodological challenges. By the time telephone surveys became common, non-coverage due to non-ownership was not an issue. But not everyone had a number that was listed in a phone book or directory, and unlisted numbers were not randomly distributed in the population. As a result, random digit dialing (RDD) methods had to be developed to incorporate unlisted numbers in samples by generating them on a computer. Initially, producing interviews from respondents with unlisted telephone numbers was inefficient and expensive because so many of the RDD numbers were neither working, in service, nor assigned to households. Eventually dual-frame designs were developed to improve efficiency.

Telephone surveys began in the 1960s, with a substantial portion of the early effort devoted to methodological studies focusing on non-coverage as a sampling issue; and by the 1970s they became the predominant mode of interviewing (Tyebjee 1979). By the end of that decade, news organizations had initiated their own collaborative polling operations. The first was the CBS News/*New York Times* poll, followed by a partnership between ABC News and *The Washington Post* and NBC News and *The Wall Street Journal*. These associations were forged in the belief that news organizations should not be subject to decisions made by commercial polling organizations about which issues to cover in polls, what were appropriate question wordings, when the study should go into the field and how the data should be analyzed. These were all decisions related to newsworthiness, ones about which news organizations should be exercising their own editorial judgments.

These partnerships and collaborations were facilitated by the fact that the technology would support short field periods of 2–4 days of interviewing (even as little as one night's worth of calling after a presidential debate); and, before the 24-hour news cycle, the two different kinds of news organizations shared approximately the same deadline of late afternoon. It was understood that the television network would get the first, brief story for its evening news show, while the newspaper would produce a longer, more analytical piece for its morning edition.

A wide variety of arrangements like this were eventually developed and modified. Some news organizations used non-partisan professionals to design their questionnaires, while others hired one Democratic and one Republican consultant for the purpose of justifying a 'bipartisan' approach. And some relationships were more complex, as Gallup formed a partnership with both a network and a newspaper (CNN and *USA Today*) that they eventually broke away from because of concerns about audience size. Some organizations had a regular partner for most of their polls but occasionally worked with different firms or news organizations for special projects.

Technological and methodological trends in the twenty-first century

However, news organizations were not free from the economic pressures that buffeted the media industry in the last 15 years. For example, the networks were spending millions of dollars each on exit polling every two years (Mitofsky 1991). By the 1990 election, they began to pool their efforts in a common exit poll project conducted by Voter Research & Surveys (VRS). ABC, CBS, CNN and NBC supported this effort; by 1992, there were 85 partner organizations consisting of newspapers, local television stations and news magazines (Mitofsky and Edelman 1995). On that Election Day, there were problems of leaked data from preliminary results that were not final and that had an impact on the US stock market and political elites. In 1993, VRS was disbanded and a new organization, the Voter News Service (VNS), was formed for the next election cycle. VNS added the functions of collecting aggregate vote returns that was formerly taken care of by the News Election Service, and the Associated Press became a sponsor. In the same year, Warren Mitofsky left CBS News to form Mitofsky International to conduct exit polls around the world.

The network exit polls encountered a number of problems in the 2000 and 2002 elections. The 2000 presidential campaign was the closest in American history, and it was not decided until a Supreme Court decision determined the outcome in Florida. Because there was only one national data source available at the time, there was no alternative check on the appropriateness of the exit poll methodology used and its relative accuracy in such a close contest. In 2002 there was a technical break-down of the exit poll operation on Election Night, and a new contract for exit poll services was awarded to Mitofsky International and Edison Research to form the National Election Pool (NEP). In 2004, there were again issues on Election Day with the leaking of preliminary results that showed John Kerry ahead of George Bush. Some interest groups tried to obtain access to the precinct-level interviews in selected states like Ohio, where they claimed the election had been stolen through fraud; but NEP never released any data at that level. Since then, NEP has established a quarantine location for network analysts to prevent data leaks, and this seems to have worked well in the elections since 2006.

Polling organizations were not buffered from further technological changes at the end of the twentieth century. The two most obvious were the advent of cell phones and the rise of the Internet. Both of these tech-nologies presented methodological challenges to pollsters as a result of differential but shifting patterns of penetration into the population that created issues of potential coverage bias, just as landline telephones had. In 1985, there were about 10,000 cell phones sold in the USA; by 1995, there were 33 million sold (Elert 2002). By mid-2011, almost one-third of US households only had a cell phone and no landline; and another one-sixth were 'primarily cell phone,' that is both kinds of phones were present but most calls were taken on the cell phone. (Blumberg and Luke, 2011).

In theory, using cell phones to contact respondents opens up new possibilities for survey research. However, regulations in the USA inhibit the use of cell phones since it is illegal to dial a cell phone number from a computer (the way most RDD samples are deployed), because both caller and recipient pay according to the American billing algorithm. In order to employ cell phone samples, pollsters have had to dial numbers by hand, often move to systems of prior contact in order to get approval for an interview and offer a financial incentive to offset the cost of the call for the respondent. As a result, it is estimated that a cell phone interview costs at least twice as much as a landline interview in the same study (AAPOR 2010b, p. 11).

The main issue with cell phones is that their adoption has not been randomly distributed throughout the population. Initially, they were more likely to be available to individuals who had a business use for them. This created unusual problems because they might be given to someone by their employer, and the area code associated with the device might not represent the residential location of that person. This presents obvious problems for drawing samples that adequately represented a region, state or the nation. As more research was conducted on patterns of use and cultural shifts in adopting such new technology, it became clear that while many people use their cell phone for continuous communication with their social network and others, a significant portion of owners think of their device as a way for them to make contact with others as they see fit but not to leave it on continuously to take calls from anyone who tries to contact them.

In 2010, there were three cautionary notes issued about the exclusion of cell phone-only (CPO) respondents in surveys based upon telephone sample designs. In the AAPOR report (2010b), the committee addressed coverage and sampling issues, non-response and weighting concerns, operational issues and associated costs, and the need for additional disclosure. As the proportion of CPO individuals increased to almost one-third of the population (Blumberg and Luke 2011), the omission of such units has become increasingly problematical. There are now alternative designs to improve estimation, including address-based sampling (ABS) procedures that allow for excellent coverage of landline households and mixed-mode designs involving self-administered or face-to-face interviews with those who rely solely upon their cell phone. These design complexities contribute to significant cost increases among this segment of the sample.

At the same time, Silver (2010b) produced a revised set of scores for pollster quality among those who conduct pre-election surveys. While the AAPOR task force on the 2008 pre-primary polls (2009) showed that pollsters using interactive voice recognition (IVR) in 2008 were as accurate as those who used standard RDD techniques, Silver noted a decline in accuracy among some of these firms in 2010. He attributes that to the fact that CPO supplements were not yet part of their designs. Unless and until firms adapt to the changing telephone landscape, their records in pre-election estimation are likely to be in danger.

Finally, the Pew Research Center (Keeter, Christian & Dimock 2010) issued a post-election report that showed an increasing Republican bias (or a Democratic underestimate) of the vote in the last two national elections from landline-only samples. For example, a landline-only sample showed a 12.7 percentage point Republican advantage in the 2010 congressional vote, while a dual-frame (landline and cell phone) sample showed a 7.6 percentage point advantage. In their 2008 surveys of presidential voting preferences, the landline-only sample showed a 5.8 percentage point Obama advantage compared with 8.2 percentage points in the dual-frame sample. The message from these analyses is clear: polling only with RDD samples of landline households risks significant estimation error in subsequent election cycles as the penetration of cell phones continues.

Web-based surveys over the Internet offer many advantages over other interviewing methods, as researchers can insert audio and video stimuli in their questionnaires. But many of the same coverage issues are associated with Internet usage in the USA. In 1997, only 18 per cent of US households had Internet access at home. By 2001 half the homes had access, and in 2009 68.7 per cent had access, predominantly by broadband (Intac 2010). By comparison, only 8.2 per cent of US households had a computer in 1984, while 80 per cent did in 2009. As a result, non-coverage issues still have to be addressed.

Economic pressures affecting polling

Since the 1990s, financial pressures have been building on news organizations. Their costs are rising due to labor and supplies, especially newsprint for newspapers. At the same time, their revenues are in a period of significant decline. With the rise of the Internet, newspapers in particular have lost their stranglehold on classified advertising in the local market in which they typically had a monopoly. The development of LISTSERV and eventually websites where individuals can advertise for free that they have a car or house for sale or where they could look for an apartment cut into this critical income stream. News aggregators began to compile and redistribute news in personalized forms without charging for access; they simply sold advertising on their sites based upon popularity (the number of hits or clicks they received).

As a result, news organizations started to look for ways to trim their costs all across the newsroom, including in their polling operations. These pressures manifested themselves in a variety of ways, including the dissolution and rearrangement of long-standing relationships between polling firms and news organizations, and the closing or reorganization of internal polling operations. These changes illustrate the range of ways in which news organizations have responded to economic difficulties, as well as their attempts to sustain audience size and demographics in straightened economic times.

For 14 years, the Gallup Organization had a collaborative polling arrangement with CNN, the cable news channel, and *USA Today*, the largest circulation newspaper in the USA. But in March 2006, a messy divorce became public through leaked emails that presented conflicting views of the breakup (Traugott 2009). A memo from the Gallup CEO suggested they were walking away from their relationship with CNN (but staying with the newspaper) because of low ratings for the segments in which Gallup poll reports appeared. While there was a disagreement about the overall audience for CNN and the audience for the Gallup segments, it was clear that Gallup felt it could find a larger audience and establish a more independent stance by having its editors appear on any number of television outlets. CNN went on to create a new set of polling arrangements and to develop an imperfect system for aggregating others' polling data for on-air use.

In other instances, leading newspapers closed their polling units entirely. *The Los Angeles Time*s closed down its internal polling unit in 2008 in order to reduce costs after severely curtailing its polling operation late in the 2006 election cycle. The primary cause was general economic conditions in the newspaper business as well as the highly leveraged purchase of The Tribune Company by an investor with no prior media industry experience; but this was also partly due to an unusual administrative and financial arrangement in the polling unit whereby they maintained their own staff of interviewers on the payroll.

In a cost-cutting environment, the director and assistant director of the poll accepted buyout offers in the spring of 2008. This was an especially difficult loss for the industry and public opinion researchers because *The Los Angeles Times* was the only unit other than the NEP that was conducting an independent national exit poll. In the 2010 election cycle, *The Los Angeles Times* teamed up with the College of Letters, Arts and Sciences at the University of Southern California to sponsor six polls. But in the same year, the McClatchy Newspapers closed down their polling unit that was part of their Washington Bureau, continuing this trend (Media Matters 2010).

In 2010, ABC News rearranged its relationship with Gary Langer, its award-winning polling director. In a mutual agreement, Langer went off the books and formed his own firm, Langer Research Associates, whose first client was ABC News (Tarran 2010). This lowered the budget line item at the network for polling, even as Langer kept an office at ABC News. But his new arrangement allowed him to pursue work for other clients as well, including the design and conduct of polls and the provision of expert witness testimony.

Future prospects for methodological change

In the polling industry, the Internet presents its own opportunities and challenges. The major attractions are a significant reduction in data collection costs as well as the possibility of using a wide range of video and audio stimuli in the questionnaire. The major concerns are again the rate of penetration of the Internet and personal computers into individual homes, and the cost differentiation between slower dial-up access and high-speed broadband connections. Again pollsters were faced with the prospect of non-coverage bias and how this could affect their estimation, at least in the early period in which about one-third of US households did not have access to the Internet at home.

Polling organizations developed various techniques to deal with the problems of uneven distribution of Internet access. One was to build very large panels of potential respondents who would be sampled and compensated in a variety of ways for participation in individual surveys. One advantage of a large panel might be that it contains a reasonable number of individuals with some unusual or infrequently occurring characteristics that would not appear in a typical RDD sample to provide enough data for analysis. Small probability samples of respondents could be drawn from the larger panels in order to produce something akin to a random sample, but a simple random sample selected from a bad frame is still an unrepresentative sample. Some firms developed sophisticated weighting schemes to adjust for this outcome, although there are suggestions that this technique created problems of its own (Rivers 2006). Another approach was to draw a probability sample of households using RDD methods and then to supply web access to those who did not already have it as long as they continue to participate in surveys as requested (DiSogra 2007). Under either circumstance, concerns also arise about the prospect of 'professional' respondents who are compensated for each completed survey and may become less representative of typical respondents who occasionally pick up their telephone and agree to participate in a poll.

AAPOR recently completed a report on online panels (AAPOR 2010a) after two years of review. The report contains ten conclusions and recommendations, starting with the notion that online panels employing non-probability designs should not be used to estimate population values because there is no generally accepted standard for weighting the results. While acknowledging that there are occasions when such designs are appropriate, as in methodological research and certain forms of market research, the impact of such designs on results will remain unclear without additional disclosure of the details of data collection.

Problems of estimating election outcomes

In general, the quality of estimating the outcome of national elections has been improving over time. In the USA, the pre-election poll estimates of the popular vote cast in the 2008 presidential election were the most accurate since such records were started after the 1948 election. This was accomplished despite concerns raised during the campaign about the pollsters' ability to account for CPO individuals or to be deceived by socially desirable over-reporting of citizens' willingness to vote for the first African-American presidential candidate (Hopkins 2009). In the same electoral sequence, however, every one of 13 pre-election polls conducted before the New Hampshire primary suggested that Barack Obama would win when Hillary Clinton actually did. Concern over the pollsters' performance caused AAPOR to appoint a committee to review the performance of the polls in the primary process. Unlike the 1948 post mortem when all of the pollsters willingly agreed to cooperate, the committee had a great deal of trouble securing detailed methodological information from them; while it eventually received minimal information from most pollsters, its report was delayed for more than eight months from its intended release date (AAPOR 2009).

Does electoral context matter?

The 2009 AAPOR report was organized around the results from testing a series of hypotheses about why the estimation errors might have occurred. By definition, this was a task complicated by post-hoc analysis of information that was not originally designed to support such testing. The report suggested a number of factors worthy of additional consideration, including information about the weighting of the data, the details of likely voter models and the level of effort to contact individuals in the original sample that could improve the estimates. Traugott and Wlezien (2009) took advantage of the availability of the extended series of pre-primary polls in 2008 due to the contest between Obama and Clinton lasting through all of the events, unlike any prior primary contest since the current system was implemented in 1976. They found the winner's share of the primary vote was almost always overestimated, a fact that was lost because of the media's emphasis on whether pollsters got the winner right or wrong. Their analysis indicated that estimation errors declined in magnitude over time, and they were related to the accumulation of delegates and closing in on achieving a majority and becoming the presumptive nominee. These results suggest that there are contextual factors in the type of election being estimated and the rules that govern the delegate selection and nomination procedures that can affect estimation. For example, likely voter models developed in the general election context might not work as effectively in the primaries, especially if there are candidates with racial, ethnic or gender appeals to specific groups in the electorate.

Since 2008, there have been electoral sequences in other countries that suggest the potential power of contextual effects to create estimation problems, especially when combined with other methodological issues. In the South Korean local elections for mayor and governor in June 2010, the polls estimated an easy victory for the ruling Grand National Party (GNP) (Cho 2010). Just before the election, a South Korean ship was sunk in disputed waters, and the reaction of the ruling GNP was thought to be overdone. It is not permitted to publish poll results in South Korea within a week of the election, but an exit poll conducted jointly by the three main television networks estimated the outcome with great precision. Research is currently underway to assess the source of the errors in the pre-election polls, all conducted with samples based upon directory frames of listed landline telephone numbers. Neither unlisted nor cell phone numbers were included, although it is currently estimated that one-sixth of Korean adults are CPO. Recent research suggests that turnout was much higher among CPO individuals or those who have both kinds of phones compared with those who are landline only (Kim, Traugott, Park, and Lee 2011). Durand (2011) suggests that equivalent sampling issues and mode effects in Quebec telephone polls presented estimation problems there as well.

In 19 Mexican gubernatorial elections in July 2010, there were a total of 51 pre-election estimates of the outcomes in which 17 indicated the wrong winner, and the size of the errors in many others were beyond the normal margin of error (Moreno, Aguilar-Pariente, and Romero 2011). These polls were all conducted face-to-face in people's homes with a secret ballot, so social desirability in responses and 'spiral of silence' effects were not likely to be largely responsible. A recent conference of commercial pollsters, government officials and academics in Cocoyoc proposed a committee to design a study for the 2012 presidential election that will evaluate a series of potential explanations through carefully designed experiments embedded in a joint pre- and post-election study. If this comes to fruition, it will represent the most significant collaborative effort between academic and commercial pollsters anywhere in the world to understand methodological issues in the estimation of election outcomes.

Does survey mode matter?

In the USA, the estimation record of polls employing *interactive voice recognition* (IVR) technology, or 'robopolls' as they are sometimes called, improved for the 2008 presidential election. The AAPOR Task Force on the pre-primary polls found that in the selected primaries they analyzed that their accuracy was equivalent to polls conducted with standard CATI techniques (AAPOR 2009). However, their accuracy record suffered in the 2010 cycle across the country (Silver 2010b), with some firms doing worse than others. Was this a mode effect or a context issue? We need to resolve this because the number of robopolls is increasing, and their methods are not fully understood. One estimate is that in a large state like California, nearly half of the polls conducted for the 2010 election cycle employed IVR techniques (DiCamillo 2010). These kinds of polls are employed in modeling a likely electorate that often takes the party identification distribution into account, something that is not known and fixed in advance in each constituency. By adjusting for this, often with large weights for some under-represented groups in the sample, there is much more room for idiosyncratic adjustments to the raw survey data and hence a greater need for disclosure of the details of such adjustments, though most pollsters employing these techniques are unwilling to disclose adjustment or modeling procedures that they consider proprietary. Taken in combination, these results from the past year from a variety of circumstances in which polls tried to estimate the outcome of sub-national elections in three different countries suggest that methodology and models developed in general election polling might not extend straightforwardly to different kinds of elections held in smaller constituencies when a presidential race is not leading the ticket.

All in all, then, these recent events suggest the need for making data collection, adjustment and analysis procedures more public. In the past year, AAPOR has initiated a 'transparency initiative' to get polling organizations to agree to provide such information. As of this date, 83 organizations have signed on to this initiative as 'supporters', but the vast majority of them are academic organizations that understand the need to disclose such details in order to facilitate the scientific process of replication and evaluation (AAPOR 2011). However, these precepts are not widely shared by commercial pollsters.

Controversies in contemporary polling

Because of technological shifts and economic pressures, there have been a number of controversies that arose in the processing of data to produce estimates of electoral outcomes and in the ways that such estimates are reported. They highlight the range and variety of issues that pollsters and survey methodologists are facing in this new environment. In a period of generally low turnout or actual turnout declines in many democracies, the problem of estimating 'likely voters' or those who will actually vote is a growing concern. This is actually a two-part problem as various procedures have been implemented to accommodate 'early' or 'absentee' voting, and an estimated 29 per cent of Americans who voted in 2010 cast their ballots before 2 November. So in current parlance, estimates of 'likely voters' now include the reported vote of those who indicated that they have already voted, as well as the candidate preference of those who say they intend to vote and are assessed as likely to do that.

This trend presents two problems for pollsters preparing pre-election estimates. First, their questionnaires have to accommodate a branching operation after they ascertain whether the respondent has voted yet or not that can distinguish between self-reported vote for a candidate and preference for a candidate when they go to the polls. Then they have to ascertain the proportions with which the two sets of estimates are combined to form the likely electorate in order to produce an estimate of the outcome of the election. This is a more onerous estimate for pre-election pollsters, especially for states that provide limited information about levels of early voting before Election Day, than it is for exit pollsters who often have more complete information on Election Day about early and in person voting based upon their two sets of interviews.

Gallup has been asking a generic congressional ballot question in American elections since 1942 that is used in various models to estimate the number of seats won and lost by each party. It is worded: 'If the elections for Congress were being held today, which party's candidate would you vote for in your congressional district – the Democratic party's candidate or the Republican party's candidate?' In 2010, Gallup produced three estimates of the outcome of the election, based upon the full sample of registered voters, a high turnout scenario and a low turnout scenario. The respective estimates of the Republican advantage were 4 percentage points among all registered voters, 15 percentage points in a low turnout scenario and 10 percentage points in a high turnout scenario. Gallup provided more detail about its likely voter models than most pollsters, but the variation that the different models produced is clear.

There were also a number of recurring issues associated with reporting poll results. Many new websites have sprung up that assemble poll results from a number of sources, providing more or less information about the sources and quality of the information they use in terms of the details of data collection. They report on public opinion and even estimate public opinion without ever conducting any of their own polls. The website for Real Clear Politics, one of the first of these 'polling aggregators', initiated a practice of reporting the average of poll results from multiple firms where they were employing essentially similar question wordings used to measure commonly used and presumably well-understood concepts such as candidate preference in an election or presidential approval. This is a dangerous and problematical approach at best because of the differences in techniques that different firms use (sampling, survey mode and the like) that comprise what are known as 'house effects' (Smith 1982), as well as differences in their estimates of the likely electorate or their sample frames. Some have argued that by combining results from multiple surveys, the estimates are more accurate – or at least have a smaller margin of error because of the combined sample sizes. However, this is a false and misleading inference for readers and viewers of the results because of other significant differences in design. And the problems only increase when the analysis involves a comparison between two readings where, for example, the president's approval rating is reported to have increased or decreased between the two estimates, but where the estimates being compared are based upon different numbers of surveys from different organizations. Under such circumstances, what does it mean to indicate that the approval rating has increased (or decreased) by 4 percentage points?

This is especially problematical when the 'poll of polls' is being used to track the horse race at the end of an election campaign. Firstly, the shifts in candidate standings can be a function of the change in the mix or even the number of polls used to calculate the two averages. Secondly, the range of dates of the surveys can be considerable, including the combination of some relatively 'old' data with the results of polls completed in the last day or two. Thirdly, the dynamics of the race are often attributed to very small shifts in the relative standing of the candidates that fall within the margin of error of any single poll and cannot even be considered statistically significant. Traugott (2009) has written an extended analysis of how CNN tried to fill the air time in its expanded news magazine show coverage of the 2008 presidential election with the 'CNN poll of polls' that employed just such an approach, and gives examples of some of the inferential errors that resulted.

In an article describing a new statistic for assessing the accuracy of pre-election polls, Martin, Traugott and Kennedy (2005) evaluated A, a measure of predictive accuracy, by comparing its value under a variety of circumstances. For published polls conducted by political parties and candidates or their campaigns, there is a clear bias in the expected direction that favored the candidates' campaign. While this element of their analysis did not receive much coverage at the time, events in the 2010 campaign prompted a statement in the form of an open letter signed by several political pollsters, about equally divided partisan affiliation, asking that journalists only pay attention to internal polls whose methodological details were fully disclosed according to AAPOR standards in order to prevent inadequate and misleading results from entering the news stream (Politico 2010; Reader 2010). They decried the 'uncritical media coverage' of internal polls released to journalists with the intent of affecting voter and donor perceptions of the race (Blumenthal 2010c). There is no meaningful way that the accuracy of such releases can be assessed, especially in the early phase of the campaign, so disclosure of methodological procedures provides a minimum standard for deciding whether to publish the results or not. Silver (2009b) describes a poll released in a New York congressional district that was apparently intended to affect the coverage of the race, and Blumenthal argues that the typical bias in a partisan poll, now more difficult to detect than ever, is almost 3 percentage points in favor of the campaign that released its results. The definition of 'partisan' extends to interest groups that promote polls that support positions they advocate.

Another new and disturbing trend is the promotion of 'do it yourself' polling whereby an individual or a group can commission a 'robopoll' of their own design for costs ranging from almost nothing to slightly more than $1000. Scott Rasmussen has reorganized his business so that his *Rasmussen Reports* contract for their data collection from another firm he owns, Pulse Opinion Research, that will also conduct a national survey using IVR technology for as little as $1,500. The entire transaction can be completed online with a credit card. This technique has begun to be used by interest groups that support or oppose specific policies or legislation, such as immigration reform. This new development is expected to draw increased attention in the 2012 presidential cycle in the USA.

Finally, mention must be made of two recent incidents in the USA that threaten the integrity and reputation of the entire polling industry. During the 2008 election cycle, the AAPOR committee on the pre-primary election polls tried to solicit information from a number of firms. The only firm not to supply any information at all was Strategic Vision, a firm located in Atlanta that claimed it paid for its own data collection without formal sponsorship. After Strategic Vision refused to cooperate, the AAPOR Council investigated and censured the firm and its president, David E. Johnson. Additional research by Nate Silver (2009a) produced an analysis suggesting that the marginals for the reported poll results had been made up, while Ben Smith of Politico (2009) revealed that the firm had neither offices in Atlanta nor a call center in Florida. After offering to produce cross-tabulations from the poll but failing to do so, Strategic Vision stopped releasing any poll results (Bishop & Moore 2010).

In a similar incident, Markos Moulitsas, the founder of the website Daily Kos, sued his pollster, Research 2000, after an independent analysis that appeared on FiveThirtyEight (Silver 2010a) suggested that the results of their polling had been made up. The analysis suggested that the marginals for the surveys had been constructed to appear 'random', when in fact analysis of the pattern in the results suggested they were contrived. Furthermore, the president of the firm, Del Ali, could not produce any individual-level data or cross-tabulations from the work he did under contract for Daily Kos (Catanese 2010). The suit has yet to be adjudicated, and the firm has taken down its website; a consent decree is in the works, and a settlement is expected early in 2012 (Kos Media LLC et al. v. Research 2000 et al. 2011).

Issues in contemporary reporting on polls

Journalists continue to have problems reporting on public opinion, partly as a function of their lack of preparation for this assignment and partly because of the way that public opinion is (mis)represented to them. This is unfortunate because journalists and their news organizations are the last gatekeepers for preventing bad data from getting into the news stream. One frequent example of this is the difference between what has come to be known as 'measured' opinion and 'considered' opinion. The former reflects answers respondents give to questions they are asked about the latest topics in the news or areas that they have not thought much about, such as foreign policy. Because an interview involves a social exchange, many respondents feel obliged to answer questions put to them, even if they are not very knowledgeable on the topic. Thus their opinions are measured through the act of being polled, although they might answer differently if they were polled again, even a short time later, on the same subject. This is different than their attitudes on topics that are matters of deep personal belief about which they have spent considerable time thinking and discussing, such as abortion; such attitudes are more deep-rooted and crystallized. But poll coverage almost never makes this distinction clear, and what may seem like a lot of volatility in public opinions and attitudes is merely the measurement of noise in an environment where the public has not reached a stable set of positions.

These reporting problems are exacerbated by the fact that reporters write about public opinion in conceptual terms, typically based upon the marginal results from a single question. This can mean that reported differences or conflicts in public opinion are often simply a function of the specific operationalization of the concept, manifested in either differences in the question wordings, the response alternatives offered in the typically dichotomous fashion or both. One way that two polls often seem to portray different public reactions to a new policy derives from the fact that one poll used a question without an explicit 'Don't know' or 'Haven't thought much about it' alternative, while another one did. The preponderance of the literature on just this simple methodological point suggests that the 'Don't know' option should be avoided when it is reasonable to expect that the public does have views on a subject so as not to provide respondents with an option to avoid expressing their views. But when this is a new policy or topic of interest, the explicit 'Don't know' option should be included so as not to force respondents to select an option that they really have not thought much about.

Finally, estimates produced for election polls, one of the most common uses of polls in the news, are increasingly based upon statistical models rather than the relatively straightforward aggregation of individual responses to a poll question (Blumenthal 2010b). Rather than simply describing the response to their question, pollsters are applying highly individualistic and often confidential proprietary models to produce their estimates. These start with constructing a definition of who a 'likely voter' is as well as how many of them will end up going to the polls on Election Day in a high or low turnout election, deciding how non-response should be accounted for and determining how weighting is applied. How much detail should journalists provide about these methods and assumptions when writing about the poll results? And what level of detail will their editors allow in their story?

Conclusions

This chapter has traced the conjoined paths of technological and methodological developments in US polling for the last 80 years. Changes in technology have allowed pollsters to conduct more frequent surveys in conjunction with their media partners. This symbiotic relationship allowed pollsters to develop their commercial market research business while establishing their own brand recognition through extensive media coverage of their public opinion research. At the same time, pollsters were satisfying the news media's need for content to assist in their coverage of electoral politics and public policy.

As new technologies have penetrated citizens' households and been adapted to polling, the field periods and costs of data collection have declined. As a result, the number of polls has proliferated, especially among local news organizations. At the same time, news organizations have faced increasing economic pressures, often because of the competing ways that new technologies affect the delivery of news and provide increased opportunities for advertising that hurt their bottom lines. Inevitably, these cost pressures have raised the prospect of associated declines in data quality.

A number of new problems in estimating election outcomes have arisen. While researchers have developed new and interesting ways to deal with them, the solutions often imply additional costs in a period when budgets have tightened. Another set of issues involve the way data are used in news stories and the responsibilities of journalists to screen data for inclusion and explain the increasingly complex ways in which estimates are being produced through statistical models rather than the simple aggregation of responses.

As pollsters develop and apply new methodologies, including increasingly sophisticated web-based surveys and polls conducted on mobile devices, each application creates fascinating possibilities for pollsters, survey methodologists and public opinion researchers. From the media's perspective, however, the issue remains how to communicate to the average citizen in a meaningful way just what the results of the latest poll mean.

References

American Association for Public Opinion Research (2009) *An Evaluation of the Methodology of the 2008 Pre-election Primary Polls*, available at http://aapor.org/uploads/AAPOR_Rept_FINAL-Rev-4-13-09.pdf.

American Association for Public Opinion Research (2010a) *AAPOR Report on Online Panels*, available at http://poq.oxfordjournals.org/content/early/2010/10/19/poq.nfq048.full.html.

American Association for Public Opinion Research (2010b) *New Considerations for Survey Researchers When Planning and Conducting RDD Telephone Surveys in the U.S. With Respondents Reached via Cell Phone Numbers*, available at http://aapor.org/AM/Template.cfm?Section=Cell_Phone_Task_Force&Template=/CM/ContentDisplay.cfm&ContentID=2818.

American Association for Public Opinion Research (2011) *Transparency Supporters*, available at http://www.aapor.org/AAPOR_Transparency_Supporters.htm.

Bellis, M. (2010) *Inventors of the Modern Computer*, available at http://inventors.about.com/library/weekly/aa120198.htm?p=1.

Bishop, G. and D. Moore (2010) *2010 Top Ten 'Dubious Polling' Awards* (February 1), available at http://www.stinkyjournalism.org/latest-journalism-news-updates-169.php.

Blumberg, S. J. and J. V. Luke (2011) Wireless Substitution: Early Release of Estimates from the National Health Interview Survey, January–June, 2011, available at http://www.cdc.gov/nchs/data/nhis/earlyrelease/wireless201112.htm.

Blumenthal, M. (2010a) *Pollsters Raise Alarm: Inaccurate Polls May Be Impacting Campaigns* (November 8), available at http://www.huffingtonpost.com/2010/11/08/pollsters-raise-alarm-ina_n_780705.html?utm_source=twitterfeed&utm_medium=twitter.

Blumenthal, M. (2010b) *Population 'Modeling:' Presuming Too Much?* (June 7), available at http://nationaljournal.com/njonline/po_20100604_8918.php.

Blumenthal, M. (2010c) *What Makes a Poll Partisan?* (March 22), available at http://nationaljournal.com/njonline/what-makes-a-poll-partisan–20100322?mrefid=site_search.

Catanese, D. (2010) *Pollster Kills Site as Critics Pile On* (July 8), available at http://www.politico.com/news/stories/0710/39497.html.

Cho, J-E (2010) *How the Polls got the Local Elections all Wrong* (June 17), available at http://joongangdaily.joins.com/article/view.asp?aid=2921960.

Converse, J. M. (1987) *Survey Research in the United States: Roots and Emergence, 1890–1960* (Berkeley, CA: University of California Press).

DiCamillo, M. (2010) *The Rise of Robopolling in California and Its Implications* (November 15), available at http://www.pollingreport.com/md1011.htm.

DiSogra, C. (2007) *Of Trains, Panel Quality, and Sample Coverage*, available at http://www.knowledgenetworks.com/accuracy/spring2007/disogra.html.

Durand, C. (2011) 'Polls at the Subnational Level: The Canadian Case.' Paper presented at the 2011 WAPOR conference, Amsterdam.

Elert, G. (2002) *Number of Cell Phones in the US*, available at http://hypertextbook.com/facts/2002/BogusiaGrzywac.shtml.

Hopkins, D. J. (2009) 'No MoreWilder Effect, Never a Whitman Effect: When and Why Polls Mislead about Black and Female Candidates', *Journal of Politics*, 71, 769–781.

Intac (2010) *Internet Usage in America by Household*, available at http://www.intac.net/internet-usage-in-america-by-household_2010-05-11/.

Keeter, S., L. Christian and M. Dimock (2010) *The Growing Gap between Landline and Dual Frame Election Polls* (November 22), available at http://pewresearch.org/pubs/1806/growing-gap-between-landline-and-dual-frame-election-polls.

Kim, S. W., Traugott, M. W., Park, S. H., and Lee, S. K. (2011) 'Why Did the Pre-election Polls in South Korean Local Elections Go All Wrong? Assessing the Sources of Errors using Dual-Frame Landline/Cell Phone Post-election Survey?' Paper presented at the 2011 WAPOR conference, Amsterdam.

Kos Media LLC et al. v. Research 2000 et al. (2011) Documents from the California Northern District Court. Available at http://dockets.justia.com/docket/california/candce/3:2010cv02894/229270/.

Martin, E. A., M. W. Traugott and C. Kennedy (2005) 'A Review and a Proposal for a New Measure of Poll Accuracy', *Public Opinion Quarterly*, 69, 342–369.

Media Matters for America (2010) *McClatchy D.C. Bureau Cuts Polling, Follows Trend* (July 8), available at http://mediamatters.org/blog/201007080012.

Mitofsky, W. J. (1991) 'A Short History of Exit Polls', in P. J. Lavrakas and J. J. Holley (eds), *Polling and Presidential Election Coverage* (Newbury Park, CA: Sage Publications).

Mitofsky, W. J. and M. Edelman (1995) 'A Review of the 1992 VRS Exit Polls', in P. J. Lavrakas, M. W. Traugott and P. V. Miller (eds), *Presidential Polls and the News Media* (Boulder, CO: Westview Press).

Moreno, A., Aguilar-Pariente, R., and Romero, V. (2011) 'The Unnatural Left-Right Coalitions: Challenges for Pre-election Polls in Mexico.' Paper presented at the 2011 WAPOR conference, Amsterdam.

Mosteller, F., H. Hyman, P. J. McCarthy, E. S. Marks and D. B. Truman (1949) *The Pre-election Polls of 1948* (New York: Social Science Research Council).

Politico (2010) Available at http://www.politico.com/news/stories/1110/45008.html.

Reader, S. (2010) *Partisan Bias in Internal Polls: Lessons from the 2010 Midterm* (November 11), available at http://www.huffingtonpost.com/scot-reader/partisan-bias-in-internal_b_782157.html.

Rivers, D. (2006) *Sample Matching: Representative Samples from Internet Panels* (Palo Alto, CA: Polimetrix Inc.), available at http://www.rochester.edu/College/faculty/mperess/srm2011/Polimetrix_Methodology.pdf.

Silver, N. (2009a) *Comparison Study: Unusual Patterns in Strategic Vision Polling Data Remain Unexplained*, available at http://www.fivethirtyeight.com/2009/09/comparison-study-unusual-patterns-in.html.

Silver, N. (2009b) *Reality Check: NY 23 Poll May Seek to Alter, Not Reflect, Reality*, available at http://www.fivethirtyeight.com/2009/10/reality-check-ny-23-poll-may-seek-to.html.

Silver, N. (2010a) *BREAKING: Daily Kos to Sue Research 2000 for Fraud*, available at http://www.fivethirtyeight.com/2010/06/breaking-daily-kos-to-sue-research-2000.html.

Silver, N. (2010b) *Rasmussen Polls Were Biased and Inaccurate; Quinnipiac, SurveyUSA Performed Strongly* (November 4), available at http://fivethirtyeight.blogs.nytimes.com/2010/11/04/rasmussen-polls-were-biased-and-inaccurate-quinnipiac-surveyusa-performed-strongly/.

Smith, B. (2009) *Embattled Pollster Defends Methods* (September 25), available at http://www.politico.com/blogs/bensmith/0909/Embattled_pollster_defends_methods.html.

Smith, T. W. (1982) 'House Effects and the Reproducibility of Survey Measurements: A Comparison of the 1980 GSS and the 1980 American National Election Study', *Public Opinion Quarterly*, 46(1), 54–68.

Squire, P. (1988) 'Why the 1936 Literary Digest Poll Failed', *Public Opinion Quarterly*, 52(1), 125–133.

Tarran, B. (2010) *ABC Polling Director Goes Independent, Bags ABC as Client* (August 2), available at http://www.research-live.com/news/people/abc-polling-director-goes-independent-bags-abc-as-client/4003278.article.

Traugott, M. W. (2009) *Changes in Media Polling in Recent Presidential Campaigns: Moving from Good to 'Average' at CNN*, available at http://www.hks.harvard.edu/presspol/publications/papers/research_papers/r33_traugott.pdf.

Traugott, M. W. and C. Wlezien (2009) 'The Dynamics of Poll Performance during the 2008 Presidential Nomination Contest', *Public Opinion Quarterly*, 73, 866–894.

Tyebjee, T. (1979) 'Telephone Survey Methods: The State of the Art', *Journal of Marketing*, 43, 68–78.

Part II

The Media's Publication of Opinion Polls

5
Opinion Polls and the Media in Germany: A Productive but Critical Relationship

Christina Holtz-Bacha

'Pollsters should say goodbye to trying to influence politics by way of public opinion research, and politicians should not succumb to the temptation to justify their decisions with the help of public opinion research.' This is what the German chancellor, Angela Merkel, said in a speech deliberating about the relationship between public opinion research and politics in early 2010 (Rede der Bundeskanzlerin . . . 2010). While pointing to the important functions of public opinion research, she also emphasized the challenges with regard to methodology and interpretation, and particularly referred to the problem of error margins.

Angela Merkel knew exactly what she was talking about. In a way, she had been the victim of polling uncertainties herself. During the parliamentary election campaign in 2005, the polls that were reported for her party had been much better than the final outcome on Election Day. In view of the major differences, the media were quick to diagnose a 'disaster of opinion polling' (Theile 2005; see also Im Vergleich 2005) and Merkel had to face considerable critique for her campaign management because she was held responsible for her party's unexpected bad performance in the election.

At the same time, she declared public opinion research to be a diagnostic rather than a prognostic instrument, and underlined that it is the exclusive task of politicians to make political decisions, maybe with the help of public opinion research but sometimes even against what appears to be public opinion. With the experience of a high-ranking politician who undergoes constant evaluation in surveys and in the media, she also cautioned her colleagues against shortsighted populism. What Merkel expressed in her 2010 speech demonstrates a certain ambiguity of politicians towards public opinion research: on the one hand, political actors seek and rely on survey findings for their decisions, their campaign planning and their image management; on the other hand, they run the risk of overestimating the validity of surveys and may be tempted to give in to short-term moods in the interest of their popularity.

The media play an important role in the relationship between politicians and public opinion research. In most cases, it is the media who report on survey findings, put them on the public agenda and might thus instigate their effects. More often than not the media themselves commission the polls. Through their decisions on the topic of polls, the time of publication and the way they interpret the findings, the media may also influence citizens' attitudes and put pressure on political actors to deal with certain issues and in a certain way. Therefore, Merkel's cautionary remarks with respect to methodology and interpretation of polls apply to the media in the same way as to the polling institutes. With the discussion about the role, the quality and the interests of the polling business continuously being brought up by the media – particularly during election campaigns – the media thus run the risk of a backlash effect that calls their own interest in the polls into question.

Against this backdrop of a sensitive relationship among the political system, the media and the pollsters, this chapter will first outline the regulation for the publication of polls in Germany and briefly describe the history and the major players of the polling business. In order to assess the relevance of polls for media reporting in Germany, it will give an overview of the extant literature, which up to now has overwhelmingly focused on election campaigns. Moreover, most studies are based on content analyses, leaving the effects of poll reporting as an open field.

Regulation and self-control

Even though discussions about some kind of regulation have been coming up from time to time, there are practically no restrictions for the publication of poll results in Germany. Critical voices usually were countered with a reference to the German constitution, which guarantees freedom of expression and freedom of information. In addition, with the possibility to bypass national restrictions by broadcasting poll results from other countries, national restrictions have become useless anyway. Thus, the publication of survey results is mostly subject to ethical appeals and self-control of the media.

The Press Code, issued by the German Press Council as a guideline for journalists working for the print media, refers in its section 2 on due diligence to the publication of poll findings (Presserat 2008). The Press Code expects the press to give information on the number of respondents, the time period of the fieldwork, who commissioned the survey and the wording of the question(s). In addition, it should be reported whether the findings are representative. If the survey was not sponsored, the reports should mention that the survey was done on the own initiative of the survey institute.

The Interstate Broadcasting Treaty, which includes provisions for national public and commercial broadcasting, appeals to compliance with general journalistic principles and due diligence in particular. If findings from surveys are reported, it should be indicated whether the data are based on a representative sample. The same provision applies to telemedia (Staatsvertrag . . . 2010).

In 1999, the Committee of Ministers of the Council of Europe, which includes 47 member states, released a recommendation on measures concerning media coverage of election campaigns (Committee of Ministers 1999). Even though the Committee of Ministers seems to be convinced that the publication of poll results could affect the election outcome, the recommendation points to freedom of the media as protected under Article 10 of the European Convention on Human Rights, which cannot easily be restricted. The Committee of Ministers, however, argues for (self-)regulation to ensure that 'the media, when disseminating the results of opinion polls, provide the public with sufficient information to make a judgement on the value of the polls' (Committee of Ministers 1999). As such, the recommendation particularly mentions the name of the political party or other organization that commissioned the poll, the organization conducting the poll and the methodology employed, the sample and margin of error of the poll and the time period when the poll was conducted. These principles were once again confirmed and extended to non-linear media services in a recommendation that the Committee of Ministers released in 2007 (Committee of Ministers 2007).

Most of the German survey institutes are members of the association ADM (Arbeitskreis Deutscher Markt- und Sozialforschungsinstitute e.V.), which represents their interests and, among other duties, promotes the self-regulation of survey research through rules of conduct and quality standards. They are also members of ESOMAR (World Association of Opinion and Marketing Research Professionals) and thus comply with its professional and ethical standards and its disciplinary procedures.

A short history of opinion research in Germany

Opinion research in Germany dates back to the nineteenth century, but representative sample methods were only introduced after the Second World War. The occupying powers used opinion research to assess the situation of the German population, the attitudes towards their policies and the progress of the democratization process (cf. Kutsch 1995; Meyen 2002). The Americans in particular also made diverse efforts to aid German researchers to acquire the scientific and technical competences for the development of survey research in Germany (Schaefer & Miller 1998). During this time, the first German survey institutes were founded that engaged in public opinion and market research. In 1945, Karl Georg von Stackelberg built up the Emnid institute in Bielefeld. He was also among a group of researchers who received grants for a trip to the USA in 1950 to study the methods of survey research (Meyen 2002, p. 64). In 1947, the Allensbach Institute started off with surveys among young people commissioned by the French military government (Noelle-Neumann 1997, pp. 42–43). Elisabeth Noelle, who founded the Allensbach Institute together with her husband Erich Peter Neumann, studied in the USA in 1937/38. There she discovered the work of George Gallup. She made opinion research the topic of her dissertation (Noelle 1940) and thus lay the grounds for what later became one of the most influential institutes for public opinion research in Germany.

Since its beginning under the occupying powers and the early years of the Federal Republic of Germany, founded in 1949, opinion research was subject to critique. Part of it was personal, directed towards the founders of the Allensbach Institute. Both of the founders had been working as journalists during the Nazi regime and therefore had to deal with suspicions concerning their role at that time. In addition, Erich Peter Neumann was an advisor of Germany's first chancellor, Konrad Adenauer, and a member of parliament for the Christian Democratic Union (CDU) from 1961 until 1965, and his wife also did not hide her preference for the conservatives (cf. Meyen 2002, pp. 64–65). However, opinion research in general was met with distrust. Many did not believe that a sample of 2000 respondents would indeed be representative of all Germans, and saw the potential for manipulation through the wording of questions. On the other hand, opinion research was regarded as a threat to democracy. Critical voices pointed to possible effects on the people as well as on the political system (Atteslander 1980; Hennis 1957). Politicians were feared to fall for populism by orienting their decisions towards short-term opinions and moods in their electorate. Only since the end of the 1960s has survey research been considered as fully established and accepted (Scheuch 1999).

While the government and the parties commissioned surveys since the early 1950s (cf. Hetterich 2000, pp. 139, 168; Kruke 2007), polls got some attention in the media during the election campaign for the first time in 1965. No survey results at all were published for the elections in 1949 and 1953. In 1957 and 1961, the Allensbach Institute for Public Opinion Research came up with a prognosis that was published in the daily newspaper *Frankfurter Allgemeine Zeitung* the day before the election. Only in 1965 did the survey business take off, and several surveys were reported during the last months and weeks of the election campaign. On Election Day, the founders of the two leading survey Institutes, Elisabeth Noelle-Neumann for the Allensbach Institute and Karl-Georg von Stackelberg for the Emnid-Institut, presented their prognoses for the election outcome on television (Kaase 1977, p. 461). This event started the first wave of discussions about the role of opinion research and the publication of survey results in the run-up to elections. The debate was kindled by the deviation of Emnid's prognosis from the actual election result. However, the fact that the Allensbach Institute had predicted a much better result for the Social Democratic Party (SDP) four weeks earlier than on Election Day gave rise to suspicions of a manipulation in favor of the CDU (Kaase 1977, p. 461).

Concerning the role of polls during campaigns, the 1976 election provided for another notable event. The electorate had been exposed to an unprecedented number of surveys covered by the media, and in many cases the media themselves also commissioned these surveys. The media thus started to create the events that they were then reporting on (Kaase 1977, p. 464).

The year 1976 was also the year in which Elisabeth Noelle-Neumann applied her spiral of silence theory to the analysis of the political process in Germany. With this theory, she introduced a social-psychological concept – the climate of opinion – into elections research (Noelle-Neumann 1976, 1980, 1990). According to Noelle-Neumann, the climate of opinion influences opinion formation at the individual level and thus has an effect on the election outcome as well. Helped by their 'quasi-statistical perception organ', individuals assess the climate of opinion by directly observing their environment and indirectly through their media use. Due to the fact that individuals fear social isolation, many tend to adapt their own opinion on issues to what is perceived as being the opinion of the majority. When Noelle-Neumann first published her spiral of silence theory in 1976, she credited television as a major influence on how voters perceive the climate of opinion. However, she hardly discussed whether and to what extent the publication of survey results on the popularity of the parties and candidates could affect opinion formation and, at last, the voting decision.

In the meantime, the number of institutes engaging in survey research increased, which provided for a competitive environment. Some of them have long-standing links with media companies. Infas was founded in 1959 and began to work for the ARD in 1965, a cooperation that lasted for almost 30 years. The year 1965 also was the year when Forschungsgruppe Wahlen started at the University of Mannheim and was established as a registered association in 1974. Today, it still regularly works for ZDF, broadcasting polls on the strength of the parties, the popularity of politicians and other relevant issues in the *Politbarometer* once a month. Electoral research for the ARD was taken over in 1996 by Infratest dimap, which was created for this purpose by merging Infratest Burke Berlin, a subsidiary of TNS Infratest, and an institute engaging in market and political research (Institut für Markt- und Politikforschung). Infratest dimap delivers the monthly *Deutschlandtrend* broadcast by ARD. Forschungsgruppe Wahlen and Infratest dimap also cooperate with ZDF and ARD for electoral reporting on election nights. Their projections at 6.00 p.m. when polling stations close have become a competitive element for the two public service television channels.

Except for Forschungsgruppe Wahlen, all survey institutes draw the major part of their revenue from market research and other surveys. Political surveys provide for only 3–20 per cent of their business (Raupp 2007, p. 134). The mass media are the most important clients for political surveys followed by political institutions and organizations. Among the political actors, the Press and Information Office, which is in charge of government communication and has its own budget for surveys, ranks second behind the media, while the political parties take third place (Raupp 2007, p. 135).

Reporting of polls in the media

As has been shown for other countries (e.g. the USA; Ladd & Benson 1992), the reporting of polls in the German media intensified over time. Brettschneider (1991, 1996, 2000, 2008) analyzed the coverage of four national quality newspapers during the last 12 weeks of 6 parliamentary election campaigns between 1980 and 1998. His findings show that there has not been a steady increase in the reporting of polls over time. Instead, the amount of articles referring to polls varied from one election to the other: While he found 65 articles in 1980 and 83 in 1983, the number of articles dropped to only 33 during the 1987 campaign but rose again to 94 in 1990. During the 1990s, however, the reporting of polls increased considerably to 168 articles in 1994 and again almost doubled to 328 articles in 1998 (Brettschneider 2000, p. 481). Other than what might be expected, he did not find an increase towards Election Day. Instead, the number of articles peaked during other weeks of the campaign. At the same time, the importance of surveys, as indicated by the centrality in the article, decreased. Whereas most articles focused on the findings if polls were reported during the election campaigns in 1980, 1983 and 1987, they were increasingly only mentioned peripherally in the later campaigns. This goes hand in hand with often only vague references such as, for instance, a hint to 'recent surveys' (Brettschneider 2000, p. 483). Concerning the quality of poll reporting, which is indicated by the information on technical data of the surveys (e.g. number of respondents, time of the interviews, question wording), it leaves a lot to be desired in survey coverage. Surprisingly, a study on poll reporting during the electoral campaign in 1994 (Donovitz 1999) found that the German news agency dpa delivered more technical information in its poll reporting than the newspapers that adopted its reports. The abandonment on the part of the newspaper journalists can only be interpreted as intentional selection behavior, but may be attributed to various reasons.

Findings by the Media Tenor for the last 90 days of the electoral campaigns in 1994, 1998, 2002 and 2005 confirmed the increasing reliance of newspapers on polls. An analysis of three newspapers (rs 2005; vb 2006) showed that the percentage of statements on survey results jumped up in 2002, particularly during the last month of the campaign. Altogether, almost 40 per cent of the statements criticized the survey institutes, while about 50 per cent did not give a clear evaluation. Media Tenor also found that among the different media, each favored certain polling firms. This led the researchers to conclude that newspapers and television stations turn to findings of those pollsters in their reporting with whom they have entered into an agreement, rather than apply quality as a selection criterion.

A content analysis of four quality newspapers (*Die Welt, Frankfurter Allgemeine Zeitung, Süddeutsche Zeitung, Frankfurter Rundschau*), a tabloid (*Bild*) and two weekly political magazines (*Der Spiegel, Focus*) identified 854 poll- and election-related articles during four months around the election in 2005 (Holtz-Bacha 2008). Almost two-thirds of the articles appeared in the political sections, while the rest were scattered all over the other parts of the newspapers and magazines. The four quality papers differed somewhat in where they offered their poll reporting. The *Frankfurter Allgemeine Zeitung* mentioned polls overwhelmingly in the politics and the economics section (93 per cent), while the other newspapers presented findings from surveys to a considerable extent in other parts as well. The *Frankfurter Rundschau* stood out with altogether 46 per cent of the articles that referred to polls published on the 'Miscellaneous' pages (18 per cent) or in other parts, such as the political, economics or feature pages. Almost one-fifth of the articles in the *Süddeutsche Zeitung* also appeared under 'Miscellaneous', whereas *Die Welt* put 23 per cent in other parts of the newspaper.

In only 23 per cent of the cases altogether, polls were the obvious reason for the article to be written. However, there were high deviations for *Bild* (61 per cent) and *Süddeutsche Zeitung* (32 per cent) in this respect. These findings were further supported by the fact that, in general, the centrality of the polls in the articles was not very high. The overall mean on a five-point scale ranging from 1 (marginal) to 5 (main focus on poll findings) was 1.97. Three newspapers, *Welt* (2.01), *Süddeutsche Zeitung* (2.18) and *Bild* (3.45) gave polls a higher emphasis, while *Frankfurter Rundschau* (1.56) and *Der Spiegel* (1.51) awarded the polls lowest centrality and mostly mentioned them only peripherally. The low centrality of poll results in the magazines, particularly in *Der Spiegel*, is reasonable because they publish longer articles in general and thus mention surveys often incidentally. Against this background, the low centrality for polls in the FR was more surprising and can probably be interpreted as an ostentatious dissociation from the survey business.

Half of all articles that reported on survey results concerned the current strength of the parties (Holtz-Bacha 2008). The interest in the performance of the parties during the election campaign seems to suggest itself in the German electoral system where the vote for a party determines the number of seats a party gets in the parliament. Nevertheless, the obsession of the media with party strength can be regarded as an indicator of the horse race character of campaign reporting, particularly when it is tracked in ever smaller intervals. In a party-oriented political system, the monitoring of the popularity of the top candidates is an even better indicator of the media's concentration on horse race aspects. In the German system, this concerns the chancellor candidates of the two big parties. Even though they usually have to form a coalition government, only SPD and CDU/CSU (Christian Social Union) can get their candidate through as chancellor, and chancellor candidates are nominated only by the two parties. In 2005, these were the incumbent chancellor Gerhard Schröder and the CDU challenger Angela Merkel. Since Merkel was the first woman ever to run as chancellor candidate in Germany, she received much attention from the media and even overcame the chancellor bonus that incumbents have enjoyed for a long time in German election reporting. All in all, poll reporting overwhelmingly did not concentrate much on the two chancellor candidates. Among all articles presenting findings from polls, only 8 per cent focused on the chancellor candidates, while another 4 per cent included other politicians. Altogether, the papers remained reluctant with evaluative comments on how the parties or candidates fared in the polls. Roughly 80–90 per cent of the articles just reported findings and did not add any positive or negative evaluations (Holtz-Bacha 2008).

In order to explore the horse race character in more detail, coders were asked to assess the framing of poll reporting. A horse race frame would be the portrayal of the election as an exciting race or the presentation of the candidates as winners and losers. However, the winner and loser schema was almost absent, and only 7 per cent of the articles on polling pictured the election as a suspenseful race. Although these findings seem to suggest that the German print media did not adhere to horse race coverage, it has to be kept in mind that the results presented here only refer to articles that somehow reported on surveys. Any other campaign coverage was excluded from this analysis. In addition, the amount of polls and poll reporting are themselves indicators for the horse race approach to elections.

The analysis of the formal features of poll reporting serves two objectives. Firstly, the findings demonstrate to what extent the newspapers and magazines comply with the recommendations of the profession, for instance the WAPOR Code of Ethics. Information on the exact wording of the question, the number of respondents, the time of the interviews and who sponsored the survey allow the reader to assess the quality, the meaning and the significance of the findings. Secondly, the absence of certain information indicates a conscious or unconscious neglect on the part of the journalists who deal with surveys and could, at least in some cases, be interpreted as a deliberate obfuscation of important background data and thus a harnessing of survey results for their own interests. In general, technical data that should help readers to assess the significance of the reported poll findings were sparsely given. If at all, the name of the polling institute was the information that was mentioned most frequently but not even in 30 per cent of the articles. Even more important data such as the sample size, the time when the interviews were done or the exact wording of the questions asked were rarely given. With a growing number of late deciders and of voters who are undecided until the last days of the election campaign, the share of respondents who say they do not yet know which party they are going to vote for would be vital information in the reporting of election surveys. However, only a few articles discuss the number of undecided voters or tell their readers how the polling institutes weigh the raw data taking account of the undecided respondents.

Findings from other studies provide further details of poll reporting in the 2005 campaign. An analysis of poll reporting in the four quality newspapers during the last three months of the 2002 and the 2005 campaign and one month after Election Day (Raupp 2007) came to the conclusion that media logic prevailed when newspapers presented survey findings. Media logic here means that the media do not spend much time and space on explaining all the intricacies of survey research, but are rather interested in presenting clear findings (p. 178). As for the context of survey reporting, the study distinguished an informational frame that reports on poll findings or uses them for prognoses for the election outcome, an instrumentalization frame that ascribes the polls certain effects, and a frame using polls within meta-coverage. With 60 per cent the informational frame that also included horse race coverage dominated survey reporting. Polls were used for instrumentalization in 27 per cent of the cases where they served to explain the causes and consequences of political actions or were disputed by either politicians or journalists, and they appeared in a meta-coverage frame in 13 per cent of the articles (Raupp 2007, p. 160).

Hohlfeld (2006) provided findings on the survey reporting in television news during the 2005 campaign. He analyzed the main evening newscasts of the four most important German television channels, two public service (ARD, ZDF) and two commercial channels (RTL, Sat.1), for the last four weeks of the campaign. The sample consisted of 658 news items that dealt with the campaign, representing a share of almost 19 per cent of all news. Polls were presented in 21 per cent (n = 136) of all news items that covered the campaign, increasing from 12 per cent four weeks before Election Day to 32 per cent during the last week. Compared with the public channels, the two commercial channels lay clearly ahead with their amount of poll reporting and its share of their political reporting.

A content analysis of news reporting on the four main TV channels during eight weeks before and one week after the election in 2009 (Krüger & Zapf-Schramm 2009) again demonstrated the increasing interest of the media in polls. Altogether, 48 surveys were mentioned in 32 days. That means poll findings were presented almost every two days. In total, the four channels devoted 160 minutes to the reporting of polls, with the two public channels (ZDF: 85 minutes, ARD: 49 minutes) far ahead of the commercial channels (RTL: 17 minutes, Sat.1: 9 minutes) (Krüger & Zapf-Schramm 2009, pp. 630–631).

All in all, as the content analyses of different media and from several elections have shown, horse race framing is by no means prevalent in German poll reporting and also has not increased considerably over time. This was once again confirmed by a study that compared poll reporting in the quality press during the hot campaign phase in 1976 and 2005 (Faßbinder 2009).

Perception and effects of polls

Over the years, with the increase of poll reporting, voters also paid more and more attention to polls (Gallus 2003, p. 128). Previous to the election in 1957, only 17 per cent of the voters indicated that they had seen or heard about poll results, while in 1965 the number of voters who came across poll findings had already risen to 35 per cent (Lupri 1969, p. 101). In the 1980s and 1990s, more than two-thirds of the voters reported that they had sometimes or regularly seen poll findings (Brettschneider 2000, p. 491), which was confirmed again during the election campaign of 2005 (Faas & Schmitt-Beck 2007, p. 236). Attention for polls is supported by socio-demographic and interest variables. Men and older people are more attentive to poll findings, as are those who demonstrate political involvement. Media use in general is conducive to attention for polls, but the use of public service newscasts, reading of regional newspapers and the use of political content on the Internet are particularly influential (Faas & Schmitt-Beck 2007, p. 240).

Brettschneider's analyses of data from German post-election surveys showed that polls may have their greatest effect on voters of the smaller parties (Free Democratic Party (FDP), Greens, and later PDS/Die Linke) and on floating voters (Brettschneider 1991, 2000). These effects are closely associated with the specificities of the German electoral system and have therefore been interpreted as rational or tactical voting. In order to get seats in the parliament, parties have to overcome a 5 per cent threshold. Thus, if the polls show that a party may have difficulties in making the threshold, voters may fear wasting their vote by voting for this party and therefore decide to cast their vote for another party even if this is not their first preference. Because this calculation functions like a self-fulfilling prophecy, the effect has also been termed the guillotine effect (Reumann 1983). Similarly, the impact of polls on the voting behavior of those voters who do not have a strong party preference and are disposed to change their ballot behavior from one election to the other is also considered to be a tactical decision. Since Germany's proportional representation system mostly leads to coalition governments, these voters seem to draw on polls for calculating how they can best use their vote to support a desired coalition or make a party strong for a future coalition. Schoen (1999, 2000, 2002), however, controlling for party identification, could not find evidence for tactical voting based on perceived election outcomes for the small parties. Similarly, the only indication for an instrumental use of poll findings in a study by Faas and Schmitt-Beck (2007) was greater attention to poll findings on the part of FDP voters.

A study of communication effects on vote choice done during the election campaign of 1990 (Schmitt-Beck 1996) revealed that media information about the strengths of the parties had an impact on the vote choice and helped the governing parties to win. This bandwagon effect was strongest among independent and less educated voters. Poll findings reported in the media play an important role for the voters to assess the electoral chances of the individual parties. The impact on vote choice as found in this study raises the demand for high quality of survey research and how results are reported in the media.

In his analysis of TV news during the 2005 campaign, Hohlfeld found that candidates were on air according to the current strength of their party. Thus, the newscasts replicated the major deviance between the polls and the final election outcome. He concluded that, consciously or not, journalists seem to construct their news items with the recent survey results in mind. Since the TV stations commissioned many of the polls mentioned in the news, the orientation towards the polls leads to a 'circle of journalistic self-conditioning' (2006, p. 16). In addition, the study showed that journalists also did quite a bit of speculating about the election outcome in their comments and presented their own prognoses, which again confirmed the impression that journalists internalize the findings from polls and let them guide their reporting.

Using a combination of data from surveys and content analyses, Jandura and Petersen (2009) ascertained that public opinion slightly preceded changes in media coverage. Thus, survey results seem to affect journalists in their coverage of the election campaign, which speaks for an indirect effect of election polls on voters.

Polls under criticism

The role of polls has again become the subject of controversial discussions after the 2002 and the 2005 election campaigns. Before the election in September 2002, poll results were published since the early summer with so far unknown density (Kaase, 2003, p. 6). For a long time, all survey institutes, except Allensbach, saw the opposition parties (CDU/CSU and FDP) in the lead. That faded away and turned in the other direction after chancellor Schröder had successfully demonstrated his commitment during floodings in the eastern part of Germany, and when he and foreign minister Joschka Fischer rejected the participation of German troops in a possible Iraq intervention. The Allensbach Institute, however, diagnosed a strong lead of the opposition parties and made an about-face only two weeks before Election Day (Kaase, 2003, p. 6). This led Michael Spreng, who acted as a consultant for the CDU/CSU's 2002 chancellor candidate Edmund Stoiber, to accuse Allensbach of having given the opposition parties a false sense of security (Allensbach hat... 2002; Gallus 2003, p. 136).

In 2005, the struggle against an unfavorable climate of opinion was even made a topic of the SPD campaign. Because chancellor candidate Schröder enjoyed a much better popularity than the SPD, it was one of the main goals of the campaign to transfer his popularity to the party. The SPD therefore embarked on a personalized strategy and Schröder made the campaign a personal challenge. He managed to raise his own popularity even more and at the same time succeeded in increasing the popular support for his party. One of the SPD's campaign posters addressed Schröder's fierce battle against the pessimistic auguries for his party: The claim that dominated the poster said *Umfrage-Sieger-Besieger*, which is a play on the German word *Sieg* (victory) with *Sieger* denoting winner and *Besieger* the one who beats someone. Thus, with this poster the SPD claimed to defeat the polls' frontrunner, which was their competitor CDU/CSU, and gave an impression of the role polls play during an election campaign and the parties' fear of the climate of opinion as conveyed by the polls.

Also in 2005, while pointing to major differences between the latest survey results before Election Day and the final outcome, the media diagnosed a 'disaster of opinion polling' (Theile 2005; see also Im Vergleich 2005). It was by no means unusual that the media denigrated the survey institutes after an election, but the critique never seemed to have been more warranted than this time. The election results were particularly disappointing for the CDU and their chancellor candidate

Angela Merkel, whom the surveys had long shown as the sure winner of the election. In fact, the CDU came out as the strongest party, but with 35.2 per cent, the party was far from the 40 per cent that had been predicted. On the other hand, the FDP experienced a pleasant surprise because the party yielded a better election result than was expected. Their share had been estimated at around 7 per cent; however, they finally obtained 9.8 per cent of the votes. The difference between the polls and the final result for the SPD was not as big as for the CDU, but they also fared somewhat better in the election than had been predicted.

Therefore, the 2005 election revived critical discussions about the voting intention question and how findings are reported (cf. Hofmann-Göttig 2005a, b). Once more, the pollsters were criticized because they do not lay open their weighting procedures (e.g. Schaffer & Schneider 2005). Each institute has its own secret recipe for dealing with the inaccuracies of response behavior or sampling errors, and it is unknown in the public how the data are processed before being published. The media in particular were criticized for not always indicating the number of undecided voters and the usual margins of error, which are even more important when the election becomes a neck-and-neck race.

German journalists also show an ambivalent stance on election polls and are also more critical than their US colleagues (Wahlumfragen... 2005; Wichmann & Brettschneider 2009). In two surveys among parliamentary journalists prior to the elections in 2002 and 2005, a total of 62 per cent of the German respondents – compared with almost 88 per cent of the White House correspondents – stated that they used survey results 'sometimes' or 'often' as basic information for an article. Whereas all US journalists indicated that they 'sometimes' or 'often' used poll findings as additional information for their articles, only 76 per cent of the German journalists said so. US journalists are also more inclined than their German colleagues to include technical information when they report on surveys. The neglect of technical information is even more surprising against the background of German parliamentary journalists being overwhelmingly convinced of an influence of published polls on voter turnout and voting decision. Among 83 per cent of those who expect survey results to exert an influence on voters, 47 per cent believe that the influence would be negative. German journalists also trust the survey institutes less than White House correspondents: 17 per cent of the German and 16 per cent of the US respondents thought that manipulation of results would occur often, and another 62 per cent of the German journalists – compared with only 42 per cent of their American colleagues – said that manipulation happens sometimes. Accordingly, 65 per cent of the German parliamentary correspondents are in favor of regulations for the publication of poll results on or prior to election days (Wichmann & Brettschneider 2009).

Conclusion

The research on poll reporting in Germany shows that the media refer to polls frequently and to an increasing extent. In particular, polls have become a major staple of campaign reporting. While the amount of survey reporting alone could give rise to a controversial discussion, the way polls are actually used in the media also casts some doubts on the relation of journalism and survey research. Polls are often mentioned incidentally and without further methodological information that would allow readers to place the results into perspective. These findings altogether raise questions about the function of survey reporting. The media may have different reasons why they do not report all background information of the surveys, but the consequences, however, are the same: without detailed knowledge of the methodological context, readers are not able to judge the quality and the importance of the findings, and journalists run the risk of being suspected of using poll data in the interest of their own argumentation.

Party strength has turned out to be the major focus of poll reporting. Concentrating on how the parties fare during the campaign seems to suggest itself in a party-oriented political and electoral system. With a 5 per cent threshold in force and coalition governments being the rule, information on the development of the popularity of the parties can even be regarded as an important guide for voters who have to decide whom they are going to support on Election Day. Knowing that their preferred party might not overcome the threshold, or in the interest of coalition mathematics, polls allow voters to make an informed decision or even result in tactical voting. Referring to the inaccurateness of polls and the 'disaster' of the election surveys in 2005 in particular, others have argued that polls may mislead voters. In addition, research has shown that the publication of polls does not prompt tactical voting.

Even though the German media first of all seem to be interested in party popularity, not much support could be found for the horse race hypothesis, neither indicated by a dominant focus on the top candidates nor in the framing. Even though personalization is undoubtedly a feature of campaigning, the fact that the winner and loser scheme is not persistent may be due to the German electoral system, which is a proportional representation system where the party vote decides the number of seats a party gets in the parliament. The extent to which the horse race scheme is identified as a major feature of poll reporting remains a question of definition. Earlier research done on poll reporting during election campaigns has identified horse race as an important attribute of poll reporting (Brettschneider 2000), while Raupp (2007) in her study included the horse race scheme in the informational frame, thus not attributing it a different quality. Therefore, differences in the coding may explain differences in the findings concerning the amount of horse race framing in poll reporting. If, however, the focus on party preferences is coded as a horse race scheme being present, this of course would boost the results for the horse race frame and deliver another picture.

In general, journalists and poll reporting in German newspapers reflect an ambivalent attitude towards polls. On the one hand, the amount of poll reporting has increased over the years, with the media themselves having a major share as sponsors, and journalists also seem to rely on polls in their selection decisions and their comments. On the other hand, several findings point to a somewhat critical stance on polling indicated for instance by the number of articles that appear under 'Miscellaneous' and the mostly peripheral reporting of polls. Considering the critical attitude of journalists towards polls and those who deliver the findings, it is even more dubious why poll findings are overwhelmingly published without the necessary information on how, when and by whom the polls were conducted. These data would provide for transparency and allow the reader to assess the quality of the polls and the significance of the findings.

Despite their mostly critical attitude towards polls, journalists increasingly use them in their reporting, and the media companies are one of, if not the, most important sponsor of surveys. In the conclusion of her study, Raupp (2007 p. 178) therefore called the relationship between journalists and opinion research a working alliance: journalists use poll results pragmatically in order to increase suspense, deliver background information, and to taper and illustrate complex issues.

In contrast to the reservations that were brought up against political polls and poll reporting in earlier years, it is now widely accepted that survey research allows people to observe their environment, assess the current strength of the parties and calculate possible coalitions (Faas & Schmitt-Beck 2007; Kaase & Pfetsch 2001). However, just like the journalists, politicians demonstrate an ambivalent attitude towards polls and do not seem to trust their colleagues for having a critical distance towards public opinion as expressed in polls. That was reflected in Merkel's speech when she referred to the former German president Richard von Weizsäcker and his remark on 'poll democracy' ('Demoskopiedemokratie') and advised politicians not to give in to short-term moods and the temptation of popularity.

References

'Allensbach hat den Schaden für die Union vergrößert' (2002, October 10) http://www.zeit.de/2002/42/Allensbach_hat_den_Schaden_fuer_die_Union_ vergroessert, date accessed October 18, 2002.

Atteslander, P. (1980) 'Demoskopie: Hilfe oder Gefahr für die Politik?', *Politische Studien*, 31, 135–142.

Brettschneider, F. (1991) *Wahlumfragen. Empirische Befunde zur Darstellung in den Medien und zum Einfluß auf das Wahlverhalten in der Bundesrepublik Deutschland und den USA* (München: Minerva).

Brettschneider, F. (1996) 'Wahlumfragen und Medien – Eine empirische Untersuchung der Presseberichterstattung über Meinungsumfragen vor den Bundestagswahlen 1980 bis 1994', *Politische Vierteljahresschrift*, 37, 475–493.

Brettschneider, F. (2000) 'Demoskopie im Wahlkampf – Leitstern oder Irrlicht?', in M. Klein, W. Jagodzinski, E. Mochmann and D. Ohr (eds), *50 Jahre empirische Wahlforschung in Deutschland* (Opladen: Westdeutscher Verlag).

Brettschneider, F. (2008) 'The news media's use of opinion polls', in W. Donsbach and M. W. Traugott (eds), *The SAGE Handbook of Public Opinion Research* (Los Angeles: Sage).

Committee of Ministers (1999) Recommendation No. R (99) 15 of the Committee of Ministers to member states on measures concerning media coverage of election campaigns (Adopted by the Committee of Ministers on 9 September 1999 at the 678th meeting of the Ministers' Deputies), https://wcd.coe.int/ViewDoc. jsp?id=419411&Site=CM&BackColorInternet=9999CC&BackColorIntranet= FFBB55&BackColorLogged=FFAC75, date accessed March 9, 2009.

Committee of Ministers (2007) Recommendation CM/Rec(2007)15 of the Committee of Ministers to member states on measures concerning media coverage of election campaigns (Adopted by the Committee of Ministers on 7 November 2007 at the 1010th meeting of the Ministers' Deputies), https://wcd.coe. int/ViewDoc.jsp?id=1207243&Site=CM&BackColorInternet=9999CC&Back ColorIntranet=FFBB55&BackColorLogged=FFAC75, date accessed March 9, 2009.

Donovitz, F. (1999) *Journalismus und Demoskopie. Wahlumfragen in den Medien* (Berlin: Vistas).

Faas, T. and R. Schmitt-Beck (2007) 'Wahrnehmung und Wirkungen politischer Meinungsumfragen. Eine Exploration zur Bundestagswahl 2005', in F. Brettschneider, O. Niedermayer and B. Weßels (eds), *Die Bundestagswahl 2005. Analysen des Wahlkampfes und der Wahlergebnisse* (Wiesbaden: VS Verlag für Sozialwissenschaften).

Faßbinder, K. (2009) 'Endspurt. Mediales Horse-Racing im Wahlkampf', *Publizistik*, 54, 499–512.

Gallus, A. (2003) 'Wahl als "Demoskopiedemokratie"? Überlegungen zur Meinungsforschung und zu ihren Wirkungen aus Anlass der Bundestagswahl 2002', in E. Jesse (ed.), *Bilanz der Bundestagswahl 2002. Voraussetzungen – Ergebnisse – Folgen* (Wiesbaden: Westdeutscher Verlag).

Hennis, W. (1957) *Meinungsforschung und repräsentative Demokratie. Zur Kritik politischer Umfragen* (Tübingen: Mohr).

Hofmann-Göttig, J. (2005a, September 9/10) *Meinungsforschung und Meinungsmache am Beispiel des Bundestagswahlkampfes 2005. Was taugt die 'Sonntagsfrage'?*, http://politische-bildung.rlp.de/fileadmin/download/2005-09-17_BTW2005_Meinungsforschung_Meinungsmache_lang.pdf, date accessed May 15, 2009.

Hofmann-Göttig, J. (2005b, September 19) *Umfragen zur Bundestagswahl vom 18. September 2005: Was taugte die 'Sonntagsfrage'?*, http://www.politische-bildung-rlp.de/fileadmin/download/2005-09-20_BTW2005_Umfragen%20zur%20Bundestagswahl%202005.pdf, date accessed May 15, 2009.

Hohlfeld, R. (2006) 'Bundestagswahlkampf 2005 in den Nachrichtensendungen', *Aus Politik und Zeitgeschichte*, (38), 11–17.

Holtz-Bacha, C. (2008, August) 'Polls and the media in Germany: a productive relationship', paper presented at the 2008 Annual Meeting of the American Political Science Association, Boston, August 28–31, 2008.

Hetterich, V. (2000) *Von Adenauer zu Schröder – Der Kampf um Stimmen. Eine Längsschnittanalyse der Wahlkampagnen von CDU und SPD bei den Bundestagswahlen 1949 bis 1998* (Opladen: Leske + Budrich).

'Im Vergleich: Letzte Umfragen und Wahlergebnisse', Frankfurter Allgemeine Zeitung. http://www.faz.net/aktuell/politik/meinungsforschung-es-fehlt-das-vertrauen-1255420.html, date accessed September 20, 2005.

Jandura, O. and T. Petersen (2009) 'Gibt es eine indirekte Wirkung von Wahlumfragen? Eine Untersuchung über den Zusammenhang zwischen der auf Umfragen gestützten und der sonstigen politischen Berichterstattung im Bundestagswahlkampf 2002', *Publizistik*, 54, 485–497.

Kaase, M. (1977) 'Politische Meinungsforschung in Bundesrepublik Deutschland', *Politische Vierteljahresschrift*, 18, 452–475.

Kaase, M. (2003) 'Die Bundesrepublik Deutschland nach der Bundestagswahl 2002 – Überlegungen eines Wahlsoziologen', *Politische Vierteljahresschrift*, 44, 3–9.

Kaase, M. and B. Pfetsch (2001) 'Polling and the democratic process in Germany – Analyses of a difficult relationship', *International Review of Sociology*, 11(2), 125–147.

Krüger, U. M. and T. Zapf-Schramm (2009, December) 'Wahlinformationen im öffentlich-rechtlichen und privaten Fernsehen 2009', *Media Perspektiven*, 622–636.

Kruke, A. (2007) *Demoskopie in der Bundesrepublik Deutschland. Meinungsforschung, Parteien und Medien 1949–1990* (Düsseldorf: Droste).

Kutsch, A. (1995) 'Einstellungen zum Nationalsozialismus in der Nachkriegszeit. Ein Beitrag zu den Anfängen der Meinungsforschung in den westlichen Besatzungszonen', *Publizistik*, 40, 415–447.

Ladd, E. C. and J. Benson (1992) 'The growth of news polls in American politics', in T. E. Mann and G. R. Ornstein (eds), *Media Polls in American Politics* (Washington, DC: The Brookings Institution).

Lupri, E. (1969) 'Soziologische Bedeutung der Wahlprognose. Über den Einfluß von Meinungsforschungsergebnissen auf die politische Willensbildung', in K. D. Hartmann (ed.), *Politische Beeinflussung. Voraussetzungen, Ablauf und Wirkungen* (Frankfurt am Main: Europäische Verlagsanstalt).

Meyen, M. (2002) 'Die Anfänge der empirischen Medien- und Meinungsforschung in Deutschland', *ZA-Information*, (50), 59–80.

Noelle, E. (1940) *Meinungs- und Massenforschung in USA. Umfragen über Politik und Presse* (Frankfurt: Diesterweg).

Noelle-Neumann, E. (1976, September 30) 'Der Einfluss des Fernsehens auf die Entscheidung der Wähler', *Die Welt*, 7.

Noelle-Neumann, E. (1980) *Die Schweigespirale. Öffentliche Meinung – unsere soziale Haut* (München: Piper).

Noelle-Neumann, E. (1990) 'Die öffentliche Meinung und die Wirkung der Massenmedien', in J. Wilke (ed.) *Fortschritte der Publizistikwissenschaft* (Freiburg/München: Alber), pp. 11–23.

Noelle-Neumann, E. (1997) 'Über den Fortschritt der Publizistikwissenschaft durch Anwendung empirischer Forschungsmethoden. Eine autobiographische Aufzeichnung', in A. Kutsch und H. Pöttker (eds) *Kommunikationswissenschaft – autobiographisch. Zur Entwicklung einer Wissenschaft in Deutschland* (Opladen: Westdeutscher Verlag).

Presserat (2008) *Publizistische Grundsätze (Pressekodex). Richtlinien für die publizistische Arbeit nach den Empfehlungen des Deutschen Presserats,* http://www.presserat.info/uploads/media/Pressekodex_01.pdf, date accessed December 6, 2010.

Raupp, J. (2007) *Politische Meinungsforschung. Die Verwendung von Umfragen in der politischen Kommunikation* (Konstanz: UVK).

Rede der Bundeskanzlerin zur Vorstellung des Allensbacher Jahrbuchs der Demoskopie 'Die Berliner Republik' (2010, March 3), http://www.bundesregierung.de/Content/DE/Rede/2010/03/2010-03-03-merkel-allensbach.html, date accessed April 11, 2010.

Reumann, K. (1983, March 9) 'Gibt es einen Fallbeil-Effekt für die kleinen Parteien?', *Frankfurter Allgemeine Zeitung*, p. 4.

rs (2005) 'Inflation statt Qualität. Über Umfrageergebnisse wird immer häufiger berichtet – doch mit welchem Mehrwert?', *Media Tenor Forschungsbericht*, (152), 58–59.

Schaefer, W. and M. Miller (1998) 'Schwierigkeiten der Umfrageforschung in den fünfziger Jahren in Deutschland: Erinnerungen und Beobachtungen', *Zuma-Nachrichten*, (43), 8–35.

Schaffer, L.-M. and G. Schneider (2005) 'Die Prognosegüte von Wahlbörsen und Meinungsumfragen zur Bundestagswahl 2005', *Politische Vierteljahresschrift*, 46, 674–681.

Scheuch, E. K. (1999) 'Die Entwicklung der Umfrageforschung in der Bundesrepublik Deutschland in den siebziger und achtziger Jahren', *Zuma-Nachrichten*, (45), 7–22.

Schmitt-Beck, R. (1996) 'Mass media, the electorate and the bandwagon: a study of communication effects on vote choice in Germany', *International Journal of Public Opinion Research*, 8, 266–291.

Schoen, H. (1999) 'Mehr oder weniger als fünf Prozent – Ist das wirklich die Frage?', *Kölner Zeitschrift für Soziologie und Sozialpsychologie*, 51, 565–582.

Schoen, H. (2000) 'Appelle zu taktischem Wahlverhalten – effektive Werbung oder verfehlte Wahlkampfrhetorik?', in J. Falter, O. Gabriel and H. Rattinger (eds), *Wirklich ein Volk?* (Opladen: Leske + Budrich).

Schoen, H. (2002) 'Wirkung von Wahlprognosen auf Wahlen', in T. Berg (ed.), *Moderner Wahlkampf. Blick hinter die Kulissen* (Opladen: Leske + Budrich).

Staatsvertrag für Rundfunk und Telemedien (2010) http://www.die-medienanstalten. de/fileadmin/Download/Rechtsgrundlagen/Gesetze_aktuell/13._RStV_01.04. 2010_01.pdf, date accessed January 6, 2011.

Theile, M. (2005, September 19) 'Dichter Nebel', *Der Spiegel. Wahlsonderheft '05*, p. 63.

vb (2006) 'Mehr als ein Spiegel der Gesellschaft. Medienpräsenz von Meinungsforschungsinstituten', *Media Tenor Forschungsbericht*, (155), 62–63.

Wahlumfragen: Was Journalisten über sie denken und wie sie auf die Wähler wirken (2005, September 8), *Informationsdienst Wissenschaft*, http://www.idw-online.de/pages/de/news?print= 1&id= 127050, date accessed September 29, 2007.

Wichmann, W. and F. Brettschneider (2009) 'American and German elite journalists' attitudes toward election polls', *International Journal of Public Opinion Research*, 21, 506–524.

6
Opinion Polls and the Media in the United States

Kathleen A. Frankovic

For all practical purposes, media polls are an American invention, and polls have been reported by the American news media as long ago as the early nineteenth century. Over the last two centuries, media polls have become an increasingly important part of the American political journalistic landscape.

Those early polls were not necessarily conducted by and for the news media itself. They were, instead, partisan efforts reported by the newspapers friendly towards the candidates or issues that these polls said the public supported.

There was a democratic reason for these polls. In the early 1800s, many states excluded the public from voting on the nation's highest office, the Presidency, and left the choice of who should cast ballots in the Electoral College to state legislatures. In 1824, the legislative choices were often not the popular choice. Newspapers of the era, which were committed to one party or faction, reported straw polls – taken in town halls, at public meetings, in books opened for the public in town halls and occasionally even in bars, and on Mississippi riverboats – suggesting that the public favored candidates who were not the choice of party leaders. The *Niles' Weekly Register*, one of the papers to publish these polls, proclaimed: 'This is something new; but an excellent plan of obtaining the sense of the people' (Frankovic 1998).

The tactic of using polls to extend the franchise was successful, as the number of states that did not have a public vote to select presidential electors dropped from seven to two between the 1824 and 1828 elections.

Beginning in 1896, newspapers became more directly involved in polling, conducting straw polls on their own. Working before scientific sampling theory was developed, their emphasis was on interviewing large numbers of potential voters to predict election results. These large-scale news polls (mostly about elections) made a virtue of these large numbers of respondents. The *Chicago Record* mailed 833,277 post-card ballots at a cost of $60,000 to all registered voters in Chicago and a 10 per cent sample in 12 Midwest states. 240,000 postcards were returned. Results were 'adjusted by mathematicians' and reported in newspapers before the election (Jensen 1971).

Other newspapers also used straw polls in 1896, although no other polling was as impressive as the *Record*'s in scope or success. The *Chicago Tribune*, the *New York Tribune*, the *Chicago Times-Herald* and even the *Omaha World-Herald* (run by William Jennings Bryan, one of the candidates) conducted and reported straw polls. In later years, more newspapers joined in. Between 1900 and 1920 nearly 20 separate news organizations conducted polls (Robinson 1922).

In its 1923 mayoral election poll, the *Chicago Tribune* tabulated more than 85,000 ballots, using a meticulously detailed interviewing plan. In the month before the April election, interviews were conducted throughout Chicago, and results were published reporting preferences of each ethnic group (including the 'colored' vote), with special samples of streetcar drivers, moviegoers (noting the differences between first and second show attendees) and white-collar workers in the Loop. Despite their lack of modern sampling theory, straw poll projects included technological innovations. The *Tribune* polled what it described as the 'white native vote', conducting 8145 telephone interviews in nine Chicago phone exchanges, covering residences and apartment build-ings where 'even the canvassers of the political parties have little or no chance to ascertain the sentiment' (*Chicago Tribune* 1923; Frankovic 1998).

The Literary Digest magazine began its polls in 1916, and sent out mil-lions of ballots – more than 10 million by 1936. It tabulated its returned ballots (usually about 10 per cent of those mailed out) by state, and had an impressive record in predicting elections until its complete failure in 1936, when it predicted a landslide victory for Republican Alf Landon over Franklin D. Roosevelt, the Democratic incumbent. In the election, Landon carried only the states of Maine and Vermont.

In the mid-1930s, American news polls emerged as we generally know them today, sampling a much smaller number of respondents, and – because of a much more inclusive sampling frame – giving a much more accurate prediction of the 1936 presidential election. The *Digest*'s frame overrepresented better-off Americans, which skewed its results for what was a class-based election (Squire 1988).

Three major news polls were established in 1935 and 1936: the Gallup Poll, established in 1935, which syndicated its results to newspapers across the country (one per media market); the Roper Poll, which Elmo Roper conducted for *Fortune* Magazine, beginning July 1935; and Archibald Crossley's polls for Hearst Publications. Dr. George Gallup became the salesman for polling, noting how important it was for democracy and for news. But of course this democratic focus, while important to the popularization of news polls, masked in part the other major use of polls – for marketing products (including movies and newspapers) and testing advertising.

The founders of these three news polls ran companies that did both. The successful election polls they produced in 1936 brought much-needed publicity to their firms, proving their methods to potential market research clients. Beating the *The Literary Digest* was critical in establishing the business of survey research.

Many newspapers jumped on the polling bandwagon. In May 1940, 118 newspapers subscribed to the Gallup Poll (Gallup and Rae 1940). *Fortune* surveys increased in frequency and appeared monthly. Between 1943 and 1948, at least 14 state organizations were conducting their own polls, using methods approximating those of the national pollsters. The *Des Moines Register* was first, in 1943, followed by the Minnesota Poll (*Minneapolis Tribune*), the Belden Texas Poll and the Field California Poll. The *Washington Post* began its own local polling in 1945 in part, it said, to supplement the Gallup poll on national affairs, but also, it claimed, 'to implement the democratic process in the only American community in which residents do not have the right to express their views at the polling booth' (*Washington Post* 1945).

The 1948 error and its aftermath

Pollsters had gained a national audience by 1948 that extended far beyond their own press releases and print media subscribers. Elmo Roper gave weekly Sunday radio talks on CBS, and both Roper and Gallup were televised. CBS broadcast both the 15-minute 'America Speaks – the George Gallup Show' on nine Sundays at 10.00 p.m., and the half-hour 'Presidential Straws in the Wind', with Elmo Roper on four Tuesdays that fall.

Many news organizations were willing to attribute more certainty to poll findings than were the pollsters themselves (Doob 1949). The front-page headline of the *Washington Post* on election morning read 'Dewey Deemed Sure Winner Today', although the last pre-election Gallup Poll had given the Republican Thomas E. Dewey only a five-point lead over the incumbent Democrat Harry Truman (49.5–44.5 per cent). In that climate, poll predictions of an easy win for Dewey made Truman's victory all the more devastating for the news polling community. *The New Yorker* magazine, which did not use polls, reacted with glee. In its 'Talk of the Town' column, it derided 'the so-called science of poll-taking' as 'not a science at all but mere necromancy' (*New Yorker* 1948). It wrote:

> The total collapse of the public opinion polls shows that the country is in good health ... although you can take a nation's pulse, you can't be sure that the nation hasn't just run up a flight of stairs, and although you can take the nation's blood pressure, you can't be sure that if you came back in 20 minutes you'd get the same reading. This is a damn fine thing ... we are proud of American for clouding up the crystal ball, for telling one thing to a poll-taker, another thing to a voting machine. This is an excellent land.

Gallup lost some subscribers. In one study, interviewing 47 editors who had used polls before the election, half said they would no longer do so (Merton and Hatt 1949). Elmo Roper spent days after the election calling his market research clients to reassure them that his commercial work was still useful.

Harry Truman himself criticized polls both before and after Election Day. He called polls 'sleeping polls' because, he said, they were like 'sleeping pills: designed to lull the voters into sleeping on Election Day'. Intelligent voters, according to Truman, were not being 'fooled. They know that sleeping polls are bad for the system. They affect the mind and the body. An overdose can be fatal' (Truman 1948).

Gallup, Roper and Crossley had ceased polling in the weeks preceding that election, convinced – like many journalists and political leaders – that New York Republican Governor Thomas Dewey would defeat the incumbent President. The expectation of a Dewey victory encouraged news organizations to declare a Dewey victory on Election Day itself, before all the returns were counted. The most famous image of that election is Harry Truman, the morning after Election Day, smiling and holding up *The Chicago Tribune*, whose eight-column headline proclaimed 'Dewey Defeats Truman'. This image is iconic: when the US Post Office issued 'The 1940s' in its series of stamps honoring the 10 decades of the twentieth century, this was among the dozen or so images of the '40s' it commemorated.

The 1948 error had much to do with the pollsters ending data collection early. It also had to do with the use of quota sampling. After the election, the Social Science Research Council sponsored an academic study of the error; its report cited last-minute changes in vote preference (as indicated in panel studies of individuals interviewed both before and after the election) as well as the use of quota, not probability, selection of respondents by individual interviewers (Mosteller et al. 1949).

The modern memory of 1948

The memory of the 1948 election mistake is still vivid. Poll mistakes continue to be compared with the 1948 mis-prediction. In 2008, polls conducted before the New Hampshire primary showed Barack Obama clearly ahead of Hillary Clinton, his principal opponent for the Democratic nomination. However, Hillary Clinton won that primary. Journalists – and even pollsters who did not conduct pre-primary polls – also reacted negatively to their colleagues' failures, even calling it a 'fiasco' (Langer 2008).

The American Association for Public Opinion Research commissioned a study of pre-election polling errors. The Committee found answers similar to those cited in 1948, including both timing and sampling issues. According to the report's summary, with the limited amount of time available to poll between the Iowa Caucuses (3 January) and the New Hampshire primary (8 January), 'polls conducted before the New Hampshire primary may have ended too early to capture late shifts in the electorate's preferences', that limited time and the survey firms' procedures did not allow for multiple attempts to reach potential respondents, 'skewing the results toward the opinions of those who were easy to reach on the phone, and who more typically supported Senator Obama', and some groups that supported Hillary Clinton, like union members and those with less education, proved more difficult to reach. In addition, the models used for estimates, which relied heavily on past voting participation as well as expressed likelihood of voting in the primary, may not have been appropriate for an election where new – and occasional – voters were drawn into the electorate (Mathiowetz 2009).

Most pre-election polls since 1948 have produced good estimates of the actual election results – at least for the general election, when the race is typically between only two candidates, and follows a long campaign through the fall. But there have been some elections where the polls have not predicted the winner's margin of victory particularly well. In 1980, most polls suggested that Ronald Reagan and Jimmy Carter were in a close election; Reagan won that contest by 10 points. And in 1996, many polls predicted a much larger margin of victory for incumbent Bill Clinton than he won. Polls in state elections and in many primaries – like New Hampshire in 2008 – have not had that level of success. In those elections, voters may not be as attentive to the campaign as they typically are for presidential elections, and the primary timetable often shortens the available time for polling. The National Council on Public Polls (NCPP), founded in 1969, regularly produces reports on how accurately the polls have predicted national and state elections, going back to 1936 and continuing to the present (reports are available on its website, www.ncpp.org). Many news organizations themselves as well as interest groups and specialized websites devoted to polls also produce measures of election polling accuracy.

After 1948: Expansion in the 1970s and the 1990s

Although slowed by the failure of the 1948 news polls to correctly predict the outcome of that presidential election, Gallup thrived, though Crossley moved almost exclusively to market research, and the *Fortune* Magazine Roper Poll (though not the Roper Poll and company) disappeared in the 1950s.

In the 1970s, television news organizations also became invested in reporting – and conducting – public opinion polls. CBS News ran telephone polls in the late 1960s and formally set up a survey unit to work with *The New York Times* in 1975. In 1975 and 1976, CBS News conducted more than a dozen national telephone opinion polls from *The New York Times* classified advertising facility, with interviewers hired and trained by *The Times*. The sampling was done using what became known as the Mitofsky-Waksberg sampling method, selecting telephone exchanges at random; if a "block" of seven digits resulted in a household when a number from it was dialed, the block would become part of the sample. There was random selection within the household, and weighting factors included size of household, sex and education. Later the interviewing would be moved to the CBS News election data intake facility, and would be conducted using Computer Assisted Telephone Interviewing (CATI).

NBC News also conducted its own polls, as did *The Los Angeles Times*. Journalistic skill sets do not normally include statistical analysis or sampling, though academics like Phil Meyer did major work in training journalists in what he titled *Precision Journalism* (1973). But units within some news organizations, which developed from advertising and marketing departments and from election coverage, did polls, too.

Public polls expanded exponentially in the 1990s when data processing no longer required the use of mainframe computers, and sampling, interviewing and data processing and analysis could all be done on PCs. CATI replaced pencil and paper questionnaires. Errors in dialing phone numbers dropped as the computer itself took control of the calling process. Smaller institutions, like colleges, could conduct national and state opinion polls for public release at minimal cost, using students to conduct most interviews.

The total number of questions archived at the Roper Center Data Archive of public polling questions at the University of Connecticut (www.ropercenter.uconn.edu) for the years 1998 and 1999 reached nearly 20,000 for each of those years, nearly half again as many questions archived for 1990 and 1991. Some of that increase is due to poll expansion, but some is due to the intense interest in one particular political scandal: Bill Clinton's relationship with Monica Lewinsky. 1710 questions were asked in 1998 and 1999 that included her name. There were 1300 questions about impeachment in those two years (with fewer than 10 per cent of the total number of items included in both counts).

But even the early 1990s was a growth era for public opinion polling: Ross Perot, who ran for President as an independent candidate in both 1992 and 1996, vowed to use public opinion to democratize decision making, going so far as to include town hall questionnaires in issues of the country's largest circulation magazine, *TV Guide*.

Pollsters were more likely to worry about their image in that decade as well. The Roper Center database contains more questions about polls themselves for the 1990s than it does for the next ten years. Excluding questions about the US Census, there were 216 public polling questions in the 1990s that asked about polls; just about half that number, 115, were asked in the following decade.

Election day polling and attempts to restrict polls

To many journalists, pre-election polling was viewed as an expansion of the news media's role in reporting elections – and to do that as quickly as possible. Even in the nineteenth century, news organizations attempted to project election results as quickly as possible. They used the technologies of the day (old tech, like carrier pigeons, and newer tech, like the telegraph) to get results quickly. As early as the 1880s, *The Boston Globe* selected certain precincts it believed represented the state and collected those vote counts as quickly as possible. From those data the paper was able to project state-wide outcomes. Some late nineteenth-century newspapers reported election results not only in special editions, but by using light projections on election nights to indicate which party had won (Littlewood 1998).

As early as 1952, television news organizations used computers to help with projections. That year, CBS linked up with the computer maker Univac for support, while NBC News called its election computer 'Mike Mono-Robot'. Projecting election outcomes did not at first include the use of exit polls to do so. Like the nineteenth-century *Boston Globe*, television news organizations gathered the votes from selected polling places when they were counted, transmitting those results to central locations to be used in projection models. Exit polls first appeared in 1969 to provide vote information in areas where votes were not counted at the polling location, but taken to a central counting facility, which delayed the media's access to the information.

By the early 1970s, some news organizations were using information collected in exit polls to analyze the results – to explain how demographic groups had cast their ballots and the reasons they gave for choosing the candidates. Each network competed to produce the best information and to project elections first. However, the costs of collecting enough data to make state-wide projections from exit polls and sample precincts forced broadcast news organizations (later joined by CNN, Fox News and the Associated Press) to combine data collection efforts, first as the Voter News Service (VNS) and later as the National Election Pool (NEP) (Mitofsky 1991).

Exit polls caused the most serious attempt to restrict polling in the USA. The First Amendment to the US Constitution includes the words: 'Congress shall make no law…abridging the freedom of speech, or of the press…'. That text has been used to insure the legal rights of any person – and any news organization – to say and publish what they wish. While there have been laws passed to limit pornography, even they are limited to subjects like child pornography, where courts have ruled that protection of the child is more important. Since broadcast television uses the 'scarce resource' of the airwaves, the Federal Communications Commission also regulates it. Certain types of speech and images – like those classified as obscene – are banned. Cable television, which does not the scarce resources of the airwaves, does not have the same restrictions.

But news coverage cannot be regulated. And polls conducted by and for the media cannot be banned. Laws that have tried to do just that have been overturned in the courts. In 1980, one network news organization, NBC News, using exit poll results to help with its projections, declared that Ronald Reagan had defeated incumbent President, Jimmy Carter, at 8.15 p.m. Eastern Time, nearly three hours before polls closed in the western part of the USA. After that election, the state of Washington restricted exit polls, legislating that voters could not be interviewed within 300 feet of the polling place. The legislature claimed that exit polling 'infringed on Washington state voters' rights by disrupting the peace, order, and decorum of the polling place, and discouraging voting' (*The Daily Herald Company* et al. v. *Ralph Munro*, 838 f2d 380).

However, the suit against the law, brought not just by *The Daily [Everett] Herald* (a Washington state newspaper), but by all broadcast network news operations and *The New York Times*, argued that 'exit polling constitutes speech protected by the First Amendment, not only in that the information disseminated based on the polls is speech, but also in that the process of obtaining the information requires a discussion between pollster and voter'.

The Court found that the state's law was too extreme. While it could regulate 'disruptive' exit polling, the law banning polling within 300 feet of a polling place could not apply to 'non-disruptive' polling. And the Court saw no evidence that conducting an exit poll was disruptive to the election process, since exit poll interviews were conducted after people had voted. In addition, if the State were trying to find a way to outlaw disruptive practices, there were less broad ways of doing that (though the Court noted that it was not clear that the examples it cited, like requiring exit pollsters to tell potential respondents that participation was voluntary, or limiting access within a smaller distance, would pass 'Constitutional muster').

The Court also noted that the law directly infringed on what the media could report on Election Night. That claim was 'impermissible'. The Court wrote that 'a general interest in insulating voters from outside influences is insufficient to justify speech regulation'. And the Court said the state had presented no evidence that any voter in Washington declined to vote because of broadcasting of early returns.

Since the Washington state case, there have been other efforts to limit exit polling. Most of those attempts have set limits on how close to the polling place those conducting exit polls can be. But, like the Washington State case, the courts have rejected all the limits on exit polling locations. In recent cases, the courts have asked those who conduct exit polling to demonstrate that keeping interviewers a significant distance away from the polling places hampers their ability to produce accurate estimates. In fact, the further away from the voting place exit pollsters are required to stand, the less accurate their estimate of the vote in that location (Edelman & Merkle 1999).

Government can summon media representatives to testify in Congressional hearings. There have been a number of such hearings, mostly following election nights where a winner has been projected before all polls were closed, including the 1980 elections and the 1964 landslide election victory of Lyndon Johnson, before exit polls were part of the reporting. And after the 2000 election, when television news media projected at 7.50 p.m. Eastern Time that Democrat Al Gore would carry the state of Florida and later retracted that projection, only to retract a late-night projection of a Bush victory there, news presidents once again appeared before Congress to apologize. News organizations conducted their own internal investigations in preparation for those hearings (Frankovic 2003; Konner, Risser & Wattenberg 2001; Mason, Frankovic & Jamieson 2001).

Most other attempts to regulate opinion and market research have been stopped by lobbying at the legislative level. For example, so far lawmakers have been willing to exclude research activities from laws that regulate sales over the telephone. A 'do not call' list was implemented in 2004. At that time telemarketers could not call those numbers registered on the list. Researchers could continue to include those numbers in their telephone samples. Lobbyists for the research industry, some representing organizations like the Marketing Research Association, continue to monitor attempts at legislation.

Self-regulation

National associations attempt self-regulation of media polls. The American Association for Public Opinion Research (AAPOR) encourages disclosure, and on occasion has condemned organizations that refuse to release detailed information about their polls. It provides Standards for Minimal Disclosure of poll results (AAPOR 2010). Many news organizations now provide much of that information – but frequently that can be found only on the organization's website, and is not contained in stories about the polls, especially when those stories are reported on television news. The National Council on Public Polls (NCPP), an organization for those who conduct or report those polls, sets similar standards for disclosure. It encourages news organizations to indicate when they release a poll that they are following those standards.

AAPOR has also established what it calls a 'Transparency Initiative', a plan to recognize those organizations that routinely disclose methodological information about their polls, and establish an archive to hold that methodological information. As of April 2011, nearly 75 organizations have signed on to the initiative; however, more than 30 of those organizations are affiliated with academic survey centers, and only five are news organizations (AAPOR 2011).

NCPP has reached out to journalists with its publication '20 Questions a Journalist Should Ask about Opinion Polls', now in its third edition (Gawiser and Witt n.d.). In addition, since 2007 NCPP has presented an award for excellence in news coverage of polls, which has been awarded to both newspaper (*Los Angeles Times*), and television poll (ABC News) reporting.

Self-regulation can be helpful in staving off government interventions. Working to be sure legislation regulating sales and marketing not applied to research has been another successful strategy. However, there are areas where the government's regulation of things outside of journalism can be applied to opinion polls. In particular, the 'content neutral' law that prohibits using automated mechanisms to dial mobile phones has had a major impact on opinion polling and on news polls. The Telephone Consumer Protection Act of 1991 prohibits the use of automated dialing systems to call a cell phone without the user's 'prior express consent'. In 2003, the Federal Communications Commission clarified the term 'automated dialing system' to include all forms of auto-dialers as well as all calls, whether between states or within a single state. Cell phones could be called, but only if the phone numbers were dialed by hand. Since that law addressed technology, and not news gathering, it applied to media polls as well as to telemarketing.

This rule could increase the costs of polling, and until the 2008 election season, news surveys excluded cell phones from their sampling frames. But by 2008, when one in five homes had no traditional landlines, and even more minorities and young adults fit that category, news polls felt required to add cell phones to their sampling frame, even though for many, that would increase the costs of their polls.

Creating public opinions

There is a widespread belief that polls affect public opinion, though direct evidence is limited. After the 1988 election, CBS News and *The New York Times* asked Americans this question: 'Some people say that news reports of polls showing who is ahead persuade people to change their minds. How many people do you think changed their minds about what they would do on election day this year because of polls – most people, many people, a few people, or hardly any at all?' 69 per cent said at least a few had; 26 per cent thought many or most had (7 per cent said most people changed their minds because of the polls). But in that same poll only 2 per cent said they personally had changed.

Belief that polls affect public opinion and voting has been long held by critics of opinion polling. These critiques are often expressed by supporters of losing candidates after elections.

Americans, too, when asked, would restrict polls and any projections made from them. A Roper Poll in 1984 found 62 per cent believing that 'television networks should not be allowed to project the final outcome of the election before polls are closed in all states'.

Some academics found an effect on Western voters of early projections (Jackson 1983); others find little or no impact (Adams 2005). But like the public research on voter impact, while many believe that people are affected by early projections, it is difficult to find individuals who admit an effect. However, there is much evidence that the media polls help to set the agenda for press coverage and in that case may affect what issues matter (Gollin 1980) and how candidates are perceived (Hardy & Jamieson 2005).

Polling today

News polling faces serious financial problems in the twenty-first century, as the media sponsors have lost advertisers to the recession and viewers and subscribers to the Internet. Those financial problems affect all aspects of their operation, including media polls. CBS News is now the only news poll that is completely controlled within the organization. Other organizations have established connections with outside firms, either for interviewing services or for full-service assistance, and sometimes at a reduced rate in return for linking the company's name with the news organization's brand. Television and print connections also continue, with links between NBC News and *The Wall St. Journal*, and ABC News and *The Washington Post*. Nearly all of the public polling done in the USA today is done – or commissioned – by the media itself, though reports of polls by non-profit research organizations, like the Pew Research Foundation, as well as special polls conducted for corporations or interest groups, are also common.

Media polls today are mainly about national politics, although state polls are frequently reported in local papers and television outlets. During presidential elections – where gathering votes in the state-based Electoral College is what will determine who is elected President, state polls are also reported, with some conducted directly for the news media. There are also polls about state races for Governor and US Senate that have national importance.

In the Roper Center archive of national public polls, there are 316 separate items that ask Americans between January and Election Day 2008 whether a person would vote for Barack Obama or John McCain 'if the election were held today'. An additional 72 items asked potential voters to choose between McCain and Hillary Clinton, who was President Obama's chief competitor during the primary campaign. In 2007, the archive shows an additional 89 questions asking how voters would choose between Hillary Clinton or Barack Obama and the eventual Republican nominee.

Of course, that is still an underestimate of the number of horse race questions asked by public polls during the campaign. There were other potential Republican and Democratic nominees frequently paired against each other in the November election. And there are ways to ask the vote question without the phrase 'if the presidential election were being held today'.

Horse race and election questions dominate news polls. And their number has grown over the decades. But it appears that their frequency may have stabilized in the last ten years. Table 6.1 shows the results from

Table 6.1 Number of questions in Roper Center archives containing the words 'presidential election' and 'today' by decade

Totals	
1930s	11 (1 election)
1940s	248 (3 elections)
1950s	191 (2 elections)
1960s	228 (3 elections)
1970s	260 (2 elections)
1980s	701 (3 elections)
1990s	1376 (2 elections)
2000s	1298 (3 elections)

Source: Roper Center Data Archives, University of Connecticut.

a Roper archive search for the terms 'presidential election' and 'today'. As Table 6.1 shows, the number of horse race questions did not increase in the 2000s.

Even with only two presidential elections occurring in the 1990s, there were more horse race questions asked in that decade than in the one that followed. The elections of 1992 and 1996 were both three-candidate elections, which may have increased the frequency of horse race questions for some polling organizations, as they asked preference for both the three-way and the two-way contests.

While horse race and other election-related items may be the most popular, other polling topics cover major news events, sometimes to an extreme degree. For example, until Hillary Clinton became a Senator from New York and a potential presidential candidate, the most famous woman in American opinion polls was Monica Lewinsky. For the 1990s, the Roper Center database contains 1710 questions that contained the name Monica Lewinsky, making her at that point the most frequently asked about woman in polling history. Just 1255 questions had been asked about the then-First Lady. But by 2010, there were more than 4000 questions naming Hillary Clinton, the presidential candidate. Hardly any questions were being asked about Lewinsky (Frankovic 2008).

News organizations may also commission polls internationally. In recent years, ABC News has joined with television networks in Great Britain, Germany and Japan to sponsor polls in Iraq and Afghanistan. The polls themselves are conducted by local interviewers, supervised first by Oxford Research International and in later years by the commercial firm D3 Systems.

The value of news polls

Polls matter. *The Washington Post* underscored that view in a late 1930s promotional pamphlet. '[T]o bring the complete story', said the pamphlet, it takes articles and pictures of what's going on, editorial analysis about the news, and 'American reactions as shown in the Gallup Poll'. *The Post* was the Gallup Poll's first subscriber, and its then-publisher, Eugene Meyer, claimed that 'the polls have changed journalism, just as the organization of press associations did, just as the advent of half-tone photo engravings did, just as the rise of the columnists and commentators did' (Meyer 1940).

Polling in or for a modern news organization does several things that matter more than ever before to a contemporary journalism that is struggling financially: a poll gives a news organization material that it owns (in other words, an exclusive story), it is expected to generate reader and viewer interest, and it helps extend the news organization's brand.

The concept of the 'exclusive' has a long history. A poll conducted by or for a particular news organization is an especially good exclusive, as a news organization not only has information that others do not, but it can control the timing of the release of the poll. News editors and reporters have praised polls. In 1916, *The Literary Digest* inaugurated its polls by saying that 'The most important piece of news-gathering... in sight at this time... [is] to find out how people are intending to vote.' Modern editors agree that polls are important and useful. They also serve to protect a news organization from being misled by politicians' descriptions of what people think or what elections mean (Kovach 1980).

In 1935, the editors of *Fortune* Magazine trumpeted the inaugural edition of their poll, conducted by Elmo Roper, linking it to impartial journalism. They wrote: 'For the journalist and particularly such journalists of fact as the editors of *Fortune* conceive themselves to be, has no preference as to the facts he hopes to uncover. He prefers, as a journalist, no particular outcome. He is quite as willing to publish the answers that upset his apple cart of preconceptions as to publish the answers that bear him out' (*Fortune* 1935).

As for stimulating public interest, the assumption has been that the public care, often in the face of contrary polling evidence. In the 1990s, *The San Francisco Examiner* included this advertisement in some of its sales boxes: 'The latest polls indicate that people like to read the latest polls.'

However, many Americans have told modern-day pollsters that there is too much emphasis on polls, especially horse race polls, but they do want government to pay attention to poll results. In October 2008, the Pew Center found a country divided over whether the reporting of polls showing which candidate was ahead was a 'good thing or a bad thing for the country'. 38 per cent called it a good thing, 43 per cent said it was a bad thing. But in the same poll, 62 per cent said the press did a good or excellent job reporting those results.

A February 2010 Harris poll found a majority of Americans said opinion polls had 'too little power and influence in Washington'. However, 31 per cent said they had 'too much'. Polls conducted 50 years apart found similar answers to this question: 'Do you believe that polls of public opinion on issues of the day have value to the people?' The Gallup Organization found 60 per cent saying they did in December

1948 (16 per cent said they did not). A CBS News poll in March 1998, during the Clinton/Lewinsky controversy received very similar responses: 68 per cent yes, 24 per cent no.

However, relatively few Americans understand how polls are conducted. In a Gallup Poll conducted as recently as September 2005, 68 per cent of the country said that a sample of 1000 adults could not accurately reflect the views of the nation's population, just about the same percentage that had thought so nearly ten years before.

There has always been a business link to news polls. Even as early as 1896, The *Chicago Record* proposed that one of the best justifications for its massive straw poll was that they 'give business... the opportunity to secure to new lines without waiting for Nov. 3'. In other words, they would provide information faster than simply waiting for election results; presumably businessmen could make plans based on those results. Similarly, The *Fortune* Poll was justified by pointing out that while large corporations could do their own research, the *Fortune* Poll would provide to smaller businesses the same type of information about the public. And in fact, the first *Fortune* poll included questions about cigarette smoking, including the brand people smoked.

The Literary Digest always included a subscription form with its millions of postcard ballots, offering respondents the opportunity to remain 'posted on the Great Presidential Poll and ALL the Issues and Results of the Campaign'.

Today, the business side of news polls comes clearly in the area of branding. News organizations do more than simply report poll results. They expect those results will be reported by others as well, extending the organization's brand. Partnerships, which continue to be created (e.g. 60 Minutes/*Vanity Fair*, Associated Press/Petside, ABC News/Yahoo), allow for reduced costs and for each news organization to receive coverage on the other's platform, whether it be print, television or the web. Poll results also can drive people to an organization's website, if they want to find out details about the conduct of a poll, and the questions it asked.

Issues for news polls today

News polls face the same difficulties all survey research does today. Current methods have problems; methods are changing, and there is no consensus about how to best carry out polls that are both legitimate and conducted in a short enough period of time to make them newsworthy. Even the most stringently conducted news polls have an interviewing period of only a few days, with the results reported the day after interviewing has been completed.

Media polls do not ask only about elections; poll questions include many about current issues. Some items have lengthy histories. Gallup asked whether or not the public approved of the way the President was handling his job on a regular basis before 1940; that question, modified only slightly since then, now serves as the thermometer for how well a president is doing. Gallup also questioned Americans in the 1930s about their assessment of the country's major problems – another question routinely asked today.

Future difficulties in conducting news polls in the USA will be similar to those all survey researchers will face: confronting lowered response rates, incorporating changing methods and changes in American behavior. Cell phone penetration will increase and the number of potential respondents who can be reached on standard landlines will continue to decline. As of mid-2010 approximately one in four households was without a landline. The percentage was even higher in some states (Blumberg et al. 2011).

Most major news organizations, including newspapers, cable and broadcast networks, and wire services, have internal rules for reporting their own polls, and for polls conducted by other which they also report. For most, those rules include outright bans on some of the newer technologies of polling: polls conducted using recorded voices and touch-tone or interactive voice response (IVR) data entry, Internet polls and other non-probability polls. Some organizations have codified those rules as part of their news reporting standards. CBS News, for example, included the basic information required to meet AAPOR and NCPP disclosure standards as information reporters should know before reporting any poll. It warns reporters to only make assertions about what 'polls say' if they can cite specific poll findings that support it. It warns reporters against reporting 'non-representative' polls like website or call-in polls.

But news polls are changing. Some news organizations report polls conducted using the IVR technique (most of which exclude cell phones from their samples). Fox News partnered with Rasmussen Reports, which conducts IVR polls, for state polls during the 2008 election. Other organizations (but by no means all) will report online panels. CBS News used poll results from Great Britain conducted among YouGov panel members to report on the 2011 Royal Wedding.

Exit polls are also facing difficulties. Like telephone polls, they suffer from declining response rates, which are now below 50 per cent. The media's desire to report more and more information about the voter's decision-making process resulted in longer and longer questionnaires, which contributed to response issues and errors in estimates. Studies of polling place interviewers have indicated that their age plays a role in response and accuracy (older interviewers have higher response rates and higher accuracy). In some elections where race has been a factor, the race of the interviewer has also affected polling accuracy when an interviewer is of a different race than the respondent (Edelman & Merkle 1999).

There are major concerns about the accuracy of American exit polls, given the sizable within precinct errors seen in recent presidential election years. The 'within precinct error' has tended to favor Democratic candidates for President, particularly Bill Clinton in 1992, John Kerry in 2004 and Barack Obama in 2008. Are Republicans less likely than Democrats to comply with the request to complete a questionnaire at the polling place? According to several public opinion polls, they may be on Election Day. A Fox News telephone poll conducted in October 2006 found 44 per cent of Democrats, but only 35 per cent of Republicans saying they were 'very likely' to complete an exit poll questionnaire. That difference would result in overestimates of Democratic voting.

Some of this appears due to varying levels of intensity among voters. Until the election of 2008, voters were most attentive to the 1992 campaign (and to that of 2004) – in both years two out of three voters paid a lot of attention to the campaign (in other modern elections before 2008, fewer than half of voters reported doing that). Both those elections had the highest errors in exit polling.

Political issues – coupled with fears of potential exit polling errors – also have affected the conduct of exit polls. There have been continued complaints about the possibility of exit poll results leaking before the polls close – and the exit poll is completed – in the age of the Internet. News organizations that participate in the National Election Pool voluntarily keep early results from all but a few individuals who are sequestered in a 'quarantine room' away from their own organizations until late afternoon on Election Day to prevent leaks to the Internet, although this lessens the value of the data to each organization.

Parties and candidates attack polls. The Republican National Committee issued a release on Election Day 2006, warning people not to trust exit polls. The increasing number of websites devoted to polls can analyze and criticize polls when they feel it necessary.

Changes in the way people vote have also altered how exit polls are conducted. Fewer people go to the polling places, choosing to vote by mail or in person before Election Day. This movement began in earnest after the 1980 election, and by 2008 more than 30 per cent of all votes were cast well before Election Day. Oregon and Washington have essentially ALL mail-in voting. In Colorado, two of three votes were cast early, and those who wanted to vote on Election Day could go to only a limited number of county 'Vote Centers', as opposed to a local polling place. More than half the vote was cast early in Texas, Nevada, New Mexico, North Carolina, Tennessee, Georgia, Arizona and Florida. Those voters need to be interviewed by telephone in the days before the election, at additional cost. In the 1980s, only three states had enough absentees to require supplemental absentee voter telephone surveys. By 2010, there were 11 state absentee phone polls, plus one national poll of absentee voters conducted in all other states. But even that does not provide full absentee and early voter coverage.

Finally, the news media in the USA is facing financial difficulties. Those difficulties have already cost some survey professionals in the news media their jobs. Continued cutbacks as revenues continue to decline may decrease the resources available for polls, or move more and more media polls to different, less expensive methodologies, like web panels. The financial difficulties will also limit resources available for exit polls at a time when costs are rising due to the changing nature of American voting.

Losing media polls would be detrimental to the polling industry and the American public. Methodological improvements have come from these polls, and the frequency of media polling provides opportunities for experiments. Exit polls (and their equivalent telephone polls for absentee and early voters) provide the only real-time assessment of what an election means from a non-partisan source. Should the media cease conducting them, there is no obvious candidate to replace them.

Methodological improvements have occurred because of the journalistic need for accurate information gathered as quickly as possible. From the 1970s through the 1990s, the most popular approach to sampling telephones had originally been developed at CBS News by Warren Mitofsky and Joe Waksberg (Waksberg 1978). Mitofsky also has been credited with the invention of the modern exit poll (see Frankovic 1992). News organizations have experimented with ways of determining who will vote and who will not, as the price of being wrong is extremely high.

The position of media polls as the current arbiter of what elections mean and what the public think about politics and issues can create its own problems. After the 2004 election, exit polls were criticized for how they asked voters the issue that mattered most to their vote. A list of items included the phrase 'moral values', which was chosen by more voters than any other item as the reason for their vote, suggesting the election was determined by those with conservative views on abortion and other social issues. Critics seized on the vagueness of the phrase, which was used on the exit poll in part because it was frequently mentioned by the Bush campaign itself (Langer & Cohen 2005).

In addition, the reliance on polls as the arbiters of what public opinion means in the USA does result in the creation of opinion by media elites, who ask questions about what interests them and not necessarily what the public care about. Susan Herbst (1993) has pointed out that, as polls became commonplace, public opinion as we understand it has become reactive, not proactive or emerging directly from public participation in spontaneous expressions of opinion, like rallies. In other words, our understanding of what people care about comes from the top down, and not from the bottom up. George Gallup once said: 'We can try out any idea – we can try out any idea in the world!'

There is one especially important democratic result of media polls: they offer the public the opportunity to learn information previously available only to elites, but that doesn't mean most people use the information about public opinion they hear or read about.

Julian Woodward, one of the founders of AAPOR, called polling a 'public utility', operating in the public interest. Polls are 'an adjunct to the ballot box, designed to make government more responsible to the electorate, and consequently, more democratic... The ballot box is inadequate,' he said. 'The poll is the continuing ballot box.'

References

AAPOR (American Association for Public Opinion Research) (2010) *Disclosure Standards*, http://www.aapor.org/Disclosure_Standards1.htm.

AAPOR (American Association for Public Opinion Research) (2011) *Transparency Initiative Supporters*, http://www.aapor.org/List_of_Supporters.htm.

Adams, W. C. (2005) *Election Night News and Voter Turnout: Solving the Projection Puzzle* (Boulder, CO: Lynne Rienner Publishers).

Blumberg, S., Luke, J. V., Ganesh, N., Davern, M. E., Boudreaux, M. H. and Soderberg, K. (2011) 'Wireless substitution: state-level estimates from the National Health Interview Survey, January 2007–June 2010', *National Health Statistics Report*, 39, April 20, 2011.

Chicago Tribune (1923) March 25, 1.

Doob, L. W. (1949) 'The public presentation of polling results', in F. Mosteller, H. Hyman, P. J. McCarthy, E. S. Marks and D. B. Truman (eds), *The Pre-election*

Polls of 1948: Report to the Committee on Analysis of Pre-election Polls and Forecasts (New York: Social Science Research Council).

Edelman, M. and D. M. Merkle (1999) 'A review of the 1996 exit polls from a total survey error perspective', in P. Lavrakas and M. Traugott (eds), *Election Polls, the News Media and Democracy* (Boulder, CO: Westview Press).

Fortune Magazine (1935) 'The *Fortune* poll', June.

Frankovic, K. A. (1992) 'Technology and the changing landscape of media polls', in T. Mann and G. Orren (eds), *Media Polls in American Politics* (Washington, DC: Brookings Institution Press)

Frankovic, K. A. (1998) 'Public opinion and polling', in D. Graber, D. McQuail and P. Norris (eds), *The Politics of News, the News of Politics* (Washington, DC: CQ Press).

Frankovic, K. A. (2003) 'News organizations' responses to the mistakes of Election 2000: why they will continue to project elections', *Public Opinion Quarterly*, 67, 19–31.

Frankovic, K. A. (2008) 'Women and the polls: questions, answers, images', in L. D. Whitaker (ed.), *Voting the Gender Gap* (Urbana, IL: University of Illinois Press).

Gallup G. and S. F. Rae (1940) *The Pulse of Democracy: The Public Opinion Poll and How it Works* (New York: Simon & Schuster)

Gawiser, S. R. and G. E. Witt (n.d.) *20 Questions a Journalist Should Ask About Poll Results*, third edition, http://ncpp.org/?q=node/4.

Gollin, A. E. (1980) 'Exploring the liaison between polling and the press', *Public Opinion Quarterly*, 44, 445–61.

Hardy, B. W. and K. H. Jamieson (2005) 'Can a poll affect the perception of candidate traits?', *Public Opinion Quarterly*, 69, 725–43.

Herbst, S. (1993) *Numbered Voices: How Opinion Polling Has Shaped American Politics* (Chicago, IL: University of Chicago Press).

Jackson, J. E. (1983) 'Election night reporting and voter turnout', *American Journal of Political Science*, 27, 615–35.

Jensen, R. (1971) *The Winning of the Midwest* (Chicago, IL: University of Chicago Press).

Konner, K., J. Risser and B. Wattenberg (2001) *Television's Performance on Election Night 2000: A Report for CNN*, http://archives.cnn.com/2001/ALLPOLITICS/stories/02/02/cnn.report/cnn.pdf.

Kovach, B. (1980) 'A user's view of the polls', *Public Opinion Quarterly*, 44, 567–71.

Langer, G. (2008) *New Hampshire's Polling Fiasco*, http://blogs.abcnews.com/thenumbers/2008/01/new-hampshires.html.

Langer, G. and J. Cohen (2005) 'Voters and values in the 2004 election', *Public Opinion Quarterly*, 65, 744–59.

Littlewood, T. B. (1998) *Calling Elections: The History of Horse-Race Journalism* (Notre Dame, IN: University of Notre Dame Press).

Mason, L., K. Frankovic and K. H. Jamieson (2001) *CBS News Coverage of Election Night 2000. Investigation, Analysis, Recommendations*, www.cbsnews.com/htdocs/c2k/pdf/REPFINAL.pdf.

Mathiowetz, N. (2009) *Report on 2008 Pre-Election Primary Polls*, http://www.aapor.org/Content/aapor/MemberConnect/Newsletters/2009SpringNewsletter/Reporton2008PreElectionPrimaryPolls/default.htm.

Merton, R. K. and P. K. Hatt (1949) 'Election polling forecasts and public images of social science', *Public Opinion Quarterly*, 13, 185–222.

Meyer, E. (1940) 'A newspaper publisher looks at the polls', *Public Opinion Quarterly*, 4, 230–40.

Meyer, P. (1973) *Precision Journalism: A Reporter's Introduction to Social Science Methods* (Bloomington, IN: University of Indiana Press).

Mitofsky, W. (1991) 'A short history of exit polls', in P. Lavrakas and P. Holley (eds), *Polling and Presidential Election Coverage* (Newbury Park, CA: Sage).

Mosteller, F., H. Hyman, P. J. McCarthy, E. S. Marks and D. B. Truman (1949) *The Pre-Election Polls of 1948. Report to the Committee on Analysis of Pre-Election Polls and Forecasts* (New York: Social Science Research Council).

The New Yorker (1948) 'Talk of the town', November 13. Roper Center Data Archive, www.ropercenter.uconn.edu.

Robinson, C. (1922) *Straw Votes: A Study of Political Predictions* (New York: Columbia University Press).

Squire, P. (1988) 'Why the 1936 *Literary Digest* poll failed', *Public Opinion Quarterly*, 52, 125–33.

Truman, H. (1948) *Address in the Cleveland Municipal Auditorium*, October 26. Truman Presidential Museum and Library, Independence, MO. http://www.trumanlibrary.org/publicpapers/index.php?pid=2009&st=&st1=

Waksberg, J. (1978) 'Sampling methods for random digit dialing', *Journal of the American Statistical Association*, 73, 40–6.

Washington Post (1945) November 11, 1.

7
Opinion Polls and the Media in Brazil

Flávia Biroli, Luis Felipe Miguel and Fernanda Ferreira Mota

The year of 1985 saw the end of a 21-year period of military dictatorship and the return to civil government in Brazil. A rather complex process *per se*, with several constraints imposed by the armed forces, which were still in control of important power resources, it suffered yet another blow with the premature death of president-to-be Tancredo Neves, who was to lead the transition to democracy. In 1988, following nearly two years of intense activity, a constitutional assembly finally concluded the new Constitution. In the following year, a new president was taken to office in a direct election, symbolizing the 'normalization' of formal democratic institutions.

The country that awoke to democracy was a complex one – be it in terms of society, economy or politics. New forms of political participation flourished, stimulated by the 1988 Constitution, which called for the establishment of councils on public policy, or as a result of pressuring social movements, which championed the adoption of 'participatory budgets' in several cities. New political forces also gained center stage, such as the Partido dos Trabalhadores (PT, the Workers' Party), comprising a coalition of union leaders, activists in the new social movements, 'progressive' Catholics and veteran leftist activists hopeful to be able to experiment beyond the Marxist-Leninist orthodoxy.

A minor party at the outset of the redemocratization process (in 1986, it saw only 16 of its members among the 487 constitutional delegates), the PT quickly moved to a more central position in Brazilian politics, thus helping to redesign the party system itself. While it is still seen by a considerable number of researchers (Kinzo 2005; Mainwaring 1999) as excessively fragmented and little institutionalized, the Brazilian party system has taken shape, at the national level, as a polarization between the PT and the Partido da Social-Democracia Brasileira (PSDB, the Brazilian Social Democratic Party). If politics in the 27 federated units (26 states plus a Federal District) is marked by plurality, at the national level the numerous political parties[1] revolve around the PT, on the one hand, and the PSDB, on the other.

Whereas in the first direct presidential election, in 1989, the winner was a small legend candidate (Fernando Collor, who would later suffer impeachment for his involvement in corruption), the PT and the PSDB polarized all following elections. The PSDB was victorious in 1994 and 1998. In 2002, it was PT leader and former unionist Luís Inácio Lula da Silva who held the presidential office. He ran for re-election, and won, in 2006, and in 2010 he succeeded in seeing his successor, Dilma Rousseff, into office. As it occupied progressively central positions in the political field, the PT slowly distanced itself from the characteristics that distinguished it in the Brazilian party system. It adapted to the dominant standards of the political game (Miguel 2006). It became a center-left alternative to the center-right politics represented by the PSDB.

A clearer understanding of the Brazilian political scenario is only possible as one considers the mass media – television, in particular. Brazilian broadcasting started in the 1950s, but massive transmissions became reality during the military regime. The military's campaign for 'national integration', which also promoted an expansion of the highways and stimulated the inward colonization of the country, drove the development of telecommunications, which included both telephone and television. In the early 1960s in Brazil, a television set was still considered a luxury appliance and only major urban centers had broadcasting capability. By the end of the dictatorship, however, five national television networks covered 99 per cent of the country, broadcasting to over 40 million television sets – an average of one set for every 3.5 inhabitants, a statistic close to the reality of more developed countries.

Media was, therefore, a central institution in the country that came out of the dictatorial regime, with all the changes this also brings to the culture, and the politics of a nation. At the same time, the means of communication in Brazil present low pluralism, being concentrated in the hands of few companies, and this has its own very relevant consequences to the configuration of public opinion in the country (Porto 2008).

One must also consider another particular characteristic of Brazil, and of other Latin American countries: a combination of far-reaching mass electronic media, at levels close to those of developed nations, and a precarious education system. In the developed world, the electronic media reaches a vast majority of homes, but access to schooling is ample and illiteracy almost non-existent. In many African and Asian countries, the school system is precarious, but radio and television, especially, are less available. Brazil combines aspects of both these realities. Schooling is deficient, in terms of both the percentage of the population it covers and of its responsibility to socialize knowledge. In 2008, illiteracy still plagued a significant 10 per cent of adults, or 19.4 per cent if one considers only the poorer northeast region of the country. The statistic is higher still if one also accounts for 'functional illiterates', who write their names, but are unable to extract meaningful information from written text. The average daily distribution of major newspapers was 4,351,000 copies, approximately 2 per cent of the population. Television, however, reached almost every family in the country; in 2006, 94.8 per cent of all homes had a television set.[2] Thus, the potential influence of electronic media remains greater than that of other media, including the Internet – which, despite its tremendous growth, was still only present in less than 30 per cent of all homes in 2009.

Rede Globo is by and large the major communications conglomerate in the country, comprising newspapers, magazines, books, music albums, computer software, cinema, home-video, radio, television (with open and cable channels), Internet portal, data communications, paging, mobile telephone services, launch and operation of satellites, communications equipment and other sectors. An unimportant group until then, Rede Globo's growth was largely due to the dictatorship. Military leaders thought it best to privilege the private broadcasting sector, which, though it was kept under censorship, benefited from public investments in infrastructure. Rede Globo was the military government's major partner, quickly becoming the largest broadcasting company in the country, be it in terms of territorial coverage, audience or advertising revenues.

Rede Globo's ranking has since then remained undisputed, though its share of audience and advertising has decreased. Its major competitors, like itself, are almost all family-run companies, which is a result of restrictions in Brazilian legislation on the presence of foreign investment and corporate bodies in control of communication companies. Despite market competition, which is often intense, all major broadcasting companies share much the same political views, and the same may be said of almost all major press (Miguel 2002; Porto 2003).

This is true of how those companies position themselves *vis-à-vis* the issues in debate – the privatization of state-owned companies, for example – and of their sympathies within the range of party options. In all presidential elections, the major press institutions have all acted in favor of the same candidates. Though the norm in Brazil is a sort of ostensive neutrality (it is not common for an editorial to officially declare a favorite for an electoral dispute), partisan politics is clearly seen in the choice of stories and special reports, framing and even, in some extreme cases, the manipulation of news materials (Kucinski 1998).

It is possible to understand the Brazilian case by making use of the three models of media systems elaborated by Hallin and Mancini for Western European countries and North America, namely polarized pluralist, democratic corporatist and liberal. These authors suggest that Latin American countries will come close to the polarized pluralist model (Hallin and Mancini 2004, p. 306; also Hallin and Papathanassopoulos 2002), which is marked, among other aspects, by a significant political parallelism – which is to say that the media mirrors the party system. It would be better, though, to define Brazilian media as a manifest adherence to the liberal model, of media neutrality and independence *vis-à-vis* political interests, although this is only imperfectly accomplished.

Media support is not a guarantee of political success. Almost all communication conglomerates rejected PT, yet this prevented neither the party's continual growth, nor its victory in the last three presidential elections. If in 2002 the media's actions were seen as an attempt, above all, to 'frame' the candidates in the hope of drawing their committed responses to key economic issues (Rubim 2004), in 2006 and 2010 the media coverage was unabashedly hostile to the PT, which nevertheless managed to obtain landslide victories (Aldé, Mendes and Figueiredo 2007; Biroli and Mantovani 2010; Jakobsen 2007). In other words, despite the low pluralism of the means of communication, the processes of production of public opinion and of electoral decision in Brazil are complex and involve also a series of other channels.

Public opinion reaches the scene

In this mediated political environment, public opinion studies and polls, particularly, have become a part of Brazilian elections. The first Brazilian polling institute was the Instituto Brasileiro de Opinião Pública e Estatística (IBOPE, Brazilian Institute of Public Opinion and Statistics), created in 1942. IBOPE gained notoriety for measuring television viewing and has been incorporated into the colloquial language as a synonym of popularity – the expression *'reach ibope'* means 'to be popular' – but it has conducted pre-electoral polls since its earliest years.

It first relevant competitor, the Gallup Institute, only appeared in 1967, already in the years of military dictatorship. This Brazilian company had the name and expertise of its North American counterpart. In 1998, the Brazilian Gallup Institute was handed over to its parent company, but it no longer conducted pre-electoral polling.

Other than its counterparts in the Southern Cone of South America, the dictatorship in Brazil chose not to close the National Congress, except for brief moments, and to allow periodical elections. The civil liberties required for public debate were withheld, Congressional powers were severely restricted, those members of parliament who dared to be more active were likely to have their political rights revoked and the most relevant offices were barred from election. However, some of the rituals of electoral democracy were maintained.

As the opposition to the dictatorship intensified, the military was forced to introduce measures to 'soften' the regime. These included amnesty to political prisoners, the reinstatement of the party system and the expansion of the electoral system. In 1982, the military oversaw the first general elections since 1965 for the offices of state governors. These were also the first elections in Brazil in which the pre-electoral polls played an important role.

Some results were controversial, such as the outcome of a survey conducted prior to elections in the state of Santa Catarina. On the eve of the election, *Veja* magazine published the numbers of a Gallup poll from earlier that week. According to that survey, government candidate Esperidião Amin was an impressive 24 percentage points ahead of his major opponent, Jaison Barreto. After tallying all ballots, however, Amin's lead was shown to be less than 0.8 percentage point. The opposition refused to accept this as mere incompetence, but, rather, denounced what they believed to be a deliberate manipulation aimed at demobilizing supporters favorable to Barreto and legitimizing an already premeditated fraud in the counting of votes (cf. Aguiar 1995).

The most notorious case, however, occurred in the state of Rio de Janeiro. The party in the government coalition was accused of planning a fraud to prevent the victory of Leonel Brizola, who had recently returned from exile and was considered a *bête noir* of the regime. According to the opposition, the data-processing company contracted by the electoral court for tallying the results was responsible for the fraud *per se*, while IBOPE and Rede Globo manipulated the public's opinion by releasing unfavorable projections that showed Brizola as a distant runner-up. All parties involved have always emphatically denied these allegations (Projeto Memória Globo 2004, pp. 109–119). Brizola denounced the scheme to the foreign press, backed by the results of a parallel tallying of votes conducted by a radio station, and was then elected.

By 1989, when the first direct presidential election following the end of the dictatorship was held, a third polling institute had already entered the scene. Datafolha, created in 1983, belongs to Folha da Manhã, S. A., a group responsible for publishing one of the three major Brazilian newspapers, the *Folha de S. Paulo*. From the outset, Datafolha refused to accept contracts from political parties, a very different policy from that of its competitors IBOPE and Gallup. Moreover, it was the only Brazilian polling institute to make use of corner sampling, rather than household samples,[3] when conducting polls. In 1984, another institute, Vox Populi, was created and, today, along with IBOPE and Datafolha, it is a major pre-electoral polling institute in Brazil.

Smaller institutes have played a role in specific contexts. This was the case of Toledo & Associates, which conducted polls for the weekly magazine *IstoÉ/Senhor* during the 1989 elections. The obvious discrepancies between the numbers released by that institute and IBOPE contributed to Leonel Brizola's accusations against the latter. Running then for the office of president, Brizola had a very clear memory of the 1982 episode and again publicly charged IBOPE with fraud. In 1991, the institute Sensus would also become part of this field, hired by the Confederação Nacional do Trabalho (National Labor Confederation) for pre-electoral polling. Along with the three major institutes, Sensus has often conducted surveys into the popularity, trust and approval of Brazilian presidents since the early years of Fernando Henrique Cardoso's first term in office (1995–1998), and its work has been widely mentioned in Brazilian political news.

In the 2010 elections, there was yet another incident involving polling institutes. As early as February of that year, the polls conducted by the Sensus, Vox Populi and IBOPE institutes showed a steady growth by PT candidate Dilma Rousseff, then the first runner-up in the electoral race. According to the polls conducted by Datafolha in the same period, however, Rousseff showed no apparent increase in votes; rather, she had dropped one percentage point. On 23 July, Datafolha showed the PT candidate only one point behind José Serra (PSDB). All other institutes had shown her in the lead as early as June and now showed her eight points ahead of Serra. It was only in mid-August that all institutes would show similar results, with Rousseff's increasing margin of votes compared with now runner-up José Serra.

Datafolha pointed to the start of the Free Airtime for Electoral Propaganda, the legislation-mandated air-time for candidates on radio and television, to explain Rousseff's extraordinary rise in their polls – Datafolha showed a 9-point increase in only a week, 24 million votes in less than a month. Previously the object of criticism by supporters of José Serra and by *Folha de S. Paulo* (the newspaper controlled by the same group),[4] all other institutes accused Datafolha of error or blatant manipulation of the numbers. Their allegations focused mainly on Datafolha's methodology and use of corner sampling, but also on important variables that, in fact, define the vote in Brazil. Datafolha had not collected data in rural areas, for example, and required interviewees to have a landline telephone for confirmation of results, which restricted samples to the strata of the population with greater purchasing power.[5] Later, all major institutes presented higher percentages of votes for Dilma Rousseff in their polls than she would actually obtain in the first election round. This was not to be repeated in the second round, when the results of the ballots were very similar to the results of the polls. Although institutes were largely criticized, the role of pre-electoral polls is now a subject of debates. Opposition parties have demands for restrictions in the use of opinion polls by the media.

The episodes mentioned above can only be understood in a scenario where the media has an increasing impact on public opinion and where polls play a very significant part in elections. Since the democratization of Brazil in the 1980s, pre-electoral polls have become an indispensible instrument for parties and candidates, interest groups, campaign finance contributors and media coverage, as well as a potential mechanism for the manipulation of public opinion. This suspicion marks both the outset of polling and the legislation that regulates it, which has ranged from measures aimed at restricting their publication to demands for transparency as to the methods employed therein.

The legislation on polling

Between 1989, when the first president was directly elected since the military coup in 1964, and December 2009, when the Superior Electoral Court's more recent resolution on the matter went into effect, Brazilian legislation suffered a series of changes with regard to how opinion polls and pre-electoral voting intention polls are registered and made known. This period saw a total of three laws and three resolutions.[6] The major changes involve the information required when polls are published by the media, the deadline for its publication prior to elections, the registry of all research and accompanying information with the Electoral Court, and, finally, the access to all research granted to political parties.

The Electoral Court has only recently required that all research institutes disclose their methodology, and the legislation on the matter is rather limited. It was only following Resolution no. 20.950 from December 2001 that the Brazilian legislation demanded that news include information such as the period when data were collected, the margins of error, the name of who contracted the research and the name of the entity or company that conducted the survey when publicizing results. In 2006, a new resolution also required the news to make known the number of interviews conducted during research and the registration number of the survey within the Electoral Court. Furthermore, this was the first resolution to determine that this information be included when such polls are mentioned by parties and candidates during propaganda on radio and television – although it did not require mentions to competing candidates.

Resolution no. 23.190 from December 2009 would add a further detail to the requirements for publicizing the results of public opinion polls in propaganda on TV and radio. It determined that 'when publicizing the results of public opinion polls during the Free Airtime for Electoral Propaganda, news must clearly inform the period when the poll was conducted and its margin of error. It is not, however, mandated to mention a candidate's competitors, as long as it presents the results in such a way that does not "push" the voter to any conclusions as to the candidate's performance in relation to his/her competitors' (Article 14).

It is the 1993 law that requires all public opinion research to be registered with the Electoral Court up to five days prior to publication. Before 1993, the media had only to make polls known to political parties that had candidates up for election. That same law brought the poll institutes under the direct inspection and scrutiny of all political parties. The Electoral Court granted political parties, upon their request, 'the power to question and confirm all data publicized, by means of random inspections of individual questionnaires, maps or equivalents' (Article 34). This article, however, was nullified by a subsequent law of 1997, and only affected the elections held in 1994.

The laws and resolutions prior to 2009 already mandated that information on research methodologies be made known to political parties (1989) and that all research be registered within the Electoral Court (1993). Since 1989, all institutes were required to inform the period when the polls were conducted and 'the method' (generically). This was very broadly understood as information on the number of interviewees per neighborhood or city, the sample population and pondered weight of variables such as sex, age, education, economic level and location, the name of the party 'sponsoring' the research and the means chosen to control and verify the collection of data. The 1993 law would add specific requirements *vis-à-vis* the identities of contracting parties. Registration with the Electoral Court guaranteed information on the cost of research and origin of the financial resources allocated to that effect, as institutes were mandated to inform who 'contracted' and who 'financed' the research. The subsequent law of 1997 would further expound the information required on methodology, as institutes would then have to produce details on the confidence interval and margin of error of results, as well as the complete questionnaire applied.

However, the distinction between methodologically oriented research and surveys lacking scientific method is only made explicit in the resolution of 2009. Article 21 thereof states that the publication of informal surveys (the so called 'enquetes' in Brazil) must be clearly characterized as a 'mere compilation of opinions, lacking a control of samples and conducted without scientific method', thus differentiated from electoral polls. Such publication is otherwise denied registration and therefore held in contempt of binding legislation, making all parties involved liable to prosecution in accordance with the law.

At present, there are no restrictions on deadlines for the publication of electoral polls in Brazil. The 1989 law prohibited the publication of electoral polls in the 30 days prior to the first round of elections and ten days prior to the second round.[7] However, the press were able to evade this with various clever expedients – one newspaper, for instance, would simply say that 'candidate X has taken the elevator up to the thirty-second floor' or 'candidate Y's thermometer is showing 27°'. The 2001 resolution finally lifted this ban and authorized electoral polls to be publicized at all times, election days inclusive. The following resolution of 2006 would maintain this, but with the restriction that all research conducted on Election Day may now be publicized only after voting has been officially closed.

Media coverage of polls during presidential elections

The surveys that gauge presidential approval ratings are a good indicator of the growing relevance of public opinion polls. Between May 1987, with José Sarney as the first civilian president since the military coup of 1964, and August 2010, with President Luís Inácio Lula da Silva nearing the end of his second term in office, the Datafolha institute conducted at least 128 surveys in which it asked whether the current president was doing a good, fair, bad or horrible job. During the Sarney administration, there were a total of nine surveys. The almost five years of the Fernando Collor-Itamar Franco presidency (15 March 1990 to 31 December 1994)[8] saw 23 surveys. This average increased in the following governments. There were 46 surveys during Fernando Henrique Cardoso's two terms, or eight years in office, and 64 surveys during his successor Lula's two administrations (Rodrigues 2010). The surveys and the news on approval of each administration have an impact on, among other things, the disputes within political parties and the nomination of candidates for the following presidential elections.

Brazilian media have also increasingly publicized the pre-electoral polls since 1989. That is what our study of the major Brazilian newspapers and weekly news magazines between 1989 and 2010 has shown.[9]

The study has considered all electoral surveys and polls published by the selected papers and magazines in a period of three months before elections (reaching first and also second round). That period considered, the newspapers have publicized 778 different polls conducted before the first round of voting in the six presidential elections since 1989. These polls have almost all been conducted by the IBOPE, Gallup, Datafolha, Vox Populi and Sensus institutes. 363 of those or 46.6 per cent made the front page, which signals their relevance in political news during elections and which allows us to infer the impact of pre-electoral polls on the public understanding of electoral scenery.

The 1989 election saw the publication of a much higher number of polls than the following elections – a total of 264 (33.9 per cent of all the polls published in this *corpus*) on the three newspapers in question. There are at least three reasons for this interest. First, their novelty: it was the first time electors could vote for president since 1960, which is to say it was the first presidential election for most voters and the first coverage of elections for most professionals in the media. Moreover, it was an unusually competitive election. Although Fernando Collor led the race from start to finish, at least four other candidates had at one point a standing chance to push the election to the second round. In the end, runner-up Luís Inácio Lula da Silva was only half a percentage point ahead of the candidate in third place.

Finally, the 1989 election was the only separate presidential election. From 1994 to the present, presidential elections have been paired with elections to other offices, namely, to the upper and lower houses of the National Congress (the Senate and the Chamber of Deputies) and to the office of State Governor. Therefore, although the media always gives the presidential race center stage, it also must cover other electoral processes, and so the polls focusing on other candidates, especially for the office of governor in the more important states, are given media attention as well.

In the subsequent elections, the number of polls that received media coverage fluctuated. There were a total of 136 polls published by the three newspapers in 1994, but only 48 in 1998. That number rose to 167 in 2002 and again dropped to 80 in 2006 and 83 in 2010. These statistics show that when the president in office is running for re-election, as was the case in 1998 and 2006, there are fewer polls published in newspapers. This is probably due to the fact that these races are potentially less competitive.

Weekly news magazines in Brazil also publish the results of electoral polls and surveys, although less frequently, due to the very nature of those weekly magazines. It is common for these magazines to reverberate the coverage already given to the polls by the daily newspapers. In these magazines, the polls are often used to support analytical articles on the general tendencies of elections. Nevertheless, they are themselves an important part of political news during elections, which can be deduced from the fact that of the universe of 266 articles focusing on the results of opinion polls in the three months prior to the six elections analyzed in our study, 84 polls, or 31.6 per cent, made front-page news.

The polls conducted in 1989 were associated with the building and success of candidate Fernando Collor, virtually unknown to the national electorate. In 1989, *Veja* was already the number-one weekly news magazine in the country and played a key role in projecting Collor's political leadership. In the three months leading up to the election, *Veja* alone published the results of polls in 38 different texts, 18 of which made the front page. Its primary competitor *IstoÉ* published only 11 polls in 1989, with only seven texts making front-page news. In the subsequent elections, *IstoÉ* showed similar numbers, with 12 texts (seven front pages) in 1994 and nine texts (three front pages) in 1998. *Veja*, however, published fewer than half as many news in 1994 (only 24, with four front pages) and 13 polls published, with zero front-page news focusing on the results of polls during the 1998 electoral race. There is, therefore, a shift, connected with the electoral juncture. In 1989, it has highlighted Collor's potential. Nine years later, *Veja* adheres to the pattern of the media coverage when Cardoso campaigned for re-election, the silence on the race (Miguel 2000). These data point to the selective publishing of opinion polls, by Brazilian media, to act within the disputes in electoral contexts.

As do the daily newspapers in question, the weekly magazines show a larger coverage of pre-electoral polls when the president in office is not campaigning for re-election. In 2002, when Luís Inácio Lula da Silva (PT) and José Serra (PSDB) ran for president, the four magazines published a total of 71 texts, more than twice the 35 texts published during the 2006 elections, when Lula was re-elected to office. Considering only the two weekly news magazines already in operation during the 1994 elections (*Veja* and *IstoÉ*), it is possible to understand this scenario as a recurrence of what happened before. In 1994, the two magazines published 36 texts on the results of polls, while in 1998, when Fernando Henrique Cardoso ran for re-election and received another four-year term, there were only 22 texts.

Not only do Brazilian newspapers, magazines and TV news publish the results of public opinion polls, but their companies also play an active part in their realization. This is the case of Folha da Manhã, S. A., which controls both the daily *Folha de S. Paulo* and the Datafolha institute. Moreover, many of these companies, such as the networks Globo and Bandeirantes, and the daily *O Estado de S. Paulo*, also often request polls and surveys. Many of them are also requested by employer entities such as the National Confederation of Labor and the National Confederation of Industry. They measure voting intentions, evaluate the different administrations and gauge public opinion. They are regularly conducted by the various institutes in question and are often seen in pre-electoral periods.

Elections as horse races

In these periods, above all, the polls focus predominantly on the 'horse race' aspects of campaigns, highlighting candidates' competition for votes (see also Porto 2008). The media further accentuate this as they often publish only the candidates' position in the polls, that is, their estimated percentage of votes, thus disregarding a more complex analysis of the patterns of voting intention in different segments, for example. Even when the underlying stratifications revealed by the polls *are* discussed by the media, they are not shown as an intricate part of those studies and are seldom highlighted in the analyses thereof. In general, however, the media will focus their attentions only on the 'horse race', with electoral projections for individual candidates.

In the three months that preceded the six presidential elections between 1989 and 2010, an overwhelming majority of the studies that made the news was of the 'horse race' type. This was a surprising

80.6 per cent of all data on public opinion published in the newspapers in question, and 68 per cent of all that was published by the weekly magazines under analysis. The remaining electoral studies published in the period presented data on candidates' rejection ratings, government approval ratings, approval of economic policy, and data on in-office presidents' influence on voting intentions, as well as data on parliament approval ratings and on the approval of inter-party alliances. Moreover, there were also surveys on the impact of religious denomination, sex and age on voters' preferences and voting intentions.

In fact, the publication of polls on vote intentions in order to feed a 'horse race' type coverage starts very early. For the October 2010 elections, the Sensus institute began to conduct research as early as October 2007, simulating races with different possible candidates. The Datafolha institute conducted polls on voting intentions regularly as of the end of 2008. Results were published at intervals of two or three months in the *Folha de S. Paulo*, where the polls were constantly given great emphasis. Although actual electoral results often differ from the various projections (the winner in the 2010 Presidential Elections, Dilma Rousseff, had more than 46 per cent of valid votes in the first round and more than 56 per cent in the second, although her position in voting intentions was 8 per cent in Datafolha's polls of the last months of 2008 and about 5 per cent in the Sensus polls of 2007), these news support the concomitant race for political and financial supporters within the various parties and entrepreneurial sectors, and, in more general terms, contribute to bring the presidential succession, albeit precociously, to the center of the political game.

In some cases, the results published are not clearly presented to the reader as the findings of proper polls, with scientific support and methodological criteria for defining samples and collection of opinions, for example, or of a merely illustrative survey of public opinion, one that does not aptly represent national electoral trends. This lack of distinction is revealing of another important characteristic of how the media presents opinion polls in Brazil; namely, it often omits relevant details on methodology – details that would allow a better and less biased understanding of the results presented.

Until 2002, when new legislation required the media to inform the public of the period when the data were collected and of the margins of error, the publication of public opinion data generally lacked any information regarding methodology. Most of these publications disregarded even the number of interviewees heard, for example (see Table 7.1).

Table 7.1 Percentage of surveys and polls published with no indication of methodology, per year of election

	Newspapers (%)	Weekly Magazines (%)
1989	76.1	79.6
1994	68.4	80.6
1998	52.1	92.5
2002	50.9	77.5
2006	36.3	71.4
2010	32.5	37.1

Note: The study considered all the electoral surveys and polls published by the three major Brazilian newspapers and the four major weekly news magazines, from a period of three months before each of the six elections. Veja and IstoÉ magazines are present in all the years in question; Época magazine is only considered as of 1998 and CartaCapital as of 2002, when they started operating.
Source: Elaborated by the authors.

The data show that, even before the new legal requirements, newspapers already published a growing number of articles in which the results of polls and surveys were followed by at least some information on the method. This is undoubtedly due to readers' greater familiarity with polls, their potentially more critical review of how they are conducted and how results may be manipulated. On the other hand, the 2001 Resolution did not legislate that *all* the news based on those results indicate the methodology used. If the primary publication of data must present information on methodology, the same does not apply to subsequent publications, however central the results of voting intention rates, for instance, may be to them. This explains the high number of publications with absolutely no indication of methodology in the weekly magazines in question. They do not commonly request opinion polls themselves; rather, they comment on results previously published on newspapers or television. *CartaCapital* magazine, however, stands out from the rest, with over 50 per cent of its news articles containing information on methodology.

It should be said, however, that the information on methodology is rather succinct. It indicates only the name of the institute that conducted the study, the registration number with the Electoral Court, which is a legal requirement, the period when the field data were collected, the number of interviewees and the number of municipalities covered.

One might consider at least part of the missing information to be self-evident. Therefore, 'a definition of the universe of the population under study which the survey is intended to represent', as suggested by the American Association for Public Opinion Research's 'Best Practices' (and, similarly, by the World Association for Public Opinion Research's 'Code of Professional Ethics and Practices'), might be deemed unnecessary, once the survey obviously refers to the Brazilian electorate. The same might also be said about the 'goals of the survey'. Nevertheless, a number of other important details lack better clarification, among which are the number of interviewees who refuse to answer the questionnaire and the questionnaire itself. Readers are unaware of how the questions were formulated or whether the voting intention rates were combined with any other surveys – for instance, on the approval of the current administration. The characteristics of the interviewers or the method used to guide the study are also lacking. Although it is unfeasible to publish this information on print material, it could certainly be made available online, for example. This, however, is unfortunately still not the case.

There is also a total lack of information on sample selection procedures, though disclosure is recommended by both the AAPOR and the WAPOR and is present also in Article 3, concerning the publication of surveys by the press, of the European Society for Opinion and Market Research's 'International Code of Marketing and Social Research Practice', which itself is rather concise and permissive. All Brazilian opinion public institutes select their samples by quotas, though this information is rarely available. Moreover, there are no details about the criteria for the stratification of quotas, nor a simple explanation to readers of the difference between this method and the use of a probabilistic sample (for a critique of the methods used by Brazilian institutes, see Ferraz 1996). In the 2010 elections, as was mentioned above, a controversy drew a line between the Datafolha institute, which makes use of corner sampling for research, and its competitors, which use household samples. However, this information is commonly absent from publications.[10]

Despite the centrality of public opinion research in political news, the growing number of institutes in Brazil, the more careful attention devoted to methodological criteria and the more detailed legal requirements for their publication, there are still several discrepancies between projections and final ballot counts. On 3 October 2010, as the first round of voting was underway, the *Folha de S. Paulo* published a poll conducted by Datafolha only two days prior to the election, while the *Estado de S. Paulo* published another poll by IBOPE conducted on 1 October. Both indicated the same results for the two major candidates: Dilma Rousseff with 47 per cent of voting intentions, followed by José Serra with 29 per cent and Marina Silva with 16 per cent. When the last ballot was counted on 3 October, however, Rousseff was shown to reach 42.9 per cent of votes – therefore outside the two-percentage-point margin of error.

Analysts alleged that the discrepancy was caused by last-minute swings in voters' moods (Mauro Paulino, *'Para que servem as pesquisas?'*, *Folha de S. Paulo*, October 5 2010, 6), which, ultimately, would guarantee that polls were never wrong or forged, placing them beyond any critical evaluation.

It must be said that, on the evening of Election Day, Rede Globo Television published an IBOPE exit poll. In that poll, if one considers only the valid votes, thus disregarding blank and null ballots, Dilma Rousseff would reach 51 per cent of all votes, José Serra 30 per cent and Marina Silva 18 per cent. In this case as well, Rousseff's 46.9 per cent of all valid votes are outside the three points margin of error.

Although this would not be repeated in the second round, when the IBOPE exit poll for Dilma Rousseff was 58 per cent and the result of the ballots was 56 per cent, it is by no means an isolated incident. On the contrary, results outside the margin of error are the norm in the opinion polls for presidential elections in Brazil. On 1 October 2006, when the first round of voting for that year's election took place, *Folha de S. Paulo* published a poll conducted by Datafolha on the two days prior to voting. One of the three major competitors had results that were outside the two-percentage-point margin of error – Geraldo Alckmin, the runner-up, had 38.1 per cent of all valid votes, whereas he only reached 35 per cent in the Datafolha poll. An IBOPE poll of the same period showed by Rede Globo evening news on the eve of the election had Alckmin with 34 per cent of the voting intentions.

In the 2002 elections, it was the winner, Luís Inácio Lula da Silva, who was outside the margin of error. On the day of the first round of elections, 6 October, *Folha de S. Paulo* published a Datafolha research conducted on the two days prior to the election showing Lula da Silva with 45 per cent of voting intention rates, a number identical to the projection of a poll conducted by IBOPE, on the three days leading up to the election. Da Silva, however, reached 41.6 per cent of all valid votes that day, a number outside both Datafolha's and IBOPE's margins of error of 2 and 1.8 percentage points respectively.

Conclusion

The media are important political actors in Brazil. Even though the pattern in Brazilian journalism is not to stand clearly for political parties or candidates, news media play an active part in conforming political and electoral agendas and defining the limits for the debate. Regardless of the sympathies of companies and journalists and of just how much these sympathies are revealed, the media are key to the meanings given to the political debate and to the political actors that take part therein. They promote, among other things, specific opinions and judgments as to the character and competency of a given politician. In a similar manner, they constantly promote or restrict his/her visibility before the public. One must account for the existence of other means to gain public visibility, such as the Internet, a growing medium in Brazil, with an ever-increasing number of users, but one to which access is still somewhat limited, or even the many networks of social movements and NGOs, or governmental communication. However, the greater public continues to see the conventional press as the most legitimate and the most prestigious, believing it to publish unbiased news material, which adds even further value to their discourse.

In Brazil, when discussing the impact of the media on the publication of public opinion researches, one must take into consideration that a large portion of the population has little or no access to newspapers and magazines. The characteristics of Brazilian society add to the potential weight of television media in the country. Some events in recent elections have been studied as a product of the influence of the media (such as in the candidacy and victory of Fernando Collor in the 1989 presidential elections, as presented in many studies[11]), while others serve as examples of the limits of that influence, namely, the episodes when the coverage of the major papers, magazines and TV news showed focus and tendencies that later proved to be incoherent with the preferences expressed by the voters (such as in Luís Inácio Lula da Silva's re-election in 2006[12] and in the election of his successor Dilma Rousseff in 2010).

The publication of electoral research by the media is part of this broader picture. The results of the polls give candidates greater notoriety, as they are 'proof' of their performance and of their potential success. In a similar manner, the thematic surveys, too, offer 'proof' of the greater public's expressed desires in a given moment of a campaign. In the first case, the polls are not only a record, but also a means by which the public may know and evaluate candidates – in general terms, by making use of the very material offered by the media. In the latter, the manner in which collective opinions are perceived reflects certain conceptions and a frame of relevance that are the very basis of how the questionnaires are created and of how public opinion is gauged.

On the other hand, as they identify different patterns of political preference according to different voters' profiles – in a more direct and much simpler manner than analysis of the voting maps would make possible – the polls promote judgments on the civic competency and, ultimately, on the legitimacy of those elected. The much higher voting intention rates for Lula da Silva, in 2006, and Rousseff, in 2010, among the less fortunate and less educated made numerous headlines and revealed a certain suspicion as to the quality of the votes of the beneficiaries of that administration's various social programs. These voters would allegedly choose to overlook the government's many corruption scandals in order not to compromise their advantages. Though obviously tainted with prejudice, these analyses gained the status of common sense among much of the press.

The news and opinion public studies do not reflect an exterior reality. They play an active part in constructing that reality. Brazil shares a lot in common with other societies where media holds a central position, where political news, surveys and voting intention polls greatly alter political debate itself and the political environment thereof. Aside from acting as intermediaries between the political field and the common citizen, the news and opinion public surveys have an impact on the relations within the political field, between competing groups and also in defining the positions of power within those groups.

Notes

1. In post-1985 elections, 12–22 parties have elected representatives in the Congress and Rae's fractionalization index is usually above 0.85.
2. For a study that considers the specificity of the influence of newspaper and television news on public opinion in Brazil, see Lima (2006).
3. Today, all major institutes in Brazil, with the exception of Datafolha, rely on door-to-door visits, based on the census conducted by the Instituto Brasileiro de Geografia e Estatística (IBGE, Brazilian Institute of Geography and Statistics).
4. In April, 2010, a court order granted the PSDB access to the Sensus institute's headquarters and questionnaires. Party representatives on site were allegedly instructed by Datafolha technicians by telephone (Cynara Menezes, 'A batalha dos números', *CartaCapital*, September 1, 2010, 28). On the other hand, *Folha de S. Paulo*'s criticism of the methodology used by the Sensus and Vox Populi institutes coincided with a media coverage that was clearly opposed to the PT's candidate.

5. At present, 41.2 per cent of all Brazilian homes have only a mobile line, not a landline (IBGE, 2009).
6. Law no. 7.773, of 8 June 8 1989; Law no. 8.713, of 30 September 30 1993; Law no. 9.504, of 30 September 1997. The latter law is the law in effect and is complemented by the following resolutions: Resolution no. 20.950, of 13 December 2001; no. 22.143, of 2 March 2006 and no 23.190, of 16 December 2009.
7. The law also prohibited 'radio and television networks from publicizing any news items on the candidates or on the behavior of voters' until 7.00 p.m. on the day of elections (Article 26, paragraph 3).
8. Vice-President Itamar Franco, elected in 1989, took office following the impeachment of President Fernando Collor.
9. The newspapers under study are the *O Globo*, from Rio de Janeiro, and *O Estado de S. Paulo* and *Folha de S. Paulo*, from São Paulo. These are the only papers with high circulation, for Brazilian media standards, nationwide distribution and seen as causing impact on public opinion. A fourth 'quality paper' with national circulation, the *Jornal do Brasil*, from Rio de Janeiro, suffered with serious financial setbacks in the 1990s and has since then drastically reduced its operations – it now has only an online edition. This newspaper was not included in this study. The magazines under study were *Veja*, *IstoÉ*, *Época* and *CartaCapital*, four major Brazilian news magazines. *Veja*, from Editora Abril, has existed since 1968 and, with a circulation of over 1 million, is today the most influential of the four. Since the 1980s, its coverage of national politics has been marked by a strong bias against the PT, though this is not admitted as an alignment with other parties or candidates. Like *Veja*, *IstoÉ* was created by journalist Mino Carta. *IstoÉ* has existed since 1976 and today has a circulation of approximately 330,000 copies. *Época*, created in 1998 as a Brazilian adaptation of Germany's traditional *Focus* magazine, belongs to Editora Globo – *Globo*'s subsidiary in the print media – and has an average weekly circulation of 400,000. *CartaCapital*, which is owned by Mino Carta, was started in 1994 as a monthly magazine, then biweekly in 1996 and weekly in 2001. With a circulation of close to 33,000 copies per week, it is aimed at an elite reader and has a more leftist orientation, sympathetic to the PT.
10. An exception to this would be the occasional news on polls conducted by telephone, when this information is present. The institutes under study do not make use of this method when surveys are requested for publication. However, telephone tracking is a resource commonly used by major campaign coordinators.
11. See Lattman-Weltman, Carneiro and Ramos (1994).
12. See the studies presented in Lima (2007).

References

Aguiar, I. (1995) *Violência e Golpe Eleitoral* (Blumenau: Editora FURB).
Aldé, A., G. Mendes and M. Figueiredo (2007) 'Imprensa e Eleições Presidenciais', in V. A. Lima (ed.), *A mídia nas eleições de 2006* (São Paulo: Fundação Perseu Abramo).

Biroli, F. and D. Mantovani (2010) 'Disputas, ajustes e acomodações na produção da agenda eleitoral', *Opinião Pública*, 16(1), 90–116.

Ferraz, C. (1996) *Crítica metodológica às pesquisas eleitorais no Brasil*. Dissertação de mestrado. Campinas: Instituto de Matemática, Estatística e Ciência da Computação, Unicamp.

Hallin, D. C. and P. Mancini (2004) *Comparing Media Systems* (Cambridge: Cambridge University Press).

Hallin, D. C. and S. Papathanassopoulos (2002) 'Political Clientelism and the Media', *Media Culture & Society*, 24, 175–95.

IBGE (2009) *Pesquisa Nacional Por Amostra De Domicílios*, http://www.ibge.gov.br, date accessed 16 September 2010.

Jakobsen, K. (2007) 'A cobertura da mídia impressa aos candidatos nas eleições presidenciais de 2006', in V. A. Lima (ed.), *A mídia nas eleições de 2006* (São Paulo: Fundação Perseu Abramo).

Kinzo, M. D. G. (2005) 'Os Partidos no Eleitorado', *Revista Brasileira de Ciências Sociais*, (57), 65–81.

Kucinski, B. (1998) *A Síndrome da Antena Parabólica* (São Paulo: Fundação Perseu Abramo).

Lattman-Weltman, F., J. A. D. Carneiro and P. A. Ramos (1994) *A imprensa faz e desfaz um presidente: o papel da imprensa na ascenção e queda do fenômeno Collor* (Rio de Janeiro: Nova Fronteira).

Lima, V. A. (2006) *Mídia: crise política e poder no Brasil* (São Paulo: Fundação Perseu Abramo).

Lima, V. A. (ed.) (2007) *A mídia nas eleições de 2006* (São Paulo: Fundação Perseu Abramo).

Mainwaring, S. (1999) *Rethinking Party Systems in the Third Wave of Democratization* (Stanford: Stanford University Press).

Miguel, L. F. (2000) 'The Globo Television Network and the Election of 1998', *Latin American Perspectives*, 27(6), 65–84.

Miguel, L. F. (2002) *Política e Mídia no Brasil* (Brasília: Plano).

Miguel, L. F. (2006) 'From Equality to Opportunity', *Latin American Perspectives*, 33(4), 122–43.

Porto, M. (2003) 'Mass Media and Politics in Democratic Brazil', in M. D. Kinzo, and J. Dunkerlez (eds), *Brazil since 1985* (London: ILAS).

Porto, M. (2008) 'Democratization and Election News Coverage in Brazil', in J. Strömbäck and L. L. Kaid (eds), *Handbook of Election News Coverage Around the World* (New York: Routledge).

Projeto Memória Globo (2004) *Jornal Nacional* (Rio de Janeiro: Jorge Zahar).

Rodrigues, F. (2010) 'Pesquisas de opinião', http://noticias.uol.com.br/politica/pesquisas/, date accessed 15 February 2011.

Rubim, A. A. C. (ed.) (2004) *Eleições Presidenciais em 2002 no Brasil* (São Paulo: Hacker).

8
Opinion Polls and the Media in Australia

Stephen Mills and Rodney Tiffen

Since 1943, every Australian election has been preceded by published opinion polls. Since 1972, every election has been preceded by at least three companies regularly conducting opinion polls for competing media groups. As early as the 1977 election, Goot and Beed (1979, p. 141) observed that 'during an election, to talk about politics is to talk about the polls', while in 2010, Young (2010, p. 186) found that in 2007, 44 per cent of election-related front page newspaper articles and 35 per cent of TV news stories contained some reference to opinion polls, a dramatic increase on the previous two elections. The prominent psephologist Peter Brent opined that 'there must be some countries more obsessed with political opinion polls than Australia, although they're yet to be found' (2007, p. 131).

Consistent with Australia's minimally regulated campaign environment (Plasser & Plasser 2002, p. 151), opinion polling has come to play this central role in an almost entirely unregulated environment and for largely commercial purposes. Pollsters may survey public opinion and conduct market research for any purpose, employ whatever survey method they choose, and operate at any time including during election campaigns, on behalf of clients in business, government and the media. Indeed, while television advertisements are banned from broadcast in the final days of a campaign (Young 2004), polls may be conducted, and published, up to, and on, Election Day (Orr 2010, pp. 176–178).

While many bemoan what they see as the influence of the polls, and there are frequent controversies about results and reporting, there has been no serious or influential proposal for any official regulation of their political role. Survey data collection is subject to a government-approved privacy code administered by the market research industry body, which also administers voluntary self-enforced guidelines on professional behavior (Association of Market and Social Research Organisations 2003, 2010); market researchers are permitted to call numbers on the Do Not Call register (Australian Communications and Media Authority 2010). An attempt by some pollsters to form an association to regulate election polling, similar to the British one, came to nothing because a principal company, Morgan Gallup, refused to participate (Goot 1988, p. 144).

The clients of these research firms are under no obligation to publish any survey results; equally, newspapers and magazines that commission and report on survey findings are subject only to voluntary guidelines issued by their self-regulatory industry body, the Australian Press Council. These guidelines recommend that poll reports include background information including 'a bedrock of who conducted the poll among whom'; they also warn against surveys that lack proper sampling, such as phone-in or Internet polls. But the Council states it is 'firmly against' any limits on the reporting of political opinion polls (Australian Press Council 2001). Adherence to the guidelines is low (Goot 2002), and even lower among 'secondary' reports summarizing the most newsworthy aspects of some other group's poll results (Mills 1999, p. 215).

The chapter proceeds by outlining the challenges to pollsters and reporters posed by the unique nature of the Australian electoral system. It then charts the growth of the media-polling relationship in Australia and traces the shifting alliances between media and polling companies. The following two sections examine the changing methods of gathering data, and the changing repertoire of survey questions. The final section examines the contemporary role of polling and the reporting of polls by reference to the politically tumultuous events of the year 2010.

The Australian electoral system and polling

'Australia has been one of the most innovative liberal democracies in the design of its electoral institutions' (McAllister 2009, p. 160). Its distinctive electoral system has both advantages and disadvantages for pollsters.

Government is determined by which party has the majority of the 150 seats in the House of Representatives, a chamber elected through single-member constituencies. Like other single-member electoral systems coming from the Anglo-American tradition, the battle to form government in Australia is essentially a two-sided contest. Since 1910, every government has been formed either by Labor or by the biggest non-Labor parties. The Labor Party, despite undergoing three major and electorally disastrous splits (in 1917, 1931 and 1955) has been a constant. But the non-Labor side has changed its identity on four occasions. Since 1944, the major party on the conservative side of Australian politics has been the Liberal Party, formed by its first leader Robert Menzies, who went on to become Australia's most successful prime minister, winning seven successive elections from 1949 to 1963, before retiring in early 1966. For all that period the Liberals were in government with the Country Party, now renamed the National Party. Although formally a coalition, the cooperation and unity between them goes far beyond a coalition between two independent parties; Sartori (1976, p. 166) famously called it a coalescence rather than a coalition. Sometimes they directly compete with each other in rural electorates, but normally a sitting member from one party is not opposed by a candidate from the other. Most importantly, voters know that the parties will govern together, so the non-Labor side is often referred to as the Coalition.

However, unlike the other Anglo-American democracies, Australia has a system of preferential voting, sometimes called the alternative vote (Hughes 2007 p. 176; Reynolds and Reilly 1997). Australian voters can express a preference for a minority party with their first vote and a second preference that may, if their preferred candidate is eliminated, influence which of the major parties wins the seat. This renders the House a more representative expression of public sentiment than would be the case under a first-past-the-post system. It also treats minor parties and independent candidates more kindly. In the 26 federal elections since the Second World War, the combined vote for Labor and the Liberal-National Parties has on all but one occasion been more than 80 per cent of the total. But the number of people voting for minor parties and independents has been increasing (Tiffen 2010). Since 1990, this has always been more than 10 per cent, and in several elections close to 20 per cent. Although there were earlier occasions when 'Others' have attracted a substantial vote, this now looks to have become a continuing feature of the Australian landscape. Between 1955 and 1972, the most important preference flow was from the Democratic Labor Party to the Coalition; now it is from the Greens to Labor.

These features create a significant headache for Australian pollsters and journalists, who have to estimate not only the primary vote each party will receive but also the pattern of support for the major parties after the distribution of preferences from minor parties and independents. The electoral scholar Malcolm Mackerras (1972) devised the concept of the 'two-party preferred' vote, which clarifies this problem by expressing the aggregate vote-split for the two major parties after the distribution of preferences. All published polls (but only since 1993, Goot 2010b, p. 71) are reported in terms of both primary vote and two-party preferred vote. The Mackerras pendulum, which ranks all electorates in a U-shape according to the two-party preferred swing necessary for the seat to change hands, has also become part of the iconography of Australian elections (Mackerras 2010). It is most useful when the basic contest is between Labor and the Coalition, less so when an electorate might be won by an Independent or a third party such as the Greens.

Like other single-member electoral systems, there is of course no guarantee that the distribution of support measured by a national survey sample will translate into parliamentary seats. Indeed in five elections, the winner actually polled less than 50 per cent of the two-party preferred vote – the lowest winning percentage was John Howard's 48.9 per cent in 1998. So to predict the winning party, pollsters need not only gauge public voting sentiments, but also which side will win the marginal seats. Further, Australian elections are perilously close. Of the 26 elections since the Second World War, in 14 the winner's share of the two-party preferred vote has been 52 per cent or less. In other words, many elections are decided on a margin less than the sampling error from a sample of 1000 respondents.

One advantage that Australian pollsters have over those in most other democracies is that registration and voting are compulsory. There is a fine if a registered voter fails to attend for the vote. The Australian electoral authorities make it easy for a voter to cast an absentee or postal ballot, or to vote in advance of Election Day if they wish. Turnout is therefore often around 95 per cent (Hill 2007 p. 126). Australian pollsters do not therefore have the problem of estimating who in their samples is likely to vote, and whether differential turnout may affect predictions.

But more than in other democracies they have a problem with informal voting. In the Australian House of Representatives, a valid vote requires numbering a vote for all candidates, and sometimes – especially when different rules apply at state level – there is accidental informal voting. However, there is also some deliberate informal voting, with ballots either left blank or spoiled in some way. In 2010, both non-attendance and informal voting spiked compared with the 2007 election. Informal voting jumped from 3.95 per cent to 5.61 per cent of the vote overall (Irvine 2010). The number not voting rose from

5.2 per cent to 6.8 per cent, so that 'more voters refused to vote than at any election since 1925, the first election at which voting was made compulsory' (Colebatch 2010). If the figures for absenteeism and informal voting are combined with the 1.4 million eligible adults who were not properly registered, then a dramatic figure of 3.2 million eligible voters – or around one-fifth of the electorate – did not cast a valid vote in 2010 (Costar & Browne 2010). This is large enough to complicate the pollsters' performance, especially when there is a possibility – and this must remain a matter of speculation – that in 2010 it told more against Labor than the Coalition.

Australian governments are made and unmade in the House of Representatives, but Australia is also a strongly bicameral system (Lijphart 1984; Tiffen & Gittins 2009, pp. 30–1). This means firstly that the composition of its two houses is incongruent, in that they are elected by different formulas and on somewhat different timetables, but that its powers are symmetrical, in that all legislation must pass both houses. The Australian Senate has multi-member constituencies, a method of proportional representation called Hare-Clark, which allows voters to choose between candidates for one party and to express preferences across parties. The pollsters pay far less attention to the Senate, and their capacity to predict the outcome is more limited.

Finally – another blessing for the polling industry – Australia has frequent elections. The maximum interval between federal elections is three years. In addition to federal elections, there are elections in the six states and two territories (plus of course local government elections, although these seldom involve any polling), so that there are typically at least a couple of elections each year somewhere in the country.

Organizational history

Public opinion polling in Australia began as a press initiative. In 1940, the head of the *Herald and Weekly Times*, Sir Keith Murdoch, father of contemporary international media mogul Rupert, arranged for one of his employees, Roy Morgan, an accountant and finance journalist by background, to go to the United States to gain experience by working with George Gallup (Goot forthcoming; Mills 1999). The first Gallup Poll, published in the *Herald* on 4 October 1941, found that 59 per cent of respondents favored equal pay for women (Mills 1999, p. 204).

This was the beginning of a remarkable association, one that monopolized national public opinion polling for more than 30 years, producing news stories on more than 3000 poll questions (Mills 1999,

p. 205). The relationship was so close that Morgan had his office in the *Herald* building.

When Murdoch died in 1952, a company valedictory hailed him as the first man to accept the value of opinion polls (Goot 2010a, p. 280). More accurately, he was the only one who had the financial capability to make it happen. Through a series of strategic acquisitions, Murdoch had built the *Herald and Weekly Times* into the first press empire in Australia. Thus he was able – through ownership and/or commercial arrangements – to publish the Morgan Gallup poll in every state (Beed 1977, p. 212; Goot 2010a, p. 274). As in other democracies, there was considerable idealism and optimism about the new venture. 'This will do a lot of good,' wrote Murdoch in 1939, when approving the approach to Gallup. The poll's newsletters carried such bold inscriptions as 'Australia Speaks' and 'What Australia Thinks' (Mills 1999, p. 206).

The astounding longevity and strength of the *Herald and Weekly Times*-Morgan Gallup monopoly was only broken in 1971. This was a period of ferment both in Australian politics, with a resurgent Labor Party led by Gough Whitlam within striking distance of its first Federal victory in a generation, and in Australian journalism. The latter was fed by many factors including generational change in the parliamentary press gallery (Lloyd 1988); new journalistic ventures in the Australian Broadcasting Commission, especially in the growth of current affairs programming to supplement news coverage (Inglis 1983) and how Rupert Murdoch's founding of the first national newspaper *The Australian* in 1964 (Cryle 2008) had helped stimulate a renewal in quality newspapers more generally (Hills 2010).

As a result, three separate companies' polls were commissioned by and reported in three different newspaper groups in the lead-up to the 1972 election (Beed 1977). Since 1972, media reporting of polls has remained competitive and dynamic, with at least three pollsters commissioned by media outlets to gauge opinion before every federal election. It has also become more unstable and complex with corporate changes in the media – most spectacularly Murdoch's takeover of the *Herald and Weekly Times* in 1987 (Tiffen 1994) – and also changing ownership and strategic permutations in the market research industry leading to several shifting alliances between pollsters and newspapers.

The most important move was the founding of Newspoll in 1985, half owned by News Limited, and managed by pollster Sol Lebovic until his retirement in 2007. The poll is now published principally in *The Australian*, although other Murdoch papers often carry a truncated report, and it is the most frequently conducted and most widely published poll in Australia. It began as a monthly poll, and became fortnightly in 1992 (Megalogenis 2010). No other newspaper has an equity investment in a polling organization, instead commissioning polls from commercial market research companies. The broadsheet newspapers in the Fairfax organization, the *Age* and *Sydney Morning Herald*, have commissioned and published polls since the 1970s including, continuously since the mid-1990s, from the Neilsen Company. Newspoll, the Neilsen poll, and Galaxy polls published in the Murdoch metropolitan tabloids constitute the three most important media polls in 2010.

A peculiarity of Australian media and polling is that it has been overwhelmingly a press affair. With the exception of a fondness for 'phone-in' polls, commercial broadcasters as well as the publicly-owned ABC have generally been content to report poll results indirectly rather than commission their own. Television has generally not been prepared to invest the necessary resources, in contrast to the USA, for example. Indeed in recent decades, polling has been primarily conducted by the relatively low-circulation broadsheets, so that one could posit that those media organizations with the largest audiences – especially commercial television – invest least in the polls (and often do the worst in reporting them).

Reporting of polls is enriched in two other principal ways. First, Australian political parties, like their counterparts elsewhere, have discovered the value of doing their own polling. By the 1980s, each party had a relationship with a pollster (Mills 1986). Interestingly, the two major parties' long periods of electoral success – the Hawke-Keating Labor government of 1983–1996 and the Howard Coalition Government of 1996–2007 – each coincided with a stable and close association with a pollster skilled in both survey and qualitative (focus group) work – Rod Cameron of ANOP and Mark Textor of Crosby Textor respectively. Excerpts from the parties' internal polling often find their way into the media, but are reported in a much more fragmentary way and much less regularly than the published polls. Typically the reports give what the parties see as the 'bottom line' of their research, but little of the supporting evidence. The reader must take their conclusions on trust, and much of the time so, presumably, must the journalist. Such trust is not always justified. Brian Dale, former press secretary to New South Wales Labor Premier, Neville Wran, confessed: 'In presenting ALP polls conducted by ANOP I always added a point or so to Wran and deducted it from (the Liberals') Willis' (Dale 1985, p. 102).

Second, the Internet has provided a significant new medium for publication and analysis of political poll results. There was already a trend in the mainstream press to do 'polls of polls'. But this reached a new peak with the rise of the blogosphere. Australia now has several psephological bloggers who bring a new level of penetration to the analysis of the polls. Internet websites such as Possum Comitatus's (the pseudonym of Scott Steel) www.pollytics.com and Peter Brent's www.mumble.com aggregate data across different published polls while contrasting and exploring their differences. This is also done by experts, for example Andrew Catsaras' influential newsletters and William Bowe's *Pollbludger* (http://blogs.crikey.com.au/pollbludger/) site. The ABC's election analyst, Antony Green, as well as becoming a fixture of every election night's television, maintains a widely cited website on all matters electoral (http://blogs.abc.net.au/antonygreen). In sum, the activities of the pollsters are more extensive than in the past, but just as importantly they are much more intensively scrutinized and analyzed.

Developing techniques

For the first decades of polling by the Morgan Gallup Poll, its contract specified that it would conduct six surveys a year, each on 11 subjects for a total of 66 separate releases each year (Goot forthcoming). Some early reports were published a month after the data had been gathered. The polls were almost never published on the front page. Only rarely were there any follow-up comments by politicians or anyone else (Goot 2010a, p. 290). The polling was all done face-to-face. This necessitated the need for a large field staff able to cover the whole country. Terry Beed, one of the founders of ANOP, described the expense and logistical difficulties of a new company organizing its field staff in the 1970s (1977).

Given its unregulated and commercially oriented nature, the growth and development of Australian public opinion polling has always been shaped by considerations of cost. Newspaper proprietors look for maximum news impact at lowest cost, and pollsters have needed to balance sample size with reliability. Face-to-face polling was always expensive and slow. Thus, once sufficient households had telephones, most market researchers leapt at this cheaper alternative means of gathering data. Yet Morgan Gallup insisted on continuing with face-to-face interviews via its field staff – and still persists with that data-gathering method today, although no longer relying solely upon it. Its principal Gary Morgan asserted that telephone polls were less accurate because respondents are more likely to nominate who they think will win rather than the party they intend to vote for (Goot 2002), but the evidence, including from his own polls, is against him (Goot 2009, pp. 124–128, 131).

Telephone polling, however, has been widely adopted – notwithstanding the sampling problems arising from, for example, younger people tending to be at home less often, or only owning mobile phones that cannot be easily included in a fixed line sample. In recent times, perhaps because of growing public irritation at the intrusions of telemarketing, there has apparently been a greater refusal rate. In practice, pollsters have an increasingly sophisticated knowledge of population parameters, and can apply this to weight their samples. Most of the time, this probably increases the accuracy of polls, but such weighting rests on the problematic assumption that the characteristics of the respondents missed are the same as the characteristics of the respondents included.

Polling by the Australian media has almost exclusively involved quantitative survey research. A rare exception was the News Ltd/Sky News collaboration in which US pollster Frank Luntz conducted two focus groups of voters in the lead-up to the 2007 elections; the sessions were broadcast on Sky and reported in *The Australian* under the banner of 'The Voters' Verdict' (Megalogenis 2007).

Three other data-gathering techniques have risen to prominence in recent years. From 2007, a public affairs consultancy Essential Media Communications (www.essential.media.com.au) has conducted a weekly survey of issues including voting intentions, drawn from an online panel and published in Australia's most successful online news service *Crikey!* This innovation is possible because an increasing proportion of households have the Internet, but the biases in inclusion are still systematic. In particular, old people and poor people, those on the wrong side of the digital divide, are excluded.

Televised debates between the two major party leaders – a feature of every Australian election campaign since 1984 (except 1987) – have also provided pollsters with new opportunities to experiment. It has been commercial broadcasting that has made the most significant contribution, through the so-called 'worm'. First deployed by Channel Nine in the 1993 debate between Keating and Hewson and progressively refined over the years, the 'worm' is generated by a small live audience, recruited by a market research company, using individual electronic devices to register their responses to the debate, on a positive-negative scale, in real time. The responses are aggregated and represented as a moving graph or 'worm' which is broadcast along with the debate itself. The technique has proven controversial but remains popular, and innovations continue. For the 2010 debate between Gillard and Abbott, the first involving a female and male candidate, audience responses were separately tracked by gender (Sawer 2010); there was also competition between Channel Nine's 'worm' and Channel Seven's 'polliegraph', the latter conducted by Roy Morgan Research Centre (Idato 2010).

In the last week of the 2010 campaign the *Sydney Morning Herald* published what it referred to as 'the most comprehensive public opinion poll ever undertaken in Australian politics' – a survey of 28,000 voters living in 54 marginal seats as well as a sample of safe seats (Brent 2010; Coorey 2010). The survey was an innovative application of automatic telephone messaging – 'robocalling' – which had been used as a campaign tool by political parties in 2004 and 2007 to disseminate their messages. In 2010, an independent research firm, JWS Research, pioneered the application of 'robopolling'. The technique lowers the cost of interviewing as respondents are speaking to an automated call centre, allowing pollsters to generate very large samples and potentially reduce the sampling error. The large JWS sample, however, was spread thin, with just 400 respondents per electorate, and this resulted in numerous incorrect predictions regarding which seats would change hands.

A developing repertoire of questions

Perhaps ironically, in the early days the Morgan Poll was centered less around parties, and certainly much less around political personalities, whereas the weight of contemporary polling is much more centered on the 'horse race'. Around nine out of ten questions Morgan asked were to do with issues. Today, the most common questions are about voting intentions, leaders and alternative leaders, and these probably constitute a majority of the questions asked and reported in the mainstream media. Moreover, when issues are canvassed, quite a high proportion do not probe respondents' perceptions or substantive attitudes, but simply which party they think would handle the issue better, typically followed by speculation on the electoral implications of this.

Morgan Gallup's questions ranged 'from the parochial to the international, from the social and humanitarian to the economic and political, from the wearing of lipstick to the dropping of atomic bombs' (Goot & Ilbery 1969, p. i). Morgan boasted that, through his partnership with the Herald group, his survey questions had 'the most newsy slant in the world' (Mills 1999, p. 206). In all this, he shared the plebiscitary idealism of George Gallup, viewing polling as a highly desirable new form of collective expression, as well as a valuable tool for democratic leaders.

While voting intentions were a staple of the polls from the beginning (Beed et al. 1978), polling about leaders was more erratic. Indeed, Morgan expressed the view that questions about the performance of political leaders was disrespectful, and only started to ask these regularly in 1968 (Goot forthcoming). Over his 23 years as prime minister, Menzies was the subject of only three approval polls, while Harold Holt, prime minister for almost two years in 1966–1967, was not the subject of any (Mills 1999 p. 209). But in 1972, Whitlam and McMahon were each the subject of 20 approval polls. Another significant step was Newspoll's introducing a regular question about the 'preferred prime minister'. In Goot's judgment, this well publicized question has helped Newspoll become the most important poll published by the Australian press in the last 25 years (2010, p. 288).

The polls' increasing focus on individual political leaders, measuring their 'popularity' or 'approval' of their performance either singly or in comparison, has been a significant contributing factor to the media's increased personalization of political reporting. Intensive polling on leadership, fuelled by news interest, fed directly into the political contest. In the late 1970s, Bob Hawke's ambitions to transfer from leading the trade union movement into parliament, and thence to leadership of the Labor Party, presented a new theme for pollsters and reporters: leader comparisons not cross-party but intra-party, comparing perceptions of an incumbent office holder such as Opposition Leader Bill Hayden with potential alternatives (if not actual challengers) such as Hawke. Such polls, especially internal party polling, became an important weapon in Hawke's campaign to destabilize Hayden's leadership and ultimately replace him in the lead-up to the 1983 Federal election (Summers 1983, pp. 29–32). This canvassing of alternative leaders has become a regular feature of Australian polling and politics; Opposition leaders appeared particularly vulnerable. Howard's first tenure as coalition Opposition leader was weakened immeasurably by a front cover of the *Bulletin* magazine in December 1988 in which he was hailed as 'Mr 18%', in reference to a new Morgan poll. Paul Kelly described opinion polls as 'handy weapons for destabilization' (Kelly 1992, p. 231).

2010: The interaction of polls and politics

The last few years have been a spectacular ride in Australian electoral politics, and in particular 2010 brought unprecedented developments. First, an elected prime minister was deposed by his own party in his first term of office. Second, for the first time since the depths of the depression in 1931, a government failed to win a majority at its first attempt at re-election. Third, for the first time since 1940, a general election produced a hung parliament with independents and minor parties holding the balance of power, leading, fourth, to the most prolonged period after an election before a new government was formed. The polls – and the reporting of them – were intricately involved in all these dramatic developments; indeed it would be impossible to explain the sequence of events without reference to opinion polling and its effect on political leaders, journalists and voters.

For its first two years after being elected in late 2007, Labor was comfortably ahead on all published two-party preferred measures; Kevin Rudd himself was reported by Newspoll, in May 2008, as 'preferred prime minister' by 72–9 over Opposition Leader Brendan Nelson. Nelson was soon replaced by Malcolm Turnbull, but at the end of 2008 the same poll showed Rudd outscored him 66–19. In a mid-October 2009 Newspoll, the two-party preferred vote hit 59–41 with the Coalition divided over its response to the proposed Emissions Trading Scheme (ETS), and Rudd still outscored Turnbull as preferred prime minister by 65–19. Such highly unusual figures would translate into an electoral wipeout for the Coalition – neatly summarized by the headline writer in *The Australian* as: 'Rudd's future assured by Coalition in chaos' (Kelly 2010). Yet the next Newspoll, at the end of October, showed a sharp and significant deterioration in Labor's position, as its lead in the two-party preferred vote fell back to 52–48, beginning a Labor slide that was never reversed. In June 2010, Rudd was ousted as prime minister by his deputy, Julia Gillard. It is possible to explain this unprecedented outcome by pointing to a sequence of government policy failures and a steady improvement in the Opposition's performance (Stuart 2010). Most significantly, the replacement of Turnbull by Tony Abbott in December 2009 reunited the Opposition around an aggressively attacking leader who immediately stymied the government's ETS legislation. But the publication of opinion polls added a crucial element, feeding the process in at least three ways.

First, opinion polls influenced the style and substance of media reporting. Polling is often said to foster 'horse race' journalism – a media preoccupation with who is winning the electoral contest rather than with the substance of policy. The truth is that polling provides several different 'form guides' for that 'horse race', and this allows journalists to choose from a diverse stream of narratives. In 2010 the major pollsters were polling on national primary voting intention, national two-party preferred vote, satisfaction ratings for prime minister and

Opposition leader, and a preferred prime minister comparison. Many of these questions were also polled within marginal electorates. Newspoll also conducted an occasional series on 'personality traits' of the prime minister and Opposition leader. This diversity should fuel a more sophisticated analysis by the media, though in the circumstances of mid-2010 nuance was replaced by a growing assault on the prime minister himself – whose slide in personal approval rating far exceeded Labor's slide in the two-party preferred vote. As the slide continued, Newspoll's fortnightly publication schedule fostered a sense of anticipation for 'Newspoll Tuesday', creating a timeframe for news reporting that was independent of the political and policy agenda and that seemingly vindicated an increasingly critical media stance towards the government and prime minister.

Second, Rudd's and Labor's deteriorating standing in opinion polls seemingly influenced the government's policy decisions as they attempted to reverse the slide, creating a negative response loop. Of all the issues, the most important was climate change. The parliamentary impasse over the ETS, along with the failure of the Copenhagen climate talks to deliver tangible progress – talks at which Rudd had tried to take a leading role – left the government without an apparent plan to address what he had earlier described as the greatest moral challenge of the age. When Rudd announced that the government would not proceed with the ETS legislation and would defer any action until 2013, the backdown fuelled public dissatisfaction and drove the polls down further. Rudd's net satisfaction rating (measuring those 'satisfied' with his performance, minus those 'dissatisfied') had been at a commanding 43 (67 minus 24) in late September 2009, but was down to 18 (52–34) at the start of 2010, and seven (48–41) in March. But in the wake of his ETS decision, Newspoll recorded a catastrophic decline. Rudd's net satisfaction rating dropped into negative territory for the first time, to –11 (39–50), while Labor's two-party preferred vote immediately fell from a winning 54–46 to a probably losing 49–51. As *The Australian* reported on its front page on 4 May, Rudd's rating had fallen 'the most in the shortest time in the 20-year history of Newspoll' (Shanahan 2010).

Third, opinion polls became the driver for the Labor Party's unprecedented decision to move against Rudd. By early June, Rudd's satisfaction rating reached –19 (36–55), and though Labor led the Coalition on a national two-party preferred vote 52–48, reports from marginal seats were worse. On 21 June Rudd was removed overnight as prime minister by Gillard in a party room movement so overwhelming that no vote was deemed necessary. The party turned to her because many of them – informed by the polls – believed that not to do so was to risk defeat in the approaching elections. *The Sunday Telegraph* reported that 'secret ALP polling in four western Sydney seats last week convinced Labor Party officials that Kevin Rudd had to go'. The paper reported that having been 'shown' the research, the MP for one of the seats 'was so concerned that he openly confronted Mr Rudd at last Tuesday's caucus meeting' (Silmalis 2010). Thus this private research has been used both to influence political decision making and to justify it after the event via leaks to the media.

Gillard explained her challenge by saying the Labor Government was a good government that had 'lost its way', and set about addressing three key policy issues – all of which had featured prominently in published polls. These efforts took place against a backdrop of continuing media attention on the polls: did Gillard give Labor a 'bounce' in the polls? Did she receive a 'honeymoon'? And did she benefit from a gender gap? Gillard called an early election for 21 August. The 2010 election was the occasion of particularly intense attention to polls – accentuating the long-term emphasis on covering the campaign as a contest (Tiffen 1989, pp. 130–1), with the dominance of horse race, sports and military metaphors framing much news coverage (Young 2010, pp. 181–2). In 2010, this was partly driven by the finely balanced state of opinion. Two-party preferred voting intentions showed parties consistently at or around the 50–50 mark. Primary voting intentions further revealed Labor's weakness and the corresponding strength of the Green vote, presenting dissatisfied Labor supporters with a credible form of protest while also highlighting the importance of the Green preference flows to determining the election outcome. The campaign was widely derided as devoid of substance or passion – a phenomenon which was itself attributed by the media to the parties' 'focus-group driven' political strategies, and in this context the published polls provided journalists with genuine news value. The main polls all performed well in their final calls: all predicted a very close outcome, although most over-estimated, but within acceptable sampling error margins, Labor's lead.

In the unprecedented post-election period – 17 days passed from Election Day until the decision of the last two Independents to support Labor in a minority government – public opinion polls continued to have prominence. Indeed, given the apparent failure of the electoral system to provide an immediate winner, some seized on the polls to play a role by providing a default evidentiary basis for determining the winner; in a hung parliament, the polls provided a potential tool to break the deadlock. For example, as the three rural independents pondered whether to support a minority Labor or minority Coalition government, Newspoll surveyed their electorates to establish what their own voters wanted them to do; *The Australian* editorialized that its poll showed the independents needed to support a minority Coalition government (*The Australian* 2010), although the crucial two opted to support Labor.

At the end of such an eventful and often problematic year, the accuracy of the polls received further vindication, when the Victorian Labor government of John Brumby was defeated. Nearly all the pundits expected Labor to be re-elected, but the late polls indicated otherwise. Betting on elections is legal in Australia, and indeed one of the staples of reporting in recent election campaigns has been the state of the betting market. Wolfers and Leigh once argued that 'the press may have better served its readers by reporting betting odds than by conducting polls' (2002, p. 223). However in Victoria, even on Election Eve, Labor was 'a barely backable favourite' and the coalition was at long odds (Bowe 2010). The polls predicted the result better than the punters.

Conclusion

Public polling in Australia is still dominated by the long-lived commercial and editorial relationship between newspapers and opinion polls. The early suspicions of polling by the left wing (Goot 2010, pp. 283–4), and accusations about the integrity of the data by politicians, such as Whitlam in 1975 (Beed 1977, p. 226; Mills 1999, p. 210) and even most recently when in 2010 Tony Abbott declared the 'worm' never favored coalition leaders in TV debates, have all proved groundless. The very public nature of the product provides incentives towards accuracy. As one of the pioneers of the industry, Ian McNair once commented: 'If we were wrong most of the time (in election polls), then sampling surveys of all kinds would be in disrepute' (Mills 1999, p. 213).

Only once did the pollsters wrongly predict an election outcome. That was in 1980. At that time the last published polls had been taken some time before Election Day, and there was almost certainly a strong swing back towards the Fraser Liberal government (Goot 1984), partly fuelled by a massive advertising campaign the government mounted when it was alerted to its position in the polls (Butler 1983; Tiffen 1989). Since then, pollsters (and party officials) have been very vigilant for late swings. The other election in which there was a dramatic swing back resulting in a government winning after being behind at the start of the campaign was in 1993. This time the polls captured the movement and pointed to a cliff-hanger. However, election outcomes, even election results, are a very limited means of holding pollsters' accuracy to account.

The longevity of the poll-media relationship suggests that both sides perceive benefits from its continuation. On the one hand, newspaper proprietors and editors are attracted to survey research because it generates news stories that are compelling, relevant and exclusive: it helps drive newspaper sales. On the other hand, polling organizations enjoy the publicity derived from their press work to market their services to commercial clients. Both sides derive a critical source of influence over policy and political matters. Sharing a vested interest in presenting their polls as significant new revelations, then, both pollsters and journalists sometimes turn a blind eye to small samples in marginal seats, report as substantial poll movements that are not statistically significant, emphasize small changes within larger stability, and maintain news interest by presenting political contests as dramatically and unpredictably close. This is compounded by another principal incentive: wanting to avoid being caught in a visible and memorable mistake. So even when their figures are fairly clear-cut, the reports are often full of caveats. This was particularly the case with the News Limited papers on the eve of the 2007 election. They all emphasized how Howard was making a comeback, and could even be on the verge of an unexpected victory (Goot 2009; Tiffen 2008). When the result was a clear victory for Rudd, their Monday morning reports stressed the inevitability of what had occurred, and the pollsters congratulated themselves.

The wish to stress the newsworthiness of their poll results was neatly captured by one former reporter from *The Australian*, who described the commercial pressures arising from Newspoll ownership as 'heavy but subtle' (Milne 2010):

> You were aware that the poll was expensive. Therefore you had better make good use of it...there was therefore an unspoken demand to dramatize the numbers within reason. You were aware that as the national flagship paper of the country, Newspoll was inextricably bound up with the prestige branding of The *Australian*. To make Newspoll count was to make the *Australian* count. That was an added pressure to maximize the impact of the poll.

In 2007, *The Australian*'s interpretation of its Newspoll became an object of controversy. The Howard government for the whole year before the election was facing what journalist Peter Hartcher described as 'polls of chilling steadiness and deadly intent' (2007), but among the multiple narratives to which any series of polling questions might lend themselves, many critics felt that the paper always sought the one most favorable to the government. Its reporting became an object of ridicule in the blogosphere (Young 2010 p. 211). In July *The Australian* (2007) editorialized against these 'sheltered academics and failed journalists who would not get a job on a real newspaper'. It concluded with an epistemological gem: 'we understand Newspoll because we own it'.

It should be stressed that it is not only newspapers, but also politicians who are prone to exaggerating the significance of the most recent polls. What Mills (1999, p. 204) called 'the three-sided relationship . . . between the pollster, the journalist and the politician' is often central to how political events unfold, as was evident above in the key events of 2010. Hartcher, analyzing the fall of John Howard, commented on the direct personal impact of the polls:

> Politicians, despite all their protestations to the contrary, live and die by the polls. Most receive them with the gravity of a judicial ruling. Especially in the run-up to an election, Howard's moods from day to day depended on the opinion polls. . . . (After poor polls) he frequently vented his frustrations on senior staff, yelling and shouting. . . . The polls ruled Howard's emotions.
>
> (2009, p. 7)

In 2010, more pollsters are reported in more media outlets, and their findings are scrutinized more intensely, than ever before in Australian history. The landscape is dynamic and competitive. For the main, the pollsters' sampling and question methodology is sophisticated and robust, and their track record over a long period has been good. There is a group of journalists who have developed considerable expertise in reporting polls, and equally importantly, on the edges of the mainstream media and outside, there is another group of experts who monitor developments closely, and whose writings feed into media discussions of the polls. Many of the dilemmas arising from the polling-media relationship are variants of the central dilemmas of democracy: the tendency of politicians to be more influenced by majority opinion than the merits of a policy; of reports of poll results to add fuel to media and political bandwagons, despite increasing evidence that voters themselves, simultaneously source and recipient, are becoming perhaps more confused, skeptical and alienated. It is wrong to hold the media reporting of polls responsible for political superficiality and conformism, but neither are they a cure for it.

Acknowledgment

This chapter has been improved by a characteristically searching critique from Professor Murray Goot.

References

Association of Market and Social Research Organisations (2003) *Market and Social Research Privacy Code*, http://www.amsro.com.au/AMSRO_wp_amsro236/wp-content/uploads/2010/12/AMSRO-Code_final_ofpc_30-June-07.pdf

Association of Market and Social Research Associations (2010) *Code of Professional Behaviour*, http://www.mrsa.com.au/files/Code_of_Professional_Behaviour.pdf

Australian Communications and Media Authority (2010) *Frequently asked Questions about the Do Not Call Register*, https://www.donotcall.gov.au/consumerfaq.cfm#exemptions.

Australian Press Council (2001) General Press release no 246, (iv) July 2001, http://www.presscouncil.org.au/pcsite/activities/guides/gpr246_4.html.

Australian, The (editorial) (2007, July 12) 'History a Better Guide than Bias'.

Australian, The (editorial) (2010, August 28) 'Time to Climb Off the Fence', p. 15.

Beed, T. W. (1977) 'Opinion Polling and the Elections', in H. Penniman (ed.), *Australia at the Polls: The National Elections of 1975* (Washington DC: American Enterprise Institute for Public Policy Research).

Beed, T. W., M. Goot, S. Hodgson and P. Ridley (1978) *Australian Opinion Polls 1941–1977* (Sydney: Hale & Iremonger).

Bowe, W. (2010, November 26) 'Pollbludger: Galaxy Poll Encourages Coalition, Bookies Say Otherwise', *Crikey*.

Brent, P. (2007) 'Poll Position: Making Sense of Opinion Polls', in C. Kerr (ed.) *The Crikey Guide to the 2007 Election* (Ringwood: Penguin).

Brent, P. (2010, August 19) 'Eyebrows Raised by March of the Robopoll', *The Australian Mumble Blog*.

Butler, D. (1983) 'Introduction', in H. R. Penniman (ed.), *Australia at the Polls: The National Elections of 1980 and 1983* (Sydney: George Allen & Unwin for the American Enterprise Institute for Public Policy Research).

Colebatch, T. (2010, September 21) 'The Great Turnoff', *The Age*.

Coorey, P. (2010, August 18) 'Poll has Abbott Reeling', *Sydney Morning Herald*.

Costar, B. and P. Browne (2010, September 24) 'Missing Votes: The 2010 Tally', *Inside Story*, http://inside.org.au/missing-votes-the-2010-tally/

Cryle, D. (2008) *Murdoch's Flagship. Twenty-Five Years of the Australian Newspaper* (Melbourne: Melbourne University Press).

Dale, B. (1985) *Ascent to Power: Wran and the Media* (Sydney: Allen and Unwin).

Goot, M. (1984) 'The Media and the Campaign', in H. R. Penniman (ed.) *Australia at the Polls: The National Elections of 1980 and 1983* (Sydney: George Allen & Unwin for the American Enterprise Institute for Public Policy Research).

Goot, M. (1988) 'Trust the Polls', in I. McAllister and J. Warhurst (eds), *Australia Votes: The 1987 Australian Federal Election* (Melbourne: Longman Cheshire).

Goot, M. (2002) 'Reporting the Polls', in S. Tanner (ed.), *Journalism: Investigation and Research* (Sydney: Pearson).

Goot, M. (2009) 'Getting it Wrong while Getting it Right: The Polls, the Press and the 2007 Australian Election', *Australian Cultural History*, 27(2), 115–33.

Goot, M. (2010a) ' "A Worse Importation than Chewing Gum": American Influences on the Australian Press and their Limits – The Australian Gallup Poll, 1941–1973', *Historical Journal of Film, Radio and Television*, 30, 269–302.

Goot, M. (2010b) 'Underdogs, Bandwagons or Incumbency? Party Support at the Beginning and End of Australian Election Campaigns, 1983–2007', *Australian Cultural History*, 28(1), 69–80.

Goot, M. (forthcoming) 'Morgan, Roy Edward', in M. Nolan (ed.), *Australian Dictionary of Biography* (Vol. 18; Carlton: Melbourne University Press).

Goot, M. and T. W. Beed (1979) 'The Polls, the Public and the Re-election of the Fraser Government', in H. R. Penniman (ed.), *The Australian National Elections of 1977* (Washington, DC and Canberra: American Enterprise Institute for Public Policy Research and the Australian National University Press).

Goot, M. and J. Ilbery (1969) *Australian Public Opinion Polls* (Occasional Monograph, Department of Government and Public Administration, no. 2, University of Sydney).

Hartcher, P. (2007, November 16) 'Howard's Instinct Let him Down', *Sydney Morning Herald*.

Hartcher, P. (2009) *To the Bitter End: The Dramatic Story Behind the Fall of John Howard and the Rise of Kevin Rudd* (Sydney: Allen and Unwin).

Hill, L. (2007) 'Compulsory Voting', in B. Galligan and W. Roberts (eds), *The Oxford Companion to Australian Politics* (Melbourne: Oxford University Press).

Hills, B. (2010) *Breaking News: The Golden Age of Graham Perkin* (Melbourne: Scribe).

Hughes, C. A. (2007) 'Electoral Systems', in B. Galligan and W. Roberts (eds), *The Oxford Companion to Australian Politics* (Melbourne: Oxford University Press).

Idato, M. (2010, July 26) 'Polliegraph Squashes Worm', *Sydney Morning Herald*.

Inglis, K. S. (1983) *This is the ABC: The Australian Broadcasting Commission 1932–1983* (Melbourne: Melbourne University Press).

Irvine, J. (2010, September 1) 'Informal Vote Makes Mockery of Democracy', *Sydney Morning Herald*.

Kelly, P. (1992) *The End of Certainty* (St Leonards, NSW: Allen and Unwin).

Kelly, P. (2010, October 7) 'Rudd's Future Assured by Coalition in Chaos', *Australian*.

Lijphart, A. (1984) *Democracies: Patterns of Majoritarian and Consensus Government in Twenty-One Countries* (New Haven, CT: Yale University Press).

Lloyd, C. J. (1988) *Parliament and the Press: The Federal Parliamentary Press Gallery 1901–1988* (Melbourne: Melbourne University Press).

Mackerras, M. (1972) *Australian General Elections* (Sydney: Angus and Robertson).

Mackerras, M. (2010, February 5) 'The Mackerras Pendulum', *The Australian*.

McAllister, I. (2009) 'Elections and Electoral Behaviour', in R. A. W. Rhodes (ed.), *The Australian Study of Politics* (London: Palgrave Macmillan).

Megalogenis, G. (2007, August 31) 'Swinging Voters Prefer to Hear Rudd Over Howard', *The Australian*, p. 7.

Megalogenis, G. (2010) 'Trivial Pursuit: Leadership and the End of the Reform Era', *Quarterly Essay*, 40, Black Inc.

Mills, S. (1986) *The New Machine Men: Polls and Persuasion in Australian Politics* (Ringwood: Penguin).

Mills, S. (1999) 'Polling, Politics and the Press 1941–1996', in A. Curthoys and J. Schultz (eds), *Journalism: Print, Politics and Popular Culture* (St Lucia, QLD: University of Queensland Press).

Milne, G. (2010, November) 'Death by Newspoll', *IPA Review*, 62(4).

Orr, G. (2010) *The Law of Politics: Elections, Parties and Money in Australia* (Annandale, NSW: The Federation Press).

Plasser, F. with G. Plasser (2002) *Global Political Campaigning, a Worldwide Analysis of Campaign Professionals and their Practices* (Westport, CT: Praeger).

Reynolds, A. and B. Reilly (1997) *The International IDEA Handbook of Electoral Design* (Stockholm: International Institute for Democracy and Electoral Assistance).

Sartori, G. (1976) *Parties and Party Systems: A Framework for Analysis* (Cambridge: Cambridge University Press).

Sawer, M. (2010, October) 'Managing Gender: The 2010 Federal Election', *Australian Review of Public Affairs*, available at http://www.australianreview.net/digest/2010/10/sawer.html.

Shanahan, D. (2010, May 4) 'Record Drop in Satisfaction after ETS Backflip as Coalition Moves Ahead', *The Australian*.

Silmalis, L. (2010, June 27) 'Why Kev had to Go', *The Sunday Telegraph*.

Stuart, N. (2010) *Rudd's Way. November 2007–June 2010* (Melbourne: Scribe).

Summers, A. (1983) *Gamble for Power: How Bob Hawke beat Malcolm Fraser. The 1983 Federal Election* (Melbourne: Thomas Nelson).

Tiffen, R. (1989) *News and Power* (Sydney: Allen and Unwin).

Tiffen, R. (1994) 'Media Policy', in J. Brett, J. Gillespie and M. Goot (eds), *Developments in Australian Politics* (Melbourne: Palgrave Macmillan).

Tiffen, R. (2008) 'Campaign Tactics, Media Bias and the Politics of Explanations: Accounting for the Coalition's Loss in 2007', *Communication, Politics and Culture*, 41(2), 8–29.

Tiffen, R. (2010, August 6) 'Polls, Elections and Australian Political History: A Primer', *Inside Story*, http://inside.org.au/polls-elections-and-australian-political-history-a-primer/

Tiffen, R. and R. Gittins (2009) *How Australia Compares*, 2nd edn (Melbourne: Cambridge University Press).

Wolfers, J. and A. Leigh (2002) 'Three Tools for Forecasting Federal Elections: Lessons from 2001', *Australian Journal of Political Science*, 37, 223–40.

Young, S. A. (2004) *The Persuaders; Inside the Hidden Machine of Political Advertising* (Melbourne: Pluto Press).

Young, S. A. (2010) *How Australia Decides: Election Reporting and the Media* (Melbourne: Cambridge University Press).

9
Opinion Polls and the Media in South Africa

Robert Mattes

When millions of South Africans lined up to vote in the country's historic founding 1994 election, public opinion polling seemed set to become a regular and important part of South Africa's new democratic system. Under *apartheid*, a flourishing private research sector had emerged and the state had developed a strong opinion research facility to monitor popular views towards political change, though both were usually prevented by a range of political and technical factors from surveying the majority of black South Africans. During the country's dramatic transition period between 1990 and 1994, a plethora of different organizations sponsored or conducted a wide range of surveys that were also widely covered by the news media. The country's main liberation movement, the African National Congress (ANC), also became increasingly acquainted with the art of survey research as part of its own transition into a modern political party. Indeed, both published polls and private polls had a number of important political impacts on South Africa's constitutional negotiations, as well as on the campaign for the crucial 1994 founding election.

Since then, however, public opinion – as expressed through opinion survey results – has failed to grow into a major force in South Africa's new democracy. While survey research results are reported in the news media, much of what is reported consists of research about consumer confidence and broad socio-political attitudes generated by commercial and academic research organizations. But because no news media outlets currently conduct or sponsor their own surveys, very little coverage consists of citizen assessments of government performance or candidates, or of political party preferences. Indeed, in probably the most telling assessment of the limited extent of political demand for data, only two political parties currently commission their own surveys.

This is surprising, not only due to the tremendous interest in public opinion in the four years leading up to the 1994 election, but also because South Africa is a democracy with a well-developed electronic and print news media. It is even more surprising given the fact that South African elections are infrequent (once every five years) and limited (one vote for a political party to run the national government, and one for a political party to run the provincial government), and that there are no direct constituency linkages between voters and members of the national Parliament or provincial legislative assemblies. This is a mixture of factors that might otherwise be expected to produce a very strong demand amongst the news media, not to mention elected representatives and party strategists for public opinion data. Yet, as will be discussed more fully at the end of this chapter, it is this very mixture of factors, when combined with additional facts of high levels of party discipline, low levels of electoral uncertainty, and other important technical and financial factors, that has had precisely the opposite effect of actually *diminishing* the demand for and the supply of public opinion data.

The apartheid heritage

Given South Africa's capitalist economy, and the size of its commercial and business sectors, it was only natural that a number of research organizations emerged to meet the growing demand for information on markets and consumer preferences. These organizations, however, were relative latecomers to the longstanding practice in other industrialized countries where commercial market research firms advertise their services by getting involved in measuring political attitudes and then publicizing these results through the news media. The 1970 white general election saw the first surveys of national samples of the white population, both commissioned by newspapers (Lever 1974, p. 400). But by the end of the 1980s, commercial firms such as Market and Opinion Surveys, Marketing and Media Research, Market Research Africa, Markinor and Research Surveys regularly asked questions about partisan politics, race relations and social and political change, and released results for publication by the news media. In addition, the state-funded Human Sciences Research Council (HSRC) began conducting regular surveys during the 1980s to monitor public opinion on various issues related to *apartheid* and the scope for social and political reform (Couper & Rhoodie 1988; De Kock 1996; De Kock, Rhoodie & Couper 1985; Rhoodie & Couper 1987; Rhoodie, De Kock & Couper

1985). The government communications agency, the South African Communications Service, also regularly commissioned surveys for the Presidency as well as for other government departments. Little, if any, of this research, however, included the attitudes of the millions of black South Africans living in the 'independent' *apartheid* Bantustans of Bophuthatswana, Ciskei, Transkei and Venda, and much of this was excluded from the other Bantustans which had not yet been granted independence, or from urban townships within 'white' South Africa by political violence or security restrictions.

Polling the transition and first election

The political significance of opinion polling grew greatly in the period between 1990 and 1994, when the *apartheid* government began informal talks and then formal negotiation with the leaders of South Africa's liberation movements and other political parties over the country's new democratic constitutional framework, as well as the structure and timing of its first election. Of fundamental importance to this bargaining were the strategic political premises upon which negotiators calculated their present and future interests. A key part of these premises consisted of judgments about levels of popular support and expectations of support in the first election. This created an increased demand for information about public opinion by the news media, by politicians wanting to win votes and find popular acceptance and support for their policies, and, most importantly, by constitutional negotiators wanting to know the relative political strengths of themselves and their bargaining partners. These demands were particularly acute because the South African political landscape was barren of any past voting records that leaders could have used as a guide or baseline to judge the relative strengths of competing actors.

Between 1990 and 1994, 23 different indigenous organizations initiated or commissioned surveys about the relative strengths of the contending political parties and leaders. These surveys were conducted by at least 15 different South African research organizations. The South African print and electronic news media were increasingly filled with reports and analyses of the current support levels of the competing political parties and their likely performance in the first election. By 1994, poll results were designated by South Africa's Electoral Act as the appropriate test for parties wishing to receive campaign finances from the State Electoral Fund (parties had to register 2 per cent support) (Mattes 1995a).

According to the philosopher John Rawls (1973), negotiations over a new constitutional dispensation would produce the fairest outcomes if they could be conducted behind a 'veil of ignorance' about how any of the negotiating parties would benefit from its outcome. All parties would attempt to protect the position of the least well off, since it could very well be any of them. However, if they could consider how the outcome might affect their fortunes, negotiators would probably choose the procedures best suited to their own particular interests. This 'ignorance' is an extreme form of uncertainty.

Uncertainty is said to be important to negotiations for a democratic constitution because contending parties need to agree to compete in such a way that electoral losers will respect the governing authority of victorious parties in return for the freedom to mobilize support and possibly win subsequent elections. This is what Guillermo O'Donnell and Philippe Schmitter (1986, p. 52) called 'contingent consent': winners and losers have to have some hope that they can keep playing under the rules of electoral competition. Constitutional negotiators haggle over how best to produce that contingent consent. Yet uncertainty is a double-edged sword. Parties need to believe that they have a chance of winning, or at least surviving an election. Otherwise, there would be no reason for authoritarian governments to hand over power, or for revolutionaries to leave the bush and join the electoral process. At the same time, stronger parties need to believe that there is at least some possibility of losing future elections so that they agree to the fairest rules of electoral competition. Viewed from this perspective, a degree of *certainty* of at least *some* electoral success and political influence is actually necessary to induce authoritarians and revolutionaries to accept elections and contingent consent. Yet this must be combined with a degree of uncertainty in order to obtain the fairest electoral and decision-making arrangements.

While no bargaining situation can ever be validly characterized by Rawls' heuristic image, in the case of South Africa, the widespread availability of survey data shredded the 'veil of ignorance', radically reducing the amount of uncertainty about present and future interests, and thus enabled what Rawls called 'present position', that is, self-interested bargaining which ultimately helped to produce a constitutional agreement that was largely in the interests of the strongest political parties. Political parties' negotiating positions on matters ranging from the timing of the first election, the rules under which those elections would be conducted and the nature of the government to be elected were all linked to their understandings of how much electoral support they could expect, when and where that support might arise, and under what conditions such support would be forthcoming.[1]

In 1990, poll results provided both the governing National Party (NP) and the ANC with increased certainty about their respective political futures, and enabled them to move closer to one another into what Timothy Sisk (1995) called a 'contract zone' and begin serious negotiations in 1991. The ANC entered negotiations secure in the knowledge that it enjoyed a far superior electoral strategic situation in relation to its competitor liberation organizations, the Pan Africanist Congress (PAC) and the Azanian People's Organization (AZAPO). Consistent with what surveys said about their electoral prospects, the PAC and AZAPO opted to stay out of the negotiations process. The NP also apparently found itself in a surprisingly strong situation, which enabled it to move away from its demands for group rights and concurrent majorities, to elections based on universal franchise. Through its awareness of survey data, especially accumulating evidence in 1990 that it might enjoy surprisingly high levels of support amongst colored, Indian and even black voters, the NP concluded that it could survive, and possibly prosper, under a democratic dispensation.

To be sure, while some key NP officials came to entertain hopes of doing very well, survey data also told the NP that the upper limit of its support base was somewhere between 30 and 40 per cent. Thus, poll-based knowledge also prevented the over-optimistic regime-led rush towards early democratic elections, which had characterized many transitions in Latin America (Huntington 1993, pp. 174–193; O'Donnell & Schmitter 1986, pp. 59–61). While it agreed to universal franchise elections, poll-based knowledge led the NP to demand strong minority vetoes (minorities being numerically defined, rather than corporately, which had been the case with early NP proposals) where winning one-third of the vote would guarantee the NP significant influence over key constitutional and policy questions.

Once the negotiations began in 1991, political parties' ability to make relatively certain calculations about their future positions led them to adopt negotiating positions which prolonged the negotiations (almost scuttling them at one point) and harmed the final constitutional product. Even as NP negotiators grew in confidence about their electoral fortunes, poll results in 1991 and 1992 showed the ANC to be significantly weaker than might otherwise have been anticipated. Thus, the NP came to believe that it was in its interests to delay elections for as long as possible in order to dissipate ANC electoral strength and possibly bring it down below 50 per cent. Its belief that the ANC was not in an electorally strong position, and simultaneous estimation that itself had not yet got to the point where it wanted to mount an election campaign, translated into an insistence on additional safeguards: an insistence which ultimately destroyed the rapidly gathering momentum towards an early settlement.

For the ANC, poll-based reports of clear majority support in 1990 enabled it to shift from its initial preference for a plurality, first-past-the-post voting system and concede to opposition party preferences for proportional representation. They also were consistent with its demand that initial negotiations amongst all political organizations be limited to preparing the ground for the first election and drafting broad principles, and leave actual constitution-drafting to an elected 'constituent assembly' (whereas the NP wanted as many issues as possible to be determined by the all-party negotiations). Its main goal was to secure majority rule through a parliamentary system where the majority party in the legislature would form the executive. But by late 1992, its failure to conclude an early agreement, along with its current standing in the polls, led it to conclude that it was also not in a strong strategic position. It resorted, in turn, to older more traditional methods of opinion demonstration – mass strikes and marches around the country – to demonstrate its anticipated popular support and force the NP to compromise its bargaining stance. Yet while widely seen to be a resounding success in popular mobilization, 'rolling mass action' ultimately failed to gain its desired negotiating goals. Thus, the ANC saw its strategic situation decline further (of which dwindling support in polls were one part) and decided in the second half of 1992 to concede on its long-held demand for a majority party cabinet and agree to the NP's demand for a power-sharing cabinet, something Nelson Mandela had explicitly ruled out just one year earlier. This decision was consistent with current surveys that showed it might not be able to get the electoral majority required to control such a cabinet, by itself or with its allies. Of course, other important factors were taken into consideration, such as mounting political violence and the fact that the NP would still dominate the army and civil service following an election. But it is highly unlikely that the ANC would have conceded on power-sharing if it had been certain, at that point, of winning 60 per cent of the vote.

Federalism was another key area in which parties' stances were consistent with their perception of the nature and distribution of their support. Its strongest proponents, the NP, the white liberal Democratic Party (DP), and the Zulu-based Inkatha Freedom Party (IFP), all realized that while they enjoyed minority support nationally, the regionally concentrated nature of their support bases offered them the ability to do quite well, and even win in some sub-national units. The ANC, anticipating a national majority, saw federalism as a ruse to deny majority rule. Once federalism was conceded by the ANC (as part of a larger deal including crucial NP concessions on their demand for permanently entrenched power-sharing), NP and ANC stances on the demarcation of the proposed federal units were consistent with evolving knowledge of their regional support. While the starting point was the nine development regions used by the Development Bank of Southern Africa, the NP and ANC proposed successive variations which split up or collapsed regions in ways that were consistent with what both parties were learning from the HSRC, who, starting in 1992, began to pool successive national samples to produce increasingly far more detailed and reliable maps of geographical variations in electoral support.

Finally, the mutually evolving belief on the part of both the ANC and NP that their respective support bases were rapidly dissipating resulted in a rush to set an election date, ahead of any agreement on the key parts of the constitution under which that election would be held – a fact which ultimately put undue pressure on the remaining negotiations. Key questions, such as the nature of the executive and legislature, and important transitional mechanism, such as the Transitional Executive Council and the Independent Electoral Commission, were rushed and badly structured (in the case of the Electoral Commission, almost destroying the founding election, see Harris (2010)).

Survey data also influenced South Africa's transition by shaping leaders' estimates of other parties' support. In a world without opinion surveys, the radical PAC might have been expected to pose a serious threat to the ANC's rural and squatter support in an 'outbidding' war of racial appeals. But polls confirmed that the ANC's extremist competitor posed no serious political threat and could safely ignore it. And while the IFP constantly attempted to portray itself as one of the 'big three' political parties to the transition, and claimed concomitant status at the negotiating table, survey results from 1990 to mid-1992 put them at 1 to 2 per cent support and almost completely undercut such claims. Yet subsequent changes in the HSRC's sampling procedures in mid-1992 produced better estimates of voter preferences in rural KwaZulu Natal and increased IFP support to around 12 per cent of the national black vote. They also began to show signs that the IFP was picking up white voters disillusioned with the NP. Several NP officials subsequently left the party and joined Inkatha, claiming it was a better vehicle for winning black votes, and the NP cabinet split over whether it should ally itself with the IFP in an anti-ANC coalition, or move quickly to an agreement with the ANC.

Ultimately, the largest set of NP concessions came in late 1993 and coincided with a rapid and drastic decline in its support base, as well as substantial rises in ANC support, which left the government trying to salvage the best possible deal and get to an election before its support completely drained away. It abandoned its demand for a permanently entrenched proportional cabinet, conceded that cabinet decisions could be made by simple majorities (obviating the entire *raison d'etre* of a proportional cabinet), agreed to a figurehead deputy presidency with no real powers, agreed to a federal arrangement which granted provinces no exclusive powers and gave the national government the ability to override provincial functions and powers, and agreed that the president could unilaterally appoint a majority of the all-important Constitutional Court.

Polls and the campaign for the first election

Besides their impact on the negotiations over South Africa's interim constitution and first election, polls also had an important impact on the campaign for that first election.[2] Perhaps the most important impact was on the nature of the ANC. As a liberation organization returning from exile, the ANC was simply not used to making strategic electoral decisions based on good information rather than on hunches or on ideological principles. Its political analysts and strategists were highly intellectual. Coming mainly from its South African Communist Party and Congress of South African Trade Union allies, its repertoire of political tactics was based on largely elite- and activist-led behaviors ranging from mass demonstrations and boycotts to armed resistance. Indeed, the ANC's initial head of electoral research was believed to be very skeptical of polling.

However, its increasing exposure to detailed survey data, first from commercial organizations, and then through its own commissioned studies research and team of analysts – a team that included then-White House pollster Stanley Greenberg – helped begin its transformation from a liberation movement into a modern political party that uses technology to develop themes and symbols to project attractive images of the party. Accumulating poll results challenged many of the preconceptions it had held about its support base and forced it to think more deeply about campaigns, elections and the nature of its constituency.

Most importantly, survey data helped erase the organization's heretofore simplistic assumption that the 'unity of the oppressed' would provide it with a ready-made support base, and that the election would simply pit the forces of liberation against the forces of oppression. Increasing evidence from various polling sources led the ANC to acknowledge and confront its serious electoral problems in the colored and Indian communities. It had previously assumed these groups would strongly support the ANC because they had also been discriminated against by *apartheid* legislation and severely oppressed during the states of emergency, and also because they had disproportionately contributed many of the leaders of the internal opposition, the United Democratic Front. Thus, the data rang alarm bells and alerted it to problems that it, in all probability, never would have realized otherwise (at least until after the votes were counted). Perhaps more importantly, such information led the ANC to treat these communities as ethnically and culturally distinct (though they did so with great clumsiness), an approach that would have been unthinkable just two years earlier.

Polls also alerted the ANC to significant problems amongst black voters. First of all, voter illiteracy and fears of intimidation threatened to limit voter turnout and severely reduce the ANC's potential margin of victory. Through a subsequent massive information and 'get out the vote' campaign, South Africa avoided the usual spoilt ballot problem associated with founding elections in the developing world and produced a voter turnout estimated conservatively at 86 per cent, but possibly even going above 90 per cent. Through its own surveys, it also discovered significant problems amongst an increasingly pessimistic black electorate stemming from growing alienation from the ANC and skepticism about the capacities of any black government to effect change. Based on this information, the ANC moved away from its initial campaign theme ('Now Is the Time') which had been intended to 'wave the bloody shirt' and portray the election as a continuation of the contest between *apartheid* and democracy. Largely as a result of Greenberg's urging, the ANC changed course and mounted a positive, forward-looking and relatively sophisticated and subtle campaign. Built around the theme of 'A Better Life for All', and the personality of Mandela, the campaign criticized current NP policies as racist, offered a plethora of policy plans and substantive promises to convince undecided voters that they were ready to govern, and utilized a series of interactive 'People's Forums' (borrowed from the 1992 Clinton Bus campaign) to send the message that it was in touch with ordinary people.

The current opinion research sector

Since the end of *apartheid*, the HSRC has continued its work on public opinion but in a more ad hoc fashion, conducting studies for different government clients on a range of specific issues such as likely voter turnout, the delivery of social services, public participation in government, or public preferences for a new electoral system (Houston, Humphries & Liebenberg 2001; Mattes & Southall 2004; Muthien 1999; Muthien Hosa & Magubane 2000). But it has also moved into a more longitudinal study of social attitudes that will be discussed below. Today, the government receives regular reports on public opinion through an in-house tracking survey conducted by the Government Communications and Information Service that was resuscitated in 2003, producing monthly briefings for the Presidency as well as special reports for other client government departments (Strydom 2010).

Since 1994, South Africa has maintained a well-developed market research sector supplying data mostly to commercial, financial and telecommunications firms, and to a much smaller extent to state agencies, and to universities and non-governmental organizations. Moreover, since 1994, fieldworkers have had access to the entire population, both urban and rural. Several major firms have also developed international linkages (e.g. TNS/Research Surveys, A.C. Nielsen, IPSOS/Markinor, Harris/Plus 94 Research). And some (e.g. IPSOS/Markinor) now conduct research in other African countries, though mostly for South African firms who are expanding their businesses across the rest of the continent.

There has been a significant presence of academically oriented survey research projects aimed ultimately at social scientific publication, but which usually release some or all of their top-line results to the news media. Non-governmental organizations such as the Institute for Multi Party Democracy (IMD), Institute for Democracy in South Africa (IDASA), Helen Suzman Foundation (HSF), South African Institute of Race Relations (SAIRR) and FW De Klerk Foundation have all commissioned commercial firms to conduct studies of public opinion on various issues related to democracy, elections and governance. University-based researchers have also commissioned a large number of studies, or fielded their own teams of fieldworkers to collect data on similar themes. Public opinion research stretches back at least as far as Henry Lever's studies of samples of white voters from specially selected marginal constituencies before the 1966 and 1970 elections (Lever 1972), and the studies of black South Africans in Johannesburg townships carried out by Theo

Hanf and his colleagues (1981), as well as a significant amount of work generated by independent researchers at Afrikaans universities (Booysen & Kotze 1985; Gagiano 1986; Gouws 1993).

While socio-political studies are carried out by a range of different universities and scholars, the most important initiatives are a series of longitudinal projects carried out as part of larger international partnerships. First, the deeper values of South African political culture have been mapped by the World Values Survey since the late 1980s through the efforts of Hennie Kotze at the University of Stellenbosch. With some limitations in sampling before the end of *apartheid*, it now provides a unique and rich record of the development of South African values over the past two decades (Kotze & Lombard 2002). Second, social values, more narrowly conceived, have been regularly mapped since 2003 by the HSRC as part of the international 'Social Attitude Survey' framework (Pillay, Roberts & Rule 2006; Roberts, Kivulu & Davids 2010). Third, attitudes about toleration and reconciliation have been measured since 1990 in a series of surveys by Amanda Gouws and James Gibson (Gibson 2004; 2009; Gibson & Gouws 2003; Gouws 1993), and subsequently on a biannual basis by the Institute for Justice and Reconciliation's 'Reconciliation Barometer'. As a result, scholars now have a valuable source of data about South Africans' attitudes towards tolerance, rule of law and legitimacy over an incredibly turbulent period of political change.

A fourth longitudinal study began with a post-election voter survey supported by IDASA after the country's historic 1994 election. As noted above, the country already had a tradition of voter studies, dating back to Lever's *The South African Voter*, and including research based on various HSRC studies, and a major pre-election study prior to the 1994 election conducted by the HSRC and the IMD (Johnson & Schlemmer 1996). However, few of these studies were explicitly set in any larger comparative framework and none of them were longitudinal. Not only was the IDASA study explicitly designed to test competing sociological, social-psychological theories of voting behaviour drawn from the international literature (Mattes 1995b; Mattes & Gouws 1995; Mattes, Gouws & Kotze 1995), but the great majority of the questions have been repeated in subsequent surveys hooked to national elections in 1999, 2004 and 2009 (Ferree 2011; Mattes & Piombo 2001; Mattes, Taylor & Africa 1999a, 1999b, 1999c). The 2004 and 2009 studies were conducted by the University of Cape Town and added a range of question modules from the Comparative National Elections Project, and the 2009 questionnaire included new modules from Comparative Study of Electoral Systems.

The last notable project was also begun by IDASA which, following its 1994 post-election study, decided to begin a series of studies to map the evolution (or lack thereof) of a democratic political culture (Mattes 2002; Mattes & Christie 1997; Mattes & Thiel 1998). After South Africa-specific surveys were carried out in 1995, 1997 and 1998, IDASA joined forces with the Ghana Centre for Development and Democracy and Michigan State University to form the Afrobarometer, the very first instance of comparative, large-scale survey political science research on the continent (Bratton & Mattes 2001a, 2001b, 2003; Bratton, Mattes & Gyimah-Boadi 2005; Mattes & Bratton 2007; Mattes & Gyimah-Boadi 2005). Since then, over 70 surveys have been conducted in four different waves of surveys that now cover 20 different countries in Sub-Saharan Africa.

So, the state is regularly informed about public policy preferences and evaluations of government performance. The academic sector produces an impressive amount of data, but a large proportion of it has to do with socio-political values, rather than evaluations of political performance and policy preferences. Some universities and NGOs are involved in opinion polling, but many of these projects consist of 'one-off' surveys. There are also several longitudinal projects, but they produce results on an infrequent basis (e.g. every two years). However, if public opinion is to play a more meaningful role in democratic politics, public attitudes about government performance and public policy preferences need to be measured and publicized on a far more frequent basis.

The frequent production and publication of public opinion results is usually accomplished around the world in one of two ways. First, commercial firms insert questions about politics into their own market research questionnaires as 'loss leaders' that gain free advertising for the company through the resulting media publicity (the Gallup Poll is clearly the most famous example of this). Yet besides the more intensely political (but less frequent) surveys such as Afrobarometer, it appears that few South African commercial research organizations regularly ask such questions (or at least publicize the results). Just two firms regularly ask questions about presidential job performance, government performance and party support (Markinor and TNS-Research Surveys). These are done no more than four times a year, and only one of these is national in scope, covering both urban and rural samples (Markinor Omnibus).

Second, news media organizations themselves can take the initiative and sponsor or commission opinion polls and publish the results as news, or use the data to add context to other reporting. As noted above, there have been numerous examples of this in South Africa, dating back at least to the 1970s when both English and Afrikaans language newspapers sponsored surveys of white opinions on party preferences, evaluations of government performance, and preferences about social and political change. However, this has occurred far less frequently in the post-*apartheid* period. In the late 1990s, the Independent Newspapers group, along with the Henry J. Kaiser Foundation, sponsored the 'Reality Check' study, which consisted of a single national survey of 3000 adults, but which produced a plethora of information that informed media reports on subjects ranging from politics to public health.

The country's most sustained cooperation between opinion researchers and the news media came in 1999 with the creation of Opinion '99, a consortium of the South African Broadcasting Corporation (SABC), Markinor, IDASA and the Electoral Institute of South Africa (EISA). Opinion '99 comprised four separate nationally representative surveys conducted in late 1998 and early 1999 with questionnaires that were wholly dedicated to government performance and election issues. The results of these surveys were used to produce almost three dozen separate media releases which were subsequently reported in several hundred different articles and electronic news pieces. In 2004, the SABC again joined forces with Markinor (but without IDASA or EISA), conducting two national surveys (October–November 2003 and January–February 2004) to provide data for SABC coverage of that campaign.

However, by the 2009 election, there was absolutely no news media involvement in initiating or sponsoring public opinion surveys. Indeed, so far as I can determine, just five organizations conducted surveys and released election-oriented results in the second half of 2008 or early 2009: MarkData (one survey), IDASA (one survey), HSRC (one survey), IPSOS/Markinor (two surveys), and Harris/Plus 94 Research (three surveys). And at least two of these (IDASA's South Africa Afrobarometer survey and the HSRC's South Africa SASAS) were part of regular studies that simply happened to coincide with this election cycle and thus carried a small number of additional election-related questions. Also, only two organizations (Markinor and Plus 94) conducted multiple surveys to enable news media, analysts and political parties to track shifts in voter preferences.

Perhaps the most telling indication of the limited and declining demand for public opinion data from South African civil society can be drawn from its political parties. As noted earlier, the ANC has regularly commissioned its own pre-election polls and focus groups ahead of each election in 1994, 1999, 2004 and 2009 (Butler 2009; Greenberg 2009; Lodge 1994, 1999, 2005; Mattes 1995a). The opposition Democratic Alliance (earlier, the Democratic Party) has also been a regular consumer of survey research, buying into ongoing syndicated surveys, and enjoying the close cooperation of sympathetic pollsters located at other commercial organizations. While it was unable to afford privately commissioned research in 1994, it now regularly commissions its own research, some of it national in scope but much of it apparently focused on specific regions (such as the Western Cape province) and specific groups of voters (such as white, colored and Indian voters) where the DA runs much more competitively than across the entire country (Booysen 2005; Jolobe 2009; Mattes 1995a). However, *no other political parties* currently conduct their own research. At most, they buy into regular omnibus surveys conducted by organizations such as Markinor, read the results in the newspapers, or simply fly by the seats of their pants (the NP, which no longer exists, also commissioned survey research in 1994 and 1999 elections; see Giliomee 1994 and Mattes 1995a).

Media coverage of public opinion polls

Unfortunately, no systematic data currently exists that would allow us to track news media coverage of public opinion polls since 1994. However, my argument about the low and declining demand and supply is corroborated by data collected by the South African media research organization Media Tenor across a roughly comparable set of news media outlets since 2004.[3] Looking only at coverage during election campaign periods, the frequency of stories mentioning poll data on political subjects (to be counted, a story had to devote at least five lines to discussing poll results or implications) was lower in the run-up to the 2009 election than in 2004 (Figure 9.1). It is true that there was a higher frequency of coverage in late 2008 than in late 2003, but – this was a reflection of the media frenzy surrounding the resignation of President Thabo Mbeki, the ongoing corruption charges against ANC presidential candidate Jacob Zuma, and the impending split within the ANC.

Since 2004, the average South African news media outlet produces an average of – in a normal year – just seven articles or reports *each year* that deal with political survey results (Figure 9.2). Again, we can see two election-related peaks in 2004 and 2009, due to national elections in those years, as well as the special circumstances of 2008. But 2010 showed a return to about the same levels as in 2004. When we break these reports down by *type* of news media (Figure 9.3), we can

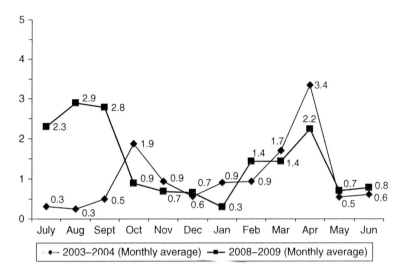

Figure 9.1 Stories discussing public opinion data, 2004 and 2009 election campaigns (average number of stories per media outlet)

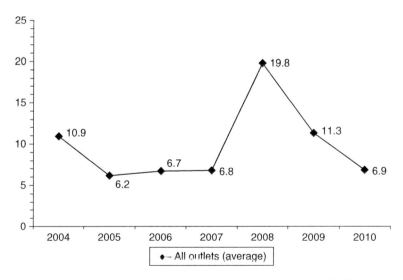

Figure 9.2 News stories reporting public opinion data, 2002–2010 (average annual number of stories per media outlet)

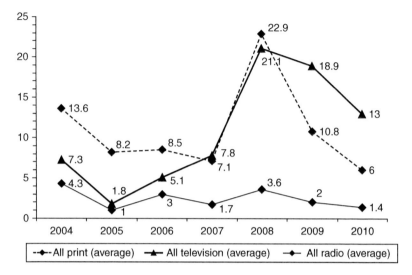

Figure 9.3 Stories reporting public opinion data annually, 2002–2010 (average number by type of media)

see that poll results are far more popular amongst print media outlets, although there is a rising trend in television news. Radio news, however, devotes scarce attention to poll results (which is significant because far more citizens listen to radio and watch TV news than read newspapers). Finally, Figure 9.4 displays the total number of poll-related stories contained in three 'quality' media that are probably the most politically influential outlets within each type of media: the independent newspaper *Business Day*, the state SABC English television news on *SABC3*, and the politically oriented SABC English radio news service *SAfm*. While *Business Day* is a relatively frequent consumer and user of poll results, the yearly average only ranges between 30 and 40 articles, meaning at most, about three articles per month. This data also reveals the very strong upsurge in interest in public opinion in the year when the split within the ANC and the personal problems of its new leader introduced a new dimension of uncertainty into the political environment. The rising interest from television is reflected in the *SABC3* data, and was probably driven by them. Yet *SAfm*, which hosts daily morning news programming that often sets the agenda for political class, hardly even mentions poll results.

Beyond the limited visibility of public opinion in the news media, the quality with which polling results are analyzed is very uneven. Based on

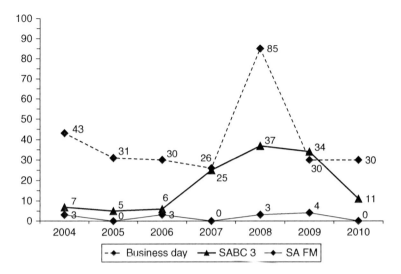

Figure 9.4 Stories reporting public opinion data annually, 2002–2010 (total stories by three influential media)

15 years of providing survey research to the media, I can say that few, if any, news reporters have developed any methodological expertise about the advantages or limitations of polling data, or how to interpret it. And a review of a non-systematic sample of newspaper articles and SABC media releases (that served as the basis of television news items) from the most recent 2009 election campaign reveals that many basic things that survey researchers struggled to convey to journalists over the past decade have not been passed on to the latest generation of reporters. Some stories failed to mention sample size. It was often difficult to know whether 'don't know' responses had been excluded from the calculation, or simply not reported. And if they were excluded, few stories ever discussed the effective sample size (e.g. the number of voters with actual preferences on which the published results were based). Some failed to mention precise survey dates, many failed to mention the confidence interval, and very few reported question wording.

Why the decline?

As indicated at the outset to this chapter, the relative paucity of publicly visible information about South Africa's evolving evaluations of government performance and public policy preferences is surprising for a variety of different reasons. In building an explanation of the present pattern of the supply of public opinion data and the demand for that data by the state, political parties, news media and civil society, several factors need to be taken into consideration. While South Africa is a democracy with a well-developed electronic and print news media, executing a nationally representative survey in South Africa is still a relatively expensive proposition. In contrast to surveys of samples of white voters, nationally representative samples require face-to-face interviews because telephone (landline) ownership is still much lower amongst black people, especially in rural areas (where large proportions of the public still live). This incurs huge costs in terms of travel and accommodation. The linguistic diversity of the population also means that questionnaires have to be translated from English into anywhere between eight and ten additional languages, depending on the size and spread of the particular sample. Paper and pencil questionnaires and data recording are still widely used because of high levels of crime, which mitigate against the use of personal or hand-held computers to record responses. This results in costly and time-consuming manual data entry.

Costs would be more manageable if survey research organizations could rely on a range of clients who buy into regular omnibus type surveys. But the necessity of doing face-to-face interviews, the size of the country, and the geographic spread of the population add an additional problem: there is a relatively long time delay between when a sponsor might want to ask a question, and when clean data is ultimately available for publication. This then becomes a factor in election polling. Survey organizations need to anticipate the dates of the election campaign and possibly adjust the fieldwork dates of their regular omnibus surveys to ensure that the survey is done within, or not too far ahead of an election campaign, but also to generate politically relevant results for the news media. But this is easier said than done, since the government usually announces the election date at the last legally possible moment, often leaving no more than six to eight weeks for the election campaign. Thus, if they do not conduct their own polls, political parties and news media often navigate the last weeks and days of the campaign on the basis of very old data.

But we also need to look to South Africa's larger political system, a system that was produced by the constitutional negotiations discussed earlier. It is true that South African elections are infrequent (once every five years) and limited (one vote for a political party to run the national government, and one vote for a political party to run the provincial government), and that there are no direct constituency linkages between voters and members of the national Parliament or provincial legislative assemblies. While one might expect those factors to conspire to produce a heightened demand for poll data, two other factors need to be considered. First of all, the combination of an almost pure List PR system with strong party discipline means that MPs have to be attuned to the wishes of their party bosses, not to the voters. They have little incentive to know what the voters think about specific policy issues. In fact, there is even a disincentive to knowing since awareness that a party position is opposed by a majority of the public (such as has been the case for years on issues such as abortion, the death penalty and immigration, and most recently in 2010 with the ANC's commitment to close down the elite 'Scorpions' crime and corruption fighting unit) simply puts any ANC MP who is at all interested in representing public opinion in an uncomfortable position. While opposition parties might be expected to relish such data, given the size of the ANC majority in Parliament, they can be used, at most, to embarrass the governing party momentarily.

Second, there was a considerable degree of uncertainty leading up to 1994 as to whether the ANC could garner, initially, a clear majority of the votes cast, and later the two-thirds majority that would allow unilateral constitutional amendment. There was also uncertainty about exactly how many seats in the proportional power-sharing cabinet (and Deputy Presidencies) would be claimed by the ANC and each opposition party. However, these interim arrangements were discarded from the final draft constitution by the Constitutional Assembly in 1996. Thus, besides the question of whether the ANC can gain a two-thirds majority (which they held anyway between 2004 and 2009, yet made no attempt to change the constitution in any major or illiberal way), the fact that the ANC has won each election with a majority ranging between 63 and 69 per cent has taken most of the uncertainty out of the electoral process. In other words, the results of South Africa's democratic elections are widely seen to a foregone conclusion with few interesting 'horse races'.

Taking all these factors together produces the following picture. Opinion polling data is expensive to produce. The state is interested in it for planning and communications purposes, and is able to afford it. While opposition political parties and news media might like to have it, given its costs, the lack of electoral uncertainty, and the political dominance of the ANC, they can do without it. Thus, with little demand from parties and news media, few polling organizations apply their minds to how to increase its public availability and use.

So what?

South Africa is clearly a democracy. It conducts regular, free and fair elections and provides its citizens with a relatively healthy degree of political rights and civil liberties. At the same time, it must be one of the most limited democracies imaginable. Elections are infrequent and ask voters to make extremely few choices. The combination of List PR and strong party discipline means that law-makers in national and provincial legislatures have little reason to respond to public preferences or shifts in those preferences if they conflict with the demands of the central party committee. Not only has the ANC won every election with over 60 per cent of the vote, no opposition party has ever won more than 20 per cent. And surveys also show that no opposition party has ever been seen as broadly representative by more than 30 per cent of the electorate. Thus, the perceived lack of choice created by the size of current ANC majorities with the lack of real alternatives provided by the country's opposition parties resulted in a drastic 30 point drop in voter turnout between 1994 (86 per cent) and 2004 (56 per cent). While there was a slight resurgence in turnout in 2009 (59 per cent) that can be attributed to the rise of the new opposition party COPE, the subsequent self-destruction of that party on the part of its leaders strongly suggests that voter participation might resume its decline in 2014. In sum, a governing party with such a huge margin of victory, such little real opposition and such strong control over its MPs might be able to ignore or even violate public preferences on a range of issues without seriously threatening its electoral prospects. In such a context, frequent and well-publicized data on voter preferences would make a valuable contribution to the democratic process by illuminating the extent and limitations of its apparent 'mandate', exposing the issues on which voters disagree with official ANC policy and thus assisting civil society and the news media to hold the governing party to higher levels of accountability.

Notes

1. The ensuing analysis of polling's impact on the negotiations process is based on Mattes (1994 and 1995a: ch. 3). For a more extended discussion of the links between parties' assessments of popular support for themselves and potential allies, on one hand, and their bargaining positions, on the other, see Sisk (1995).
2. The ensuing analysis of polling's impact on the first election is based on Mattes 1995a, ch. 4. Also see Greenberg 2009, ch. 3.

3. I would like to thank Wadim Schreiner and Chris Van Coppenhagen of Media Tenor for providing this data.

References

Booysen, S. (2005) 'The Democratic Alliance: Progress and Pitfalls', in J. Piombo and L. Nijzink (eds), *Electoral Politics in South Africa: Assessing the First Democratic Decade* (New York: Palgrave Macmillan).

Booysen, S. and H. Kotze (1985) 'The Political Socialization of Isolation: A Case Study of the Afrikaner Student Youth', *Politikon*, 12(2), 23–46.

Bratton, M. and R. Mattes (2001a) 'Support for Democracy in Africa: Intrinsic or Instrumental', *British Journal of Political Science*, 31, 447–474.

Bratton, M. and R. Mattes (2001b) 'Africans' Surprising Universalism', *Journal of Democracy*, 12, 105–121.

Bratton, M. and R. Mattes (2003) 'Support for Economic Reform? Popular Attitudes in Southern Africa', *World Development*, 31, 303–323.

Bratton, M., R. Mattes and E. Gyimah-Boadi (2005) *Public Opinion, Democracy and Market Reform in Africa* (Cambridge: Cambridge University Press).

Butler, A. (2009) 'The ANC's National Election Campaign of 2009: *Siyanqoba!*', in R. Southall and J. Daniel (eds), *Zunami! The 2009 South African Elections* (Johannesburg: Jacana/Konrad Adenauer Foundation).

Couper, M. and N. Rhoodie (1988) 'White Attitudes Toward Desegregation', in D.J. Van Vuuren et al. (eds), *South Africa: The Challenge of Reform* (Pretoria: Owen Burgess Publishers).

De Kock, C. (1996) 'Movements in South African Mass Opinion and Party Support to 1993', in R.W. Johnson and L. Schlemmer (eds), *Launching Democracy In South Africa: The First Open Election, April 1994* (New Haven, CT: Yale University Press).

De Kock, C., N. Rhoodie and M. Couper (1985) 'Black Views on Socio-Political Change in South Africa', in D.J. Van Vuuren et al. (eds), *South Africa: A Plural Society in Transition* (San Diego, CA: Butterworth-Heinemann).

Ferree, K. (2011) *Framing the Race in South Africa: The Political Origins of Racial-Census Elections* (Cambridge: Cambridge University Press).

Gagiano, J. (1986) 'Meanwhile, 'Back on the Boerplaas': Student Attitudes to Political Protest and Political Systems Legitimacy at Stellenbosch University', *Politikon*, 13(2), 3–23.

Gibson, J. (2004) *Overcoming Apartheid in South Africa: Can Truth Heal a Divided Nation?* (New York: Russell Sage Foundation).

Gibson, J. (2009) *Overcoming Historical Injustice: Land Reconciliation in South Africa* (Cambridge: Cambridge University Press).

Gibson, J. and A. Gouws (2003) *Overcoming Intolerance in South Africa: Experiments in Democratic Persuasion* (Cambridge: Cambridge University Press).

Giliomee, H. (1994) 'The National Party's Campaign for a Liberation Election', in A. Reynolds (ed.), *Election '94 South Africa: The Campaigns, Results and Future Prospects* (New York: St. Martin's Press).

Gouws, A. (1993) 'Political Tolerance and Civil Society: The Case of South Africa', *Politikon*, 20(1), 15–31.

Greenberg, S. (2009) *Dispatches from the War Room: In the Trenches with Five Extraordinary Leaders* (New York: St. Martin's Press).

Harris, P. (2010) *Birth: The Conspiracy to Stop the '94 Election* (Johannesburg: Umuzi).

Houston, G., R. Humphries and I. Liebenberg (eds) (2001) *Public Participation in Democratic Governance in South Africa* (Pretoria: HSRC Publishers).

Huntington, S. (1993) *The Third Wave: Democratization in the Late Twentieth Century* (Norman, OK: University of Oklahoma Press).

Johnson, R.W. and L. Schlemmer (eds) (1996) *Launching Democracy in South Africa: The First Open Election, April 1994* (New Haven: Yale University Press).

Jolobe, Z. (2009) 'The Democratic Alliance: Consolidating the Official Opposition', in R. Southall and J. Daniel (eds), *Zunami! The 2009 South African Elections* (Johannesburg: Jacana/Konrad Adenauer Foundation).

Kotze, H. and K. Lombard (2002) 'Revising the Values Shift Hypothesis: A Descriptive Analysis of South Africa's Value Priorities Between 1990 and 2001', *Comparative Sociology*, 1(3–4), 413–437.

Lever, H. (1972) *The South African Voter: Some Aspects of Voter Behaviour With Special Reference to the General Elections of 1966 and 1970* (Cape Town: Juta and Co.).

Lever, H. (1974) 'Opinion Polling in South Africa: Initial Findings', *Public Opinion Quarterly*, 38, 400–408.

Lodge, T. (1994) 'The African National Congress and Its Allies', in A. Reynolds (ed.), *Election '94 South Africa: The Campaigns, Results and Future Prospects* (New York: St. Martins Press).

Lodge, T. (1999) 'The African National Congress', in A. Reynolds (ed.), *Election '99 South Africa: From Mandela to Mbeki* (New York: St. Martin's Press).

Lodge, T. (2005) 'The African National Congress: There is No Party Like It; Ayikho Efana Nayo', in J. Piombo and L. Nijzink (eds), *Electoral Politics in South Africa: Assessing the First Democratic Decade* (New York: Palgrave Macmillan).

Mattes, R. (1995a) *The Impact of Public Opinion Polling on South Africa's Transition to Democracy*. A Report to the 'Investigation into Research Methodology Project' of the South African Human Sciences Research Council. Pretoria: Human Sciences Research Council.

Mattes, R. (1995b) *The Election Book: Judgment and Choice in the 1994 South African Election* (Cape Town: Idasa).

Mattes, R. (2002) 'South Africa: Democracy Without the People', *Journal of Democracy*, 13(1), 22–36.

Mattes, R. and M. Bratton (2007) 'Learning About Democracy in Africa: Performance, Awareness and Experience', *American Journal of Political Science*, 51, 192–217.

Mattes, R. and J. Christie (1997) 'Personal Versus Collective Quality of Life and South Africans' Evaluations of Democratic Government', *Social Indicators Research*, 41(1–3), 205–228.

Mattes, R. and A. Gouws (1998) 'Race, Ethnicity and Voting Behavior', in T. Sisk and A. Reynolds (eds), *Elections and Conflict Resolution in Africa* (Washington, DC: United States Institute of Peace).

Mattes, R. and E. Gyimah-Boadi (2005) 'South Africa and Ghana', in L. Diamond and L. Morlino (eds), *Assessing the Quality of Democracy* (Baltimore, MD: Johns Hopkins University Press).

Mattes, R. and J. Piombo (2001) 'Opposition Parties and the Voters in South Africa's 1999 Election', *Democratization*, 8(3), 101–128.

Mattes, R. and R. Southall (2004) 'Popular Attitudes Toward the South African Electoral System', *Democratization*, 11(1), 51–76.

Mattes, R. and H. Thiel (1998) 'Consolidation and Public Opinion in South Africa', *Journal of Democracy*, 9, 95–110.

Mattes, R., A. Gouws and H. Kotze (1995) 'The Emerging Party System in the New South Africa', *Party Politics*, 1, 379–393.

Mattes, R., H. Taylor and C. Africa (1999a) 'Hegemony, Dominance or Weak Opposition? The Partisan Situation on the Eve of South Africa's Second Election Campaign', *Transformation: Critical Perspectives on Southern Africa*, 38, 1–19.

Mattes, R., H. Taylor and C. Africa (1999b) 'Judgment and Choice in the 1999 South African Election', *Politikon: The South African Journal of Political Studies*, 26, 235–247.

Mattes, R., H. Taylor and C. Africa (1999c) 'Public Opinion and Voter Preferences 1994–1999', in A. Reynolds (ed.), *Election '99 South Africa: From Mandela to Mbeki* (Cape Town: David Philip).

Muthien, Y. (1999) *Democracy South Africa: Evaluating the 1999 Election* (Pretoria: HSRC Publishers).

Muthien, Y., M. Khosa and B. Magubane (2000) *Democracy and Governance Review: Evaluating Mandela's Legacy, 1994–1999* (Pretoria: HSRC Publishers)

O'Donnell, G. and P. Schmitter (1986) *Transitions from Authoritarian Rule: Tentative Conclusions About Uncertain Democracies* (Baltimore, MD: Johns Hopkins Press).

Pillay, U., B. Roberts and S. Rule (2006) *South African Social Attitudes: Changing Times, Diverse Voices* (Pretoria: HSRC Publishers).

Rawls, J. (1973) *A Theory of Justice* (Cambridge, MA: Harvard University Press).

Rhoodie, N. and M. Couper (1987) 'Whites' Perceptions of the Fundamental Issues Surrounding the Election of 6 May 1987', in D.J. Van Vuuren (ed.), *South African Election, 1987* (Pretoria: HSRC Press).

Rhoodie, N. and M. Couper (1988) 'South Africans' Perceptions of Political Reform', in D.J. Van Vuuren et al. (eds), *South Africa: The Challenge of Reform* (Pretoria: Owen Burgess Publishers).

Rhoodie, N., C. De Kock and M. Couper (1985) 'White Perceptions of Political Change in South Africa', in D.J. Van Vuuren et al. (eds), *South Africa: A Plural Society in Transition* (San Diego, CA: Butterworth-Heinemann).

Roberts, B., M.W. Kivilu and Y.D. Davids (eds) (2010) *South African Social Attitudes: Reflections on the Age of Hope* (Pretoria: HSRC Publishers).

Sisk, T. (1995) *Democratization in South Africa: The Elusive Social Contract* (Princeton, NJ: Princeton University Press).

Strydom, M. (2010, September 24) Remarks to the 'Afrobarometer Policy Users Conference,' Accra Ghana.

10

The Good, the Bad and the Ugly: Public Opinion Polling in Taiwan

Lars Willnat, Ven-hwei Lo and Annette Aw

Introduction

The development of public opinion polling in Taiwan is closely linked to the democratization process that started in the late 1980s. The lifting of martial law in 1987 not only allowed pollsters to work more freely, but also enabled Taiwan's media to grow and develop an appetite for public opinion data. However, decades of one-party rule by the Kuomintang (KMT, the Nationalist Party) severely stunted the development of polling in Taiwan. The mostly pro-government media did not criticize the authorities, and polls mainly served to document public support for official policies. As a result, polling organizations in Taiwan had to catch up with similar institutions in other industrialized nations throughout the 1990s. A general lack of experience was especially obvious in early political polls, which emerged during the 1993 elections for county magistrates and city mayors.

Throughout the past two decades, Taiwan's media and polling organizations have experienced three general stages: an adjustment to political freedom, a move into commercialization and, finally, a period of extreme market competition (Huang 2009). The public opinion industry in Taiwan today is heavily criticized by academics, politicians and journalists who object to its overtly commercial nature and the manipulation of polls during elections (Chu & Chang 2004). Taiwan's opinion polls also have been criticized for oversimplifying issues and for producing pseudo-opinions (Lo 1991). Hence, the public have serious reservations about the quality and credibility of polls in Taiwan.

The goal of this chapter is to evaluate the current state of professional polling in Taiwan. It begins with a summary of how Taiwan's history has influenced the practice of public opinion polling, especially after Taiwan's democratization in the late 1980s. Then it discusses how the frequent misuse of polls in Taiwan might have affected people's perceptions of them and subsequently undermined the perceived legitimacy of polls in this young democracy. Finally, in order to evaluate the current practice of polling, this chapter analyzes the reporting of public opinion polls in two leading Taiwanese newspapers during the past decade.

A short history of polling in Taiwan

Shortly after the Kuomintang regime's retreat to Taiwan in 1950, martial law was imposed to suppress any potential resistance to the rule of the Chinese Nationalist Party (KMT). Taiwan's authoritarian government not only controlled all political and economic resources, such as government administration, law making and the judicial system (Huang 2009), but it also established the Government Information Office to regulate print and broadcast media. To suppress the development of an independent media, the KMT restricted how many pages a newspaper could print and where it could be distributed. Only government-sponsored media were free from these limits (Chai 2000).

Because of the tight restrictions on media and research organizations, polling methodology and the overall quality of the infrequent surveys conducted at this time remained crude. In addition, pollsters were afraid to investigate politically sensitive topics that might have drawn the attention of the authorities, or could have led to high refusal rates among a frightened public (Cheng 1991). Appleton (1977) also notes that early efforts to modernize the polling industry in Taiwan were undermined by a general lack of Chinese-speaking survey experts who were familiar with contemporary research methods. However, familiarity with both Mandarin and the most recent survey methods was essential for developing culturally appropriate questions and accurate translations of test items into Chinese.

According to Lo (1991), the first public opinion poll was conducted in 1952 by *Hsin Sheng Daily* with questions about the Sino-Japanese Peace Treaty, then under negotiation. On 14 February of that year, the newspaper distributed 283,600 survey questionnaires to its readers – of which 81,238 were returned. Two years later, *United Daily News* followed with a survey on whether simplified Chinese characters should be adopted in Taiwan. Pollsters for the *Daily News* asked its readers to cut the printed questionnaire from the newspaper, complete it and then return it by mail. In all, 17,480 valid questionnaires were returned (Lo 1991).

Although the methods used in these two surveys would be considered inadequate by today's standards, they represent the first attempts by the Taiwanese press to use more accurate public opinion data in news reports on important public issues.

Encouraged by the results of earlier surveys, *Hsin Sheng Daily* set up Taiwan's first Survey Research Center in 1956. Although the center closed six years later, it produced nearly 100 polls, of which 36 were published (Lo 1991). In 1958, legislator Wu Wang-chi established the Society of Public Opinion Polls, which remained the only active force in the polling business for almost 20 years after the dissolution of *Hsin Sheng Daily*'s survey center in 1962. In conjunction with its polling efforts, the organization also started the journal *Public Opinion Monthly* in 1972 to provide readers with reports on polling theory, survey methodology and poll results (Chu & Chang 2004).

In 1978, the Taiwanese government joined the field of public opinion research and initiated a series of national opinion polls with samples that ranged between 4000 and 6000 respondents. These polls, which were used by the KMT for policy-making, covered a variety of topics such as the public's evaluation of government policies, satisfaction with government performance, and voting intentions. Unfortunately, the findings of these polls were available only to government officials and were never published. Moreover, polls conducted and published by other organizations during the early 1980s remained amateurish and received very little attention from the public. According to one media observer:

> This may have been due as much to the homogeneous climate of opinion during that period as to the lack of knowledge concerning the role of polls as an important institution in a democracy. Until recent years, there was a tendency to equate public opinion with the opinion of the mass media and legislators; no felt need thus existed for other channels of opinion. The majority of the polls dealt with essentially noncontroversial issues such as attitudes toward health insurance, railroad services, and disco dancing.
>
> (Chung 1987)

In 1983, however, the *United Daily News* set up an internal polling division and began publishing surveys that focused on people's perceptions of political candidates. Two years later, the *China Times* launched its own polling department, which started its operation with a series of pre-election polls on the 1985 mayoral election in Taipei. Encouraged by the favorable reception of these polls among its readers, the *Times* expanded its polling operations during the 1986 elections for the Legislative Yuan with the help of social scientists who introduced sophisticated statistical methods and election forecasts (Chung 1987). Overall, the *Daily News* and the *Times* published 138 polls between 1985 and 1987 (Lo 1991). Given the scarcity of public opinion polls in Taiwan during the 1980s, the two newspapers should be credited with making polls an important new mechanism for public discourse in Taiwan.

The end of martial law in 1987 brought sweeping political changes to Taiwan. All restrictions on newspapers were lifted and political opposition parties were allowed to form and organize for the first time in almost four decades. The sudden liberalization of media and politics also created new public spheres for political communication, discussion of important political and social issues, and the mobilization of voters (Rawnsley 2004). This also freed Taiwan's public opinion researchers from political restraints, allowing them to choose which issues they wanted to investigate and which questions they would ask. In 1989, National Chengchi University (NCCU) established the Election Study Center (http://esc.nccu.edu.tw), which quickly established itself as the leading institution for electoral research in Taiwan (Chu & Chang 2004). In 1994, the center also launched a new Chinese-language *Journal of Electoral Studies*, which is now ranked as one of the top Chinese-language journals in political science (http://esc.nccu.edu.tw/english/modules/tinyd7).

During the 1990s, a series of new public opinion organizations – both profit-oriented and non-profit – emerged in Taiwan. Following the model of NCCU's Election Study Center, National Taipei University, Shih Hsin University, Tunghai University, National Chung Cheng University and National Sun Yat-sen University all opened their own academic polling centers (Chu & Chang 2004). The number of polling operations affiliated with Taiwan's media increased when three cable TV news services – TVBS, ETTV and SETN – established their own survey departments. This growth in public opinion polling further accelerated when political candidates in the early 1990s began integrating survey research into their election campaigns, which, in turn, increased the demand for methodologically sophisticated research.

A true milestone for public opinion research, however, was the 2000 presidential election campaign, which ended the KMT's monopoly on political power that had lasted for more than 50 years. Both the KMT and the Democratic Progressive Party (DPP) used public opinion polls extensively during the 2000 presidential election campaign to measure voters' issue preferences and perceptions of the candidates. Sensing the historic relevance of the 2000 election, television and newspaper organizations conducted a record number of election polls. However, many of the polls came from the parties themselves and were conducted with questionable methodologies and political goals in mind. Chu and Chang (2004) noted that 'both the candidates and political parties have learned how to manipulate survey results during the nomination process or during electoral competition, even going so far as to plant false survey results in order to misinform the voters ...' (p. 748). In the end, the proliferation of manipulated polls during the election quickly eroded the public's trust in professional pollsters. According to Chu and Chang (2004):

> Survey research has become a booming industry, yet there has been no concomitant development of professional ethics. Many for-profit institutes, under the intense market competition, simply degraded themselves as hired guns. They sacrificed professional ethics and produced dubious figures to meet their clients' demands.
>
> (p. 747)

National identity and independence

Two of the most significant issues that have been polled since the early 1990s are Taiwanese national identity and independence from Mainland China. Most of Taiwan's 23 million citizens identify themselves as Taiwanese, Chinese or both. As Figure 10.1 shows, the number of people who consider themselves Taiwanese increased from about 18 per cent in 1992 to 53 per cent in 2010. Those who consider themselves Chinese, on the other hand, dropped dramatically from about 26 per cent in 1992 to 4 per cent in 2010. Although most of the population considered itself both Taiwanese and Chinese in the early 1990s, the percentage of people with such a dual national identity decreased slightly from 46 per cent in 1992 to about 40 per cent in 2010. Overall, these trends show that a growing number of Taiwanese have developed a distinct national identity during the past 18 years that might ultimately separate them from Mainland Chinese. As Sobel, Haynes and Zheng (2010) point out, the 1996 Taiwan Straits Crisis and the ongoing political tensions between China and Taiwan might have inadvertently supported this development.

Public opinion data collected during the past two decades also show that most Taiwanese favor maintaining a political status quo between

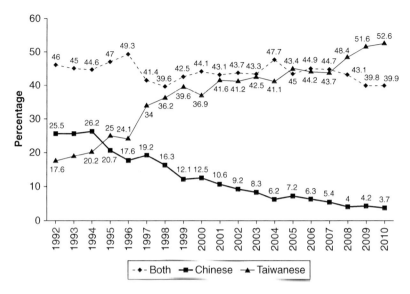

Figure 10.1 Changes in the Taiwanese/Chinese identity of Taiwanese, 1992–2010

Source: Election Study Center, National Chengchi University, http://esc.nccu.edu.tw/english/modules/tinyd2/content/TaiwanChineseID.htm.

Mainland China and Taiwan. As Figure 10.2 shows, the percentage of citizens who prefer a permanent status quo increased from about 10 per cent in 1994 to 25 per cent in 2010. In addition, more than a third (36 per cent) of the population in 2010 prefers to maintain the status quo while leaving the door open to potential changes down the road. At the same time, the percentage of people calling for Taiwan's unification with Mainland China never exceeded 4 per cent between 1994 and 2010. Similarly, those who call for Taiwan's immediate independence remained a small minority that increased only slightly from 3 to 6 per cent during the last 16 years.

Overall, this means that in 2010, about six in ten Taiwanese choose a 'maintain and wait' attitude when it comes to the question of national independence. It should be noted, though, that citizens who prefer the status quo with a slow move towards independence doubled from 8 per cent in 1994 to 16 per cent in 2010, while those who prefer the status quo with a slow move towards unification dropped from about 16 per cent in 1994 to 9 per cent in 2010. These subtle trends in public opinion might indicate a slow drift towards national independence rather than unification.

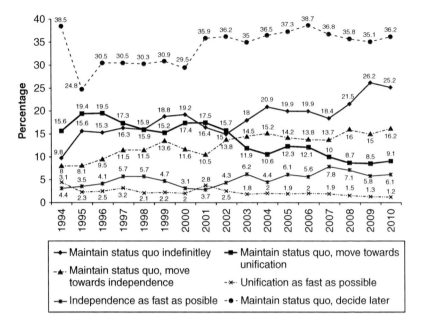

Figure 10.2   Changes in unification–independence stances of Taiwanese, 1994–2010
Source: Election Study Center, National Chengchi University, http://esc.nccu.edu.tw/english/modules/tinyd2/content/tonduID.htm.

Polls and elections in Taiwan

Throughout the 1990s, competition among media outlets increased exponentially and led to an intense battle for readers and viewers. Public opinion polls were used to draw attention to media coverage and became a major weapon in the fight for larger audiences.

Because of such competition the overall quality of public opinion polls in Taiwan suffered – especially during elections. According to political scientist Christian Schafferer (2009), who specializes in the analysis of Taiwan's elections, 'most opinion polls are either fake or unprofessionally conducted. The media are biased and often misinterpret poll results or use unreliable data' (p. 384). During the 2000 presidential election campaign, for example, the KMT placed advertisements in leading newspapers that were disguised to look like regular poll stories that indicated only the KMT candidate could save Taiwan from war with China (Rawnsley and Fell, n. d.). The proliferation of such fake, doctored or inaccurate poll reports from unknown polling organizations, as Schafferer (2009) observes, has 'become a serious problem in Taiwan and led to several disputes after media-declared winners lost elections' (p. 384).

This general lack of high-quality polls is partly explained by the fact that independent polling organizations only play a marginal role in Taiwan. Institutions such as National Chengchi University's Election Study Center, which regularly publishes independent polls and analyses on a variety of political issues, are still the exception in Taiwan. Moreover, their work is often overlooked amid the deluge of polls from Taiwan's many commercial and media-related polling organizations. Reputable polls also have been undermined by party-owned organizations such as the DPP Survey Center, which regularly runs election-related polls to investigate the party's public support, voters' ratings of DPP officials, and the public's issue preferences (Rigger 1999). As mentioned earlier, surveys conducted by these party-owned polling organizations have become important strategic tools in Taiwan's election campaigns and frequently stir controversies over their methods and conclusions (Rawnsley 2006).

The often questionable quality of opinion polls in Taiwan is exacerbated by decreasing levels of trust in the media among the public – as indicated by surveys conducted in 2003 and 2008 by the Institute of Sociology at Academia Sinica (Chang & Liao 2004, 2009). In 2003, about a quarter (25.2 per cent) of respondents said that newspapers are 'not reliable'. By 2008, this group swelled to more than half (51.4 per cent). Similarly, public perceptions of TV news reliability deteriorated between 2003 and 2008. While two half of the respondents (22.1 per cent) thought TV news was 'not reliable' in 2003, almost half of the respondents (48.1 per cent) thought so by 2008. Overall, it is safe to conclude that Taiwanese media have lost a significant portion of the public's trust and confidence in recent years.

As a result, some local media observers have concluded that Taiwan's media often play a negative role in the nation's democratization process. Despite being freed from political control more than two decades ago, 'Taiwan's media in general have been unable to abide by professional ethics and are – with a few notable exceptions – no longer capable of fulfilling the responsibilities of the fourth estate' (Lu 2006).

In an attempt to reduce the perceived disruptive power of polls during elections, Taiwan's lawmakers enacted the Election and Recall Law in 1995, which prohibits the release of poll results in the last ten days of presidential campaigns. This has drawn heavy criticism from politicians and pollsters – mostly because it contradicts Article 11 of Taiwan's Constitution, which guarantees freedom of speech, teaching, writing and publication.

While the ban does not apply to local elections in Taiwan, presidential candidates quickly found creative ways to circumvent the law. According to public opinion researcher Robert Chung (2004), polls are still conducted shortly before elections, but the results are not released to the public. Instead, pollsters privately brief political parties and the media on the results. Once the pre-election ban on publishing poll results takes effect, candidates start flooding the media with advertisements citing polls that show they need additional votes to ensure their victory. During the close race in the 2000 presidential election, for example, the KMT used such poll-advertisements (known as 'saving ads') to draw voters away from the independent candidate and unite them behind the KMT's candidate. The KMT hoped that the combined number of voters would be enough to defeat DPP candidate Chen Shui-bian (Rawnsley and Fell n.d.).

The 2000 presidential election

The misuse of opinion polls by politicians and the media peaked during the 2000 presidential election. Chen Shui-bian won the election with only a 2.5 per cent lead in the final ballots, which ended more than half a century of Kuomintang rule in Taiwan. While most of the reputable, pre-election polls showed a statistical tie among the top three candidates, many voters remained undecided late into the election. As a result, media coverage of the 2000 presidential election was saturated with opinion polls (see also Figure 10.3) – some allegedly bought in order to create a so-called 'watermelon effect', which refers to the Chinese expression that a watermelon always leans towards its heavier side (Mangahas 2000). Political observers agree that these manipulations greatly undermined the legitimacy and reputation of Taiwanese pollsters. Interviewed about the role of public opinion polls during the election, Liu I-Chou, former director of National Chengchi University's Election Study Center, concluded that 'by using polls as a publicity tool, the public opinion research environment has been polluted, and people have lost confidence in surveys. I don't know how long it will take to rebuild people's trust. In fact, I can't even think of a way to fix it' (cited in Hwang 2000).

The 2004 presidential election

Liu I-Chou's pessimistic comments about the future of public opinion polling in Taiwan proved visionary. During the 2004 presidential election, 'faked and misinterpreted opinion polls contributed to social unrest, when incumbent president Chen Shui-bian officially won the election with a margin of 0.3 per cent of the vote and the media, nevertheless, proclaimed rival candidate Lien Chan as the winner, since he had "led" in opinion polls' (Schafferer 2009, p. 384). As shown in Table 10.1, most reputable polls released shortly before the legally mandated cut-off date (10 March 2004) indicated a statistical dead-heat between the two contenders with an average spread of 1.3 per cent. According to Taiwan's Central Election Commission, the 2004 presidential election 'had to be considered a close call', but it also noted that 'there is no evidence of any significant last-minute shift'. The report concluded that 'the assertion that Lien was "clearly leading" in the pre-election polls cannot be justified' (Central Election Commission 2004).

However, the real controversy focused on how Taiwan's television stations covered Election Day. According to *Strait Times* reporter Theresa

Table 10.1 Gaps in polls between Chen Shui-bian (DPP) and Lien Chan (KMT) in the 2004 presidential election (%)

Date	News organization	Chen Shiu-bian (DPP)	Lien Chan (KMT)	Undecided	Gap
1 March 2004	*China Times*	39.8	38.1	22.1	1.7
4 March 2004	Shih Shin University	37.6	42.6	19.8	−5.0
4 March 2004	Focus Survey Research	40.4	39.5	20.1	0.9
7 March 2004	*United Daily News*	38.0	41.0	21.0	−3.0
7 March 2004	Set TV	38.3	36.7	25.0	1.6
8 March 2004	TVBS	36.0	40.0	24.0	−4.0
	Average	−	−	−	−1.3

Source: Official Report by the Central Election Commission on the 2004 Presidential Election in Taiwan. http://www.asiamedia.ucla.edu/print.asp?parentid–9436. The gap is expressed relative to Chen Shiu-bian's poll numbers. Thus, a positive number indicates Chen Shiu-bian in the lead, and a negative one indicates Lien Chan in the lead. Official vote outcome: Chen Shiu-bian: 50.11 per cent and Lien Chan: 49.89 per cent. The legally mandated cut-off for poll publications was 10 March 2004.

Tan, 'nearly a dozen commercial TV stations exaggerated and massaged the ballot count in their relentless battle to win viewers and increase ratings' (Tan 2004). Just minutes after the polls closed on at 4.00 p.m. on 20 March 2004, stations started showing vote counts that quickly surpassed the 100,000 mark. Around 4.20 p.m., the vote count by the Central Election Commission (CEC) was still in the hundreds of votes, while tallies shown on television news channels had passed the 1 million mark. By 4.45 p.m., Taiwan's election authority announced that only about 180,000 votes had been counted, but many TV stations already were reporting more than 6 million votes for each camp – with opposition candidate Lien Chan leading all the way (Tan 2004). Once the stations finally caught on to what the real situation was around 6.00 p.m., they quickly fixed their ballot tallies to show Chen Shiu-bian taking the lead.

The most likely explanation of this rush to report the latest vote estimates (which might remind some readers of how US television networks reported the 2000 US presidential Election Night) is that stations simply exaggerated the numbers in the early counting period, then gradually changed them to the real figures once the CEC started releasing the official tallies. Huang (2009) notes that 'due to the news channels' manipulations, many citizens did not trust the results presented by the CEC later that night and thus they were open to suggestions by KMT candidate Lien Chan to his supporters to protest the exceptionally close election result' (p. 15).

The 2006 Taipei mayoral election

While the reputable polls did a fairly good job in predicting actual voter preferences during the 2004 presidential election, polls conducted during the 2006 Taipei mayoral election proved much less reliable. As Table 10.2 shows, the results of polls conducted just days before the election differ markedly from votes cast on 9 December 2006. While poll results for KMT candidate Hau Lung-pin deviated from the actual election results by 8 percentage points on average, poll results for DPP candidate Frank Hsieh were off by a whopping 22 percentage points on average – a much larger deviation and fairly unlikely in polls that are based on representative samples. Meanwhile, poll numbers for independent candidate James Soong had an acceptable range of deviations from actual results (three percentage points).

Considering the large number of undecided voters, one might argue that these poll numbers are not that far off the mark. Yet assuming that

Table 10.2 Deviations from election results in polls conducted during the 2006 mayoral election in Taipei (%)

Date	News organization	Hau Lung-pin (KMT)	Frank Hsieh (DPP)	James Soong (Independent)	Undecided
4 Dec 2006	TVBS	52 (−2)	21 (−20)	7 (+3)	14
5 Dec 2006	*China Times*	44 (−10)	17 (−24)	5 (+1)	22
2 Dec 2006	*United Daily News*	48 (−6)	17 (−24)	8 (+4)	26
27 Nov 2006	ERA TV	41 (−13)	20 (−21)	8 (+4)	26
9 Dec 2006	Election results	54(−8)[*]	41(−22)[*]	4 (+3)[*]	–

Notes: Percentages are rounded.
[*]Average poll deviation from actual vote on 9 December 2006.
Source: EastSouthWestNorth. http://www.zonaeuropa.com/20061209_1.htm

most undecided voters eventually voted for the two main candidates, the poll numbers still exhibit a fairly large underreporting bias for Frank Hsieh, the main candidate *not* affiliated with the KMT. This might indicate that the media and their affiliated pollsters decided to create a climate of opinion that favored the KMT candidate.

This suspicion was pursued in an editorial published on Election Day by the Taiwanese newspaper *Apple Daily*, which complained that 'the biased media cooperated with the KMT to protect Hau Lung-pin' (*Apple Daily* 2006). Irrespective of whether or not these fairly unreliable poll results document systematic vote manipulation, what they do show is that Taiwan's political opinion polls can be extremely unreliable and deceiving.

Public perceptions of polls in Taiwan

The proliferation of manipulated, fake or methodologically questionable surveys in Taiwan's media has left most voters with low levels of trust in political poll results. In an attempt to understand how Taiwanese people think about presidential election polls, Hu, Tsai and Hsie (2000) conducted a national telephone survey of 1078 respondents in March 2000. As expected, the authors found that respondents were very skeptical about the credibility of such polls. Nearly 76 per cent of respondents said they did not trust presidential election polls, while only 17.1 per cent said they did trust such polls. In a similar telephone survey of 1079 Taiwanese voters, Lo and Lu (2008) found that 61 per cent of respondents did not trust polls that were published during the 2008 presidential election. Only 16.3 per cent of the respondents explicitly said that they 'trusted' those poll results.

Past research in the USA has identified various factors that influence the perceived credibility of public opinion polls. According to a Kaiser Family Foundation study (2001), 66 per cent of respondents said that polls are not useful for officials to understand how the public feels about issues because 'the results of polls can be twisted to say whatever you want them to say'. Similarly, 64 per cent questioned the usefulness of polls because 'polls don't accurately reflect what the public thinks', and 61 per cent thought that 'polls don't ask for the public's opinion on the right issues'. When asked how often they thought public opinion polls accurately reflect what the public think, only a third (33 per cent) of respondents said that they do so most of the time.

How much people trust public opinion polls is, of course, related to how they actually use them. The earlier mentioned survey by Hu, Tsai and Hsie (2000), for example, found that almost half (47.7 per cent) of respondents paid no attention to election poll reports. In a similar study conducted in 2008, Lo and Lu (2008) found that more than a third (38.5 per cent) of respondents said they did not follow presidential election poll stories 'at all', and 18.4 per cent claimed they followed them only 'rarely'.

Hu, Tsai and Hsie's (2000) analysis identified several significant predictors of attention to election polls. First, respondents who claim higher levels of political interest tend to pay more attention to poll stories. Second, respondents with more education and a greater degree of political involvement are more likely to pay greater attention to presidential election polls. These findings have been supported by research in the USA, where trust in polls was found to be related to basic characteristics of citizens, such as political ideology and education. Currin-Percival's (2005) analysis of 1997 survey data collected by the Pew Research Center, for example, found that people who are politically more conservative trust polls less, while higher levels of education and more exposure to news on television increased trust in polls.

Although most Taiwanese people do not trust election polls, Wei, Lo and Lu (2011) found in a recent study that citizens perceive others as being more susceptible to the influence of polling news than themselves. More specifically, their findings indicate that Taiwanese generally perceive news about election polls to have a greater influence on other people's voting decisions than their own voting decisions. Most citizens also believe that other people's understanding of election campaigns is misled more by poll-based stories than their own understanding. The authors also found that poll credibility was significantly related to perceived effects on self and others. The less credible that election polls were perceived to be, the larger the 'self-other' perceptual gap became.

Media coverage of public opinion polls in Taiwan

Another explanation of the public's skepticism about polls might be related to the fact that media outlets often do not disclose the information the public needs to know about polls (Welch 2002). Several studies have shown, for example, that the vast majority of poll-based stories do not provide even basic methodological information such as sample size, survey method, question wording, and other information essential for understanding and evaluating the significance of the findings discussed (Chang 1999; Larson 2003; Welch 2002).

Chang's (1999) analysis of 187 poll stories published in two Singaporean newspapers between 1993 and 1996 concluded that 'public opinion surveys in Singapore are fraught with theoretical and methodological problems' and that their reporting in the news media 'leaves much to be desired' (p. 21). The author found that only about 66 per cent of survey-based news stories reported the sampling method, 6 per cent mentioned the polls' response rates, and none provided information about the margin of error. In a similar study of poll stories published in US newspapers during the 2000 US presidential election, Welch (2002) found that almost none of the articles disclosed important methodological information. Only about two in ten stories published in *The New York Times* (18 per cent) and *The Washington Post* (22 per cent) reported the sampling errors of the polls they discussed. Two items that the newspapers consistently reported were the sponsor of the poll and the poll's results.

Insufficient information about survey methodology has been documented in televised poll reports as well. Larson's (2003) study of evening network news during the 2000 US presidential election found that only 55 per cent of poll stories addressed the sampling error. Moreover, 47 per cent of the stories were 'inaccurate' – either because they claimed that one candidate was ahead when the results were within the margin of error, or because results were said to be 'outside of the margin of error' when they were not.

Content analysis of published public opinion polls in Taiwan

To analyze the quality of poll reporting in Taiwan's media, the authors of this chapter conducted a content analysis of all poll stories published in the *China Times* and *United Daily News* between 1999 and 2009. The two newspapers were selected because they are the largest and most influential newspapers in Taiwan. In the 1990s, they shared 60 per cent of the nation's daily newspaper circulation – each claiming around 1 million readers – and more than 75 per cent of newspaper advertising (Wang & Lo 2000). Both are privately owned and considered to be pro-Kuomintang. While all newspapers lost readers during the past decade, the *United Daily News* and *China Times* are still among the four most widely read newspapers in Taiwan (Chang & Liao 2009).

All news stories containing references to public opinion polls were retrieved from the newspapers' archives, which are available for paying subscribers. To be considered for inclusion in the analysis, stories had to be based on a public opinion poll of individual respondents and their opinions (Chang 1999). Excluded were stories that featured popularity contests and those based on journalists' interviews with a few people only.

The unit of analysis was the news story. Following closely the American Association for Public Opinion Research Code of Professional Ethics & Practice (AAPOR 2011), each article was coded to indicate whether it contained information on the (1) date of story, (2) length of story, (3) focus of poll, (4) conductor of poll, (5) sponsor of poll, (6) polling method, (7) type of respondents, (8) sampling method, (9) sample size, (10) response rate, (11) sampling error, (12) studied period, (13) question wording and (14) sample population. The purpose of this analysis was to determine whether the stories contained adequate information for readers to judge the content and quality of the polls.

Two graduate students fluent in Chinese (native speakers) were trained as coders. Using Holsti's formula, an intercoder reliability check (Holsti 1967) was performed by asking both students to code an identical set of 67 randomly chosen poll stories. The reliability coefficients for each variable were: length of story =.89, focus of poll =.88, conductor of poll =.87, sponsor of poll =.85, polling method =.89, type of respondents =.86, sampling method =.89, sample size =.88, response rate =.87, sampling error =.90, studied period = 1.00, question wording =.91, and sample population =.89. The overall average was 89.

Findings

The two newspapers published 1335 poll stories, 501 of which came from the *China Times*, and 834 from the *United Daily News*. As Table 10.3 shows, the most frequently covered topic in the analyzed stories was politics (65.1 per cent). In fact, between 1999 and 2009, the amount of poll stories that focused on politics consistently ranged between 60 and 70 per cent. Other contemporary issues such as life style (4.9 per cent), economics (3.9 per cent), education (3.4 per cent), crime (2.5 per cent) and transportation (2.4 per cent) received much less attention in the polls. Overall, between 1999 and 2009, a slight decrease was found in the number of poll stories about politics (–4.2 per cent), crime (–1.5 per cent), economics (–1.1 per cent) and quality of life (–0.9 per cent). By contrast, more poll stories were found for topics such as lifestyle (+4.4 per cent), transportation (+3.7 per cent), health (+1.9 per cent) and entertainment (+.07 per cent).

Conductor of polls. The relatively short history of public opinion polling in Taiwan has led to a shortage of independent polling organizations able to conduct and analyze surveys with a politically independent eye. Instead, Taiwan's polls are conducted mostly by media organizations and commercial pollsters who keep in mind the potential profit of the polls they run. It is therefore not a big surprise that more than half

Table 10.3 Focus of polls in the *China Times* and the *United Daily News*, 1999–2009 (%)

Focus of polls	1999–2000	2001–2002	2003–2004	2005–2006	2007–2009	Total
Politics	67.2	59.8	66.9	70.2	62.5	65.0
Lifestyle	2.7	6.1	5.2	3.5	7.1	4.9
Economics	4.4	5.6	3.0	2.2	3.3	3.9
Education	3.0	3.6	3.0	4.4	3.3	3.4
Crime	2.0	2.5	3.0	3.9	0.5	2.5
Transportation	1.7	2.2	1.9	1.8	5.4	2.4
Entertainment	2.0	1.1	1.9	3.1	2.7	2.0
Health	1.4	1.7	2.6	1.3	3.3	1.9
Environment	0.7	2.2	1.9	0.0	1.1	1.3
Life quality	1.4	2.0	0.4	0.9	0.5	1.1
Others	13.5	13.2	10.2	87	10.3	11.6
N (# of poll stories)	296	358	269	227	185	1,335

Table 10.4   Conductor of polls in the *China Times* and the *United Daily News*, 1999–2009 (%)

Conductor of polls	1999–2000	2001–2002	2003–2004	2005–2006	2007–2009	Total
Media organization	48.3	52.0	61.3	63.4	42.4	53.7
Commercial polling	14.2	10.9	6.3	9.2	22.3	12.0
Government	4.7	5.0	7.4	7.9	12.0	6.9
Education institution	7.4	5.0	7.4	3.9	3.3	5.6
Research/poll institutes	3.7	5.0	2.6	3.5	6.5	4.2
Business/Marketing	1.4	1.7	1.1	2.6	2.7	1.8
Interest groups	2.0	2.5	1.5	0.0	2.7	1.8
Community organizations	3.0	0.8	0.4	0.9	0.0	1.1
Others	11.1	10.6	4.1	4.8	3.8	7.5
Not clear	4.2	6.5	7.9	3.8	4.3	5.4
N (# of poll stories)	296	358	269	227	185	1,335

Note: Conductor of the polls refers to the group or organization that carried out the poll; the conductor may be different from the sponsor.

(53.7 per cent) of all the published polls in both Taiwanese newspapers were conducted by media organizations (see Table 10.4). Polls conducted by commercial services (12.0 per cent), the government (6.9 per cent), educational institutes (5.6 per cent), and research or professional institutes (4.2 per cent) are much less common. Interestingly, the number of polls done by media organizations shrank significantly between 1999 and 2009 (–5.9 per cent). Yet the number of surveys by commercial pollsters (+8.1 per cent) and the government (+7.3 per cent) grew notably during the same time period.

While this might indicate that commercial and government pollsters are replacing work not done by media pollsters, it is important to note that the total number of polls published per year have decreased significantly since 2001. As shown in Figure 10.3, the number of published poll stories peaked in 2001 with 207, then dropped to a low of 36 stories in 2009. This dramatic drop is due partly to the rapidly declining economy in Taiwan, especially after the 2000 presidential election. As a result, Taiwan newspapers have suffered serious financial difficulties because of declining readership and advertising revenue and subsequently decided to cut polling expenses. These budget cuts after 2001 were so severe that

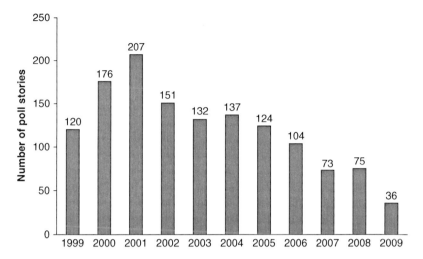

Figure 10.3 Number of poll stories in the *China Times* and the *United Daily News*, 1999–2009

Source: Authors' content analysis of all poll stories in *China Times* and *United Daily News* 1999–2009. Total *N* = 1,335.

the total number of published polls kept declining over the years despite two presidential elections in 2004 and 2008.

Sponsor of polls. Overall, only about 65 per cent of the poll stories in both newspapers identified the sponsors of the surveys – those individuals or organizations that paid for the surveys. While this low number is discouraging, it should be noted that stories without a clear indication of poll sponsorship has decreased from 38.8 per cent in 1999–2000 to 26.8 per cent in 2007–2009. As shown in Table 10.5, the most frequent poll sponsors were media organizations (37.8 per cent), followed by the government (11.5 per cent), community organizations (2.4 per cent), educational institutions (2.0 per cent) and interest groups (1.8 per cent). As expected, polls sponsored by media organizations increased from 34.8 per cent in 1999–2000 to 43.9 per cent in 2007–2009. During the same period, government sponsorship jumped from 8.1 per cent to 14.1 per cent. Yet sponsorship of polls by educational and community organizations decreased between 1999 and 2009. Overall, these trends seem to indicate that while the media organizations have reduced the total number of in-house polls conducted between 1999 and 2009, sponsorship of contracted polls has increased slightly.

Table 10.5 Sponsor of polls in the *China Times* and the *United Daily News*, 1999–2009 (%)

Sponsor of polls	1999–2000	2001–2002	2003–2004	2005–2006	2007–2009	Total
Media organization	34.8	38.0	38.7	36.0	43.9	37.8
Commercial polling	0.0	0.8	0.7	0.9	1.6	0.7
Government	8.1	14.2	11.5	9.2	14.1	11.5
Education institution	2.4	1.7	3.0	1.8	1.1	2.0
Research/poll institutes	1.0	1.1	1.1	3.5	2.7	1.7
Business/marketing	0.7	0.6	1.1	0.9	1.6	0.9
Interest groups	0.7	2.8	2.2	0.4	2.7	1.8
Community organizations	4.7	2.2	1.1	1.8	1.6	2.4
Others	8.8	10.9	3.3	3.9	4.9	6.9
Not clear	38.8	27.7	37.3	41.6	26.8	34.3
N (# of poll stories)	296	358	269	227	185	1,335

Note: Sponsor of the polls refers to the group that paid for the survey or asked other to do the survey for it; the sponsor may be different from the conductor.

Table 10.6 Method of polls in the *China Times* and the *United Daily News*, 1999–2009 (%)

Method of polls	1999–2000	2001–2002	2003–2004	2005–2006	2007–2009	Total
Telephone survey	52.4	52.5	56.9	60.1	52.4	54.6
Online survey	1.7	1.7	1.1	2.2	5.4	2.2
Personal interview	1.7	0.3	0.4	0.0	1.1	0.7
Mixed-method survey	0.7	0.8	1.1	0.0	0.0	0.6
Street survey	0.0	0.0	0.4	0.4	0.0	0.1
Others	3.0	6.7	3.7	3.5	3.3	4.3
Not clear	40.5	38.0	36.4	33.8	37.8	37.5
N (# of poll stories)	296	358	269	227	185	1,335

Polling methods. As shown in Table 10.6, only about six in ten news stories that contained polls also indicated the method on which the polls were based. Thus, a significant proportion of stories did not allow readers to assess how the poll was conducted. In stories that identified the polling method, telephone surveys dominated between 1999 and 2009. Other methods such as online surveys (2.2 per cent), personal interviews (0.7 per cent), or mixed-method (0.6 per cent) and street surveys (0.1 per cent) were used only in rare cases. Overall, these trends in polling methodology have not changed much between 1999 and 2009, except for a slight increase in the number of online polls during 2007–2009.

Methodological information provided. Table 10.7 presents the percentage of poll stories that included relevant methodological information. The most frequent types of information were conductor of polls (94.6 per cent), type of respondents (76.8 per cent), sample size (74.9 per cent), study period (69.4 per cent), polling method (62.5 per cent) and question wording (68.2 per cent). Between 1999 and 2009, the frequency of reporting these methods consistently increased. The only exception was the reporting of sample size, which dropped from 81.1 per cent in 1999–2000 to 72.4 per cent in 2007–2009.

By contrast, the percentage of stories that included information on sampling error was much lower (56.5 per cent) and actually dropped seven percentage points between 1999 and 2009. Overall, only 42.4 per cent of the polls published in the two newspapers were based on random-sampling methods. The rest relied on non-random or unidentified sampling methods. Similarly, the response rate of polls (1.6 per cent) and the original sample population (16.4 per cent) were mentioned only in a few stories.

Conclusions

Public opinion polling in Taiwan has a short and turbulent history. The long period of political control that ended in 1987 left the Taiwanese polling industry with little professional experience and only a rudimentary understanding of how to conduct reliable public opinion polls. The subsequent democratization process allowed pollsters to catch up with their Western counterparts during the 1990s, but also resulted in the rampant misuse of election polls by political parties and their candidates. This development was due to a lack of independent polling organizations in Taiwan, which until today have played only a marginal role in the creation and publication of reliable public opinion polls.

Table 10.7 Percentages of stories reporting methodological information, 1999–2009

Methodological information provided	1999–2000	2001–2002	2003–2004	2005–2006	2007–2009	Total
Sponsor provided	61.2	72.3	62.7	58.4	73.2	65.7
Conductor provided	95.8	93.5	92.1	96.2	95.7	94.6
Method of poll provided	59.5	62.0	63.6	66.2	62.2	62.5
Sampling error provided	53.8	57.8	61.0	60.1	46.7	56.5
Sample size provided	81.1	72.0	74.8	74.0	72.4	74.9
Response rate provided	2.7	2.0	1.5	0.4	0.5	1.6
Sample population provided	8.1	13.2	21.6	25.4	16.8	16.3
Study period provided	53.9	68.2	69.5	70.5	64.9	69.4
Respondent type provided	75.9	72.6	77.3	79.4	82.7	76.8
General population	28.7	35.8	28.6	33.8	39.1	32.9
Likely voters	33.1	24.9	36.4	36.8	9.3	31.7
Other	13.9	12.0	12.3	9.2	14.1	12.3
Not clear	24.3	27.4	22.7	20.1	17.4	23.1
Question wording provided	64.4	75.4	68.0	63.2	65.8	68.2
For all questions	2.0	2.8	5.2	7.9	4.9	4.3
For some questions	8.4	6.1	4.1	6.6	7.1	6.4
Paraphrased questions	54.4	66.5	58.7	48.7	53.8	57.5
Sampling method provided	34.1	40.5	53.6	45.2	39.1	42.4
Random digit dialing	26.7	28.2	46.5	42.1	34.8	34.8
Random sampling	2.0	4.2	2.6	2.6	2.2	2.8
Systematic sampling	1.4	6.1	1.9	0.4	0.0	2.4
Stratified sampling	3.0	2.0	2.6	0.0	1.6	1.9
Other random method	3.0	4.2	2.6	2.6	2.7	3.1
Not clear	65.9	59.5	46.4	54.8	60.9	57.6
Graph provided	3.7	5.0	16.0	6.6	5.4	7.3
Table provided	12.8	20.7	20.4	22.8	20.1	19.2
N (# of poll stories)	296	358	269	227	185	1,335

Note: In stories that reported the polls' sample sizes, the median number of respondents was 999.

As this study has shown, most of the polls published by Taiwan's media today are conducted or sponsored by media organizations. While this is not necessarily a huge problem given the aggressiveness and independence of Taiwan's media, growing competition between more and more media outlets has encouraged newspapers and television stations to use polls to attract more audiences. In addition, political parties and campaign managers quickly recognized the power of polls to manipulate the voting public. As a consequence, polls in Taiwan often focus on controversial topics that attract large audiences or might sway voters. The situation is compounded by the fact that many polls are based on questionable methods and samples that undermine their representativeness.

Of course, the ongoing commercialization of polling has affected other nations as well. In a recent critique of the US polling industry, for example, Rosenstiel (2005) wrote that 'the proliferation of outlets offering news, which has resulted in greater competition for audience, has also intensified the motivation of using polls in part for their marketing value rather than purely their probative journalistic value' (p. 698). He concludes that 'the landscape of political polling and the press might be thought of as an ecosystem in distress. The press culture represents a marketplace. With fewer barriers to entry, there are more pollsters who will move in whatever ways they can to fill that market' (pp. 714–715).

Thus, in response to the growing competition of media outlets in the USA, the US media have been using polls as a marketing tool to attract audiences – similar to what has happened in Taiwan. Interestingly, this strategy seems to work despite the fact that a majority of the people – both in Taiwan and the USA – generally do not trust polls. While it is difficult to quantify the additional readers or viewers a media organization might attract by publishing poll stories, it is clear that many people enjoy following the polls, especially during elections.

The proliferation of non-scientific online polls on websites of large media organizations such as CNN.com or *USA Today* certainly is a reflection of this recognized interest. The goal of such 'quick polls' is not to inform people about an important issue, but to attract audiences by exploiting their desire to 'see their vote being counted'. The fact that these polls are self-selective, and therefore carry no relevant information, is conveniently ignored by those who design and publish such surveys to attract audiences.

The problems observed in Taiwan's polling environment, however, run much deeper. Due to the often questionable survey methodologies employed by Taiwan's pollsters, especially the polls conducted during elections have been notoriously inaccurate in their predictions. Moreover, most surveys in Taiwan are conducted by media organizations or political pollsters who care very little about the democratic value of their work, which, in turn, has severely undermined people's trust in public opinion polls overall. It is reasonable to assume that this loss in trust has been accelerated by the fact that most poll stories in Taiwan do not contain crucial information about survey methodology. As this study has documented, only about four in ten poll stories published between 2007 and 2009 were based on random-sampling methods – a fact that was not clearly discussed in most stories. It is highly unlikely that media audiences understand the difference between 'good' representative samples and 'bad' convenience samples on which the majority of polls published in Taiwan's media are based.

Ultimately, the only way to improve the quality of polls in Taiwan is to support the growth of politically independent polling organizations that are able to conduct surveys on topics that are truly relevant to the public. Such organizations must be independent from the government, political parties and the media, and, ideally, should be funded by academic institutions or endowments to ensure their competitiveness with commercial pollsters. While such a request might seem blue-eyed to some, especially during a global recession that has undermined funding for independent research in most nations, Taiwan's short polling history has prevented the development of independent pollsters with a reputation for high-quality work. Thus, a coordinated effort to support Taiwan's independent pollsters must be a priority. Given the importance of opinion polls for a functioning democracy, it seems a small price to pay for a true reflection of what the public thinks in such a young democracy.

References

American Association for Public Opinion Research (AAPOR) (2011) *AAPOR Professional Code of Ethics & Practice*, http://www.aapor.org/AAPOR_Code.htm, date accessed 27 February 2011.

Apple Daily (December 9, 2006) *Public Opinion Polls, Gambling Odds and Democracy Gone Astray*. Translated by EastWestSouthNorth, http://www.zonaeuropa.com/20061209_1.htm, date accessed 27 February 2011.

Appleton, S. (1977) 'Survey research on Taiwan', *Public Opinion Quarterly*, 40, 468–481.

Central Election Commission Report on the Presidential Election (March 26, 2004), http://www.asiamedia.ucla.edu/print.asp?parentid=9436, date accessed 27 February 2011.

Chai, W. (2000) 'The transformation of the mass media in Taiwan since 1950: Introduction', *Asian Affairs*, 27(3), 133–140.

Chang, T. K. (1999) 'Reporting public opinion in Singapore: Journalistic practices and policy implications', *The Harvard International Journal of Press/Politics*, 4, 11–28.

Chang, L. Y. and L. S. Liao (2004) *The Basic Survey Project of Taiwan Area's Social Change* (Taipei: Academia Sinica).

Chang, L. Y. and L. S. Liao (2009) *The Basic Survey Project of Taiwan Area's Social Change* (Taipei: Academia Sinica).

Cheng, C. M. (1991) *Public Opinion and Survey* (in Chinese) (Taipei: Sanmin).

Chu, Y. H. and Y. T. Chang (2004) 'Taiwan', in J. Geer (ed.), *Public Opinion and Polling Around the World: A Historical Encyclopedia* (Santa Barbara, CA: ABC-CLIO, Inc).

Chung, T. Y. R. (2004) *Let Taiwan Election Surveys Grow*, http://hkupop.hku.hk/english/columns/columns68_tw.html, date accessed 27 February 2011.

Chung, W. W. (1987) Opinion polls come of age. *Taiwan Review*. 12/01/1987, http://taiwantoday.tw/ct.asp?xItem=109639&ctNode=122&mp=9, date accessed 27 February 2011.

Currin Percival, M. (2005) *In Polls We Trust: Individual Assessments of Representations of Mass Opinion*. Paper presented at the annual meeting of the American Political Science Association, Washington, DC, http://www.allacademic.com/meta/p_mla_apa_research_citation/0/4/2/1/3/pages42133/p42133-1.php, date accessed 27 February 2011.

Holsti, O. R. (1967) 'Computer content analysis in international relations research', in E. A. Bowles (ed.), *Computers in Human Research* (Englewood Cliffs, NJ: Prentice-Hall).

Hu, Y. W., C. C. Tsai and C. C. Hsie (2000) *Election Polls: Who Cares? Who Believes? Affect Who?* Paper presented at the annual convention of the Chinese Communication Society, Taipei, June 26–27, 2000.

Huang, C. L. (2009) *The Changing Roles of Media in Taiwan's Democratization Process*. The Brookings Institution. http://www.brookings.edu/papers/2009/07_taiwan_huang.aspx#_ftn4, date accessed 27 February 2011.

Hwang, J. (February 5, 2000) By the numbers. *Taiwan Review*. http://taiwanreview.nat.gov.tw/ct.asp?xItem=507&CtNode=1348, date accessed 27 February 2011.

Kaiser Family Foundation (2001) *National Surveys of the Role of Polls in Policymaking*, http://www.kff.org/kaiserpolls/3146-index.cfm, date accessed 27 February 2011.

Larson, S. G. (2003) 'Misunderstanding margin of error. Network news coverage of polls during the 2000 general election', *The International Journal of Press/Politics*, 8(1), 66–80.

Lo, V. H. (1991) *Precision Journalism* (Taipei: Cheng Chung Book Co.).

Lo, V. H. and H. Y. Lu (2008) *Third-Person Effect of News Reports About Presidential Polls*. Unpublished manuscript.

Lu, S. H. (November 21, 2006) 'The great Taiwanese media failure', *Taipei Times*. http://www.asiamedia.ucla.edu/print.asp?parentid=58140, date accessed 27 February 2011.

Mangahas, M. (2000) *Opinion Polling and Young Democracies*, Keynote address given at the annual conference of the World Association for Public Opinion Research in Portland, OR, May 2000.

Rawnsley, G. (2004) 'Treading a fine line: Democracy and the media in Taiwan', *Parliamentary Affairs*, 57, 209–222.

Rawnsley, G. (2006) 'Democratization and election campaigning in Taiwan: Professionalizing the professionals', in K. Voltmer and S. Splichal (eds), *Political Communication, the Mass Media and Transitions to Democracy* (London: Routledge).

Rawnsley, G. and D. Fell (n.d.) *Democratization, Liberalization and the Modernization of Election Communication in Taiwan*. Working paper. School of Oriental and African Studies, University of London, www.soas.ac.uk/taiwanstudies/workingpapers/file24472.pdf, date accessed 27 February 2011.

Rigger, S. (1999) *Politics in Taiwan: Voting for Democracy* (London: Routledge).

Rosenstiel, T. (2005) 'Political polling and the new media culture: A case of more being less', *Public Opinion Quarterly*, 69, 698–715.

Schafferer, C. (2009) 'Evolution and limitations of modern campaigning in East Asia: A case study of Taiwan', in D. W. Johnson (ed.), *Routledge Handbook of Political Management* (London: Routledge).

Sobel, R., W. A. Haynes and Y. Zhen (2010) 'The polls – trends. Taiwan public opinion trends, 1992–2008: Exploring attitudes on cross-strait issues', *Public Opinion Quarterly*, 74, 782–813.

Tan, T. (April 24, 2004) Taiwan: Taiwan's TV polls coverage a big hoax. *The Strait Times*. Retrieved on February 27, 2011 from http://www.asiamedia.ucla.edu/print.asp?parentid=10576.

Wang, G. and V. H. Lo (2000) 'Taiwan', in S. Gunaratne (ed.), *Handbook of the Media in Asia* (New Delhi: Sage).

Wei, R., V. H. Lo and H. Y. Lu (2011) 'Examining the perceptual gap and behavioral outcomes in the perceived effects of polling news in the 2008 Taiwan presidential election', *Communication Research*, 38, 206–217.

Welch, R. L. (2002) 'Polls, polls, and more polls: An evaluation of how public opinion polls are reported in newspapers', *The Harvard International Journal of Press/Politics*, 7(1), 102–114.

Part III

Effects and Consequences of Published Opinion Polls

11
Attitudinal and Behavioral Consequences of Published Opinion Polls

Patricia Moy and Eike Mark Rinke

It is a truism to speak of the key normative role that public opinion polls play in contemporary democratic societies. Theorists and practitioners have long extolled how polls inextricably link citizens to their elected officials. Indeed, public opinion polls not only offer citizens a mechanism with which to express their sentiment on key issues of the day but also provide policy makers with information about what their constituents might or might not desire. Citizens may be able to express their views on a particular issue through individual acts such as donating money to a cause or writing a letter to the editor of a local newspaper, but along with voting polls are one of the few opportunities that offer the mass public equal voice. Moreover, the role that polls play in the citizen–policy maker relationship hinges upon their dissemination by the mass media.

This chapter explores the attitudinal and behavioral consequences of public opinion polls portrayed in the media. We focus not on how policy makers respond to poll results, but on how the consumption of content from published polls can influence citizens. We begin with a review of the types of information imparted by published opinion polls, and discuss their effects both within and outside the voting context. In doing so, we discuss two theories of influence – the spiral of silence and impersonal influence – and articulate the mechanisms of influence that may be at play.

Media portrayals of polls

Media portrayals of public opinion travel in many guises, none more explicit than straightforward statements about how a representative sample of citizens stands on an issue. Polling organizations often take snapshots of opinion on a controversial issue, and these results are disseminated to the larger public by the news media. The almost guaranteed publication of polls is facilitated by the symbiotic relationship between polling organizations and the news media (Traugott 2008): polling organizations need the media to promote their work, and the news media need content that is timely, deals with conflict and is generally newsworthy. This symbiotic relationship has morphed over the years such that news organizations have built or expanded their own polling operations by pooling resources (e.g. CBS News and the *New York Times*) or entered into partnerships with research companies (e.g. *The Guardian* and ICM in the UK).

In election campaigns, polls constitute a significantly larger portion of news media coverage, termed horse race coverage. Scholars, pundits and citizens alike have expressed concern over this type of media content, which focuses on which candidates are winning, losing and doing better than expected (Bartels 1988). These portrayals prioritize candidates' relative popularity over their policy issue stances, and depict politics as a game involving a series of elaborate strategies. Although the advent of television brought with it a focus on image, this norm of campaign coverage existed among newspapers for a century prior to the broadcast medium's appearance on the media landscape (Sigelman & Bullock 1991), though levels of horse race coverage vary depending on cultural and institutional contexts (Strömbäck & Kaid 2008). Moreover, this norm of coverage is dictated by journalists, not the candidates or parties; in fact, in the context of the USA, the national media have been shown to be relatively unreceptive to covering substantive messages (Flowers, Haynes & Crespin 2003).

Three types of election polls provide much of the fodder for horse race coverage (Asher 2007). Cross-sectional surveys often include a *trial heat question*, which asks respondents the candidate or party for whom they would vote if the election were held today. Despite its reliance on a single poll, media coverage of trial heat survey results typically reference how the candidates or parties fared relative to other recent polls. More formal comparisons often are made in *tracking polls*, which utilize rolling averages of consecutive days' worth of interviews with slightly smaller samples (Traugott & Lavrakas 2007). *Exit polls* are surveys conducted with voters as they depart from their balloting location, and are used by the news media to project election outcomes as well as to explain why citizens cast their vote a particular way.

As we illustrate later, horse race coverage, as represented by public opinion polls, has serious implications for how citizens think and act regarding politics. But the concern is not merely academic. Governments around the globe are apprehensive about the ramifications of the publication of pre-election poll results. Data collected in 2002 from 66 countries indicated that just under half (46%) had embargoes on the publication of pre-election poll findings (Spangenberg 2003). These embargo periods ranged from one day in countries such as Argentina, France and Israel, to 30 days in the case of Luxembourg. Most of the restrictions involve questions regarding vote intention, and the top reason cited for these restrictions was the need to protect the dignity of the democratic process. In over two-thirds of the countries studied, media organizations could publish exit polls only after all polls had closed (see also Chapter 3).

The assumption that undergirds this set of popular and academic concerns as well as the governmental measures against the publication of poll results is that poll data help constitute part of citizens' information environment. And certainly, the nature of the environment, which includes mediated information, interpersonally communicated information as well as first-hand experience, is a major factor in determining how individuals respond to the world around them (Shamir & Shamir 1997). Against this backdrop, we now turn to the effects of published opinion polls within and outside the electoral context.

Effects of published opinion polls

Effects on voting

One of the most frequently researched areas of poll effects is their impact on citizens' political voting decisions. Preoccupation with understanding these voting effects dates back to the earliest days of scientific public opinion polling, when concerns loomed over a possible 'bandwagon effect' of such information, that is, a tendency of polls to boost support for the political option (candidate, party or policy) shown to be favored by a majority of people (Robinson 1937). There were heated debates about the possibility of such a phenomenon early on (Gallup 1965; Gallup & Rae 1940), which continue until this day, with the aforementioned media bans motivated by such concerns. The classic works in this area revolved mostly around conceptualizing and measuring the bandwagon assumption (Baumol 1957; Henshel & Johnston 1987; Simon 1954; Zech 1975). From these works emerged the development of formal models of poll effects to more accurately predict voting behavior (Henshel 1995; Simon 1997).

Today, voting-related research of poll effects can be broadly categorized by the criterion variable of interest – namely, whether the scholar is interested in the effects of published polls on *turnout* (i.e. whether to vote, a behavioral effect) or on *voting preferences* (the question of what or whom to vote for, which can be an attitudinal and/or behavioral effect). We briefly address both domains of research in turn.

Effects on turnout

Effects of published polls on turnout among citizens can be classified simply as either mobilizing or demobilizing. Based on Downs' (1957) theoretical position that individuals are rational beings and engage in cost-benefit analyses, both types of effects turn on two key factors – their assessment of the situation and their sense of political efficacy. Specifically, will citizens' expectations about the likely outcome of a referendum or election change due to the information retrieved from published polls? And, given the perceived closeness of the race, what do citizens believe to be the electoral utility of voting?

The literature provides evidence for both possible consequences. Studies investigating the demobilizing effects of polls on turnout often focus on the consequences of media coverage of exit polls, since these are believed to lower one's propensity to turn out. Despite some evidence of such effects (Delli Carpini 1984), a research summary by Sudman (1986) indicates that these are likely to be small and occur only if the polls show a clear winner of an election that previously has been shown to be close. In addition, some studies find similar effects of pre-election polls (de Bock 1976).

On the flip side, a slightly larger body of work has produced findings showing the mobilizing effects of published opinion surveys. These studies typically assume that the closeness of an election is positively related to the perceived utility of casting one's ballot and thus the magnitude of turnout. Though there are studies that do not find support for this hypothesis (Kunce 2001; Matsusaka 1993; Matsusaka & Palda 1999), recent findings from a large-scale meta-analysis of empirical studies (Geys 2006), formal election modeling (Taylor & Yildirim 2010), and natural (Indridason 2008) and participation game experiments (Großer & Schram 2010) consistently point to a strong positive effect of election closeness on voter turnout. It is important to note that turnout studies often assume that citizens are aware of the closeness of an election as indicated by pre-election polls. But this assumption is by no means self-evident and in need of further investigation, especially in light of some null findings in the published literature (Ansolabehere & Iyengar 1994) and the contradictory results reported in a meta-analysis of poll effect studies (Hardmeier & Roth 2003). For example, politically predisposed citizens might engage in 'wishful thinking', thereby diminishing the effects of poll exposure on election predictions (Babad 1995, 1997; Granberg & Brent 1983). However, to the extent that polls are received by citizens and shape their perception of election closeness, the available evidence suggests that they have an independent influence on the size of election turnouts.

Effects on voting preferences

Three types of poll effects on voting intention can be broadly distinguished from one another: the *bandwagon effect* mentioned above, sometimes also referred to as the *contagion effect* (Blais, Gidengil & Nevitte 2006); its converse, the *underdog effect*, in which polls lead people to support a trailing party, candidate or policy position; and *strategic voting*, which involves the possibility of voting for a viable 'second-best' solution if one's preferred candidate or party has little chance of success in the election or referendum.

Similar to the turnout effects of polls, studies on the bandwagon effects of poll information draw from a distinct strand of research on rational choice theory, resulting in the development of predictive 'bandwagon curve' models of voting behavior (Gartner 1976; McKelvey & Ordeshook 1985; Meirowitz 2005; Straffin 1977). Moreover, evidence of bandwagon effects has emerged in a number of experimental (Ansolabehere & Iyengar 1994; de Bock 1976; Mehrabian 1998) and survey studies (Abramowitz 1987; Nadeau, Cloutier & Guay 1993; Skalaban 1988), mostly in the USA but also in European countries (McAllister & Studlar 1991; Schmitt-Beck 1996), in primary (e.g. Kenney & Rice 1994) and presidential (Gimpel & Harvey 1997) election contexts, and in the context of general multi-party elections (Faas, Mackenrodt & Schmitt-Beck 2008) and referendum campaigns (Tyran 2004).

Regardless of the contexts in which bandwagon effects have been shown to occur, studies show either aggregate or individual level effects of polls in the opposing direction of an increase of support given to a party, candidate or policy position trailing in published pre-election/referendum polls. For example, in their survey experiment, Lavrakas, Holley, and Miller (1991) find underdog effects of polls three times as large as bandwagon effects. Similarly, in her early review of the poll effects literature, Marsh (1984) concludes that there is a persistent suggestion of possible underdog effects but no support for the bandwagon hypothesis. Despite its breadth, the extant literature can hardly conclude whether bandwagon or underdog effects are generally stronger or more widespread. The inability to do so stems primarily from theoretical and operational inconsistencies: researchers not only study different contexts but also emphasize different processes underlying these effects. Yet, a relatively recent meta-analysis (Hardmeier & Roth 2003) yielded a seeming preponderance of a moderate bandwagon effect. However, this finding should not be accepted at face value, as it is impossible to control whether it is due to imbalances within the sample of studies conducted (e.g. the vast majority of studies focused on US contexts). At this point, we must note that more process-oriented, cumulative research rather than premature generalizations about relative frequencies and sizes of these two effect forms is in order.

The third voting preference effect, strategic voting, is concerned with whether voters use pre-election poll information to inform their voting behavior in such a way so as to maximize the utility of their vote in producing a favorable election outcome. Research in this domain has surged as scholars study poll effects in multi-party or candidate elections where such voting behavior is particularly relevant. Consuming information from published polls can be particularly effective in improving election forecasts of politically unaware citizens (Andersson, Gschwend, Meffert & Schmidt 2006; Meffert & Gschwend 2011). It is important to note that the promotion of strategic voting by published polls represents an influence on behavioral voting preferences, but not on the attitudes of citizens (Blais, Gidengil & Nevitte 2006; Forsythe, Myerson, Rietz & Weber 1993).

Non-electoral effects

The attitudinal and behavioral effects of published opinion polls outside the electoral realm are no less significant than those related to voting. Undergirded by normative assumptions that a healthy populace is one in which citizens are engaged in political discussion with each other, exchanging ideas, and being exposed to differing viewpoints, a spate of political communication and public opinion studies has shown that perceptions of public opinion can shape individual attitudes and behaviors. This section presents research related to how published polls can foster political distrust, increase political engagement and constrain opinion expression.

Effects on political trust

The ubiquity of published polls during an election campaign makes them virtually impossible to ignore. As noted earlier, media coverage of polls contributes much to the culture of horse race journalism, and as Patterson (1993) noted, 'the game schema dominates the journalist's outlook' (p. 60). This game schema, or strategy coverage, is characterized, among other things, by language related to games, war and conflict, with voters seen as audience members and candidates/parties as performers; a focus on candidates' or parties' standings in the polls; and a central concern with winning and losing (Jamieson 1992). Extrapolating from the election to controversies in general, published polls often reflect at least two competing sides, whether they are Republicans and Democrats, or those who favor military intervention overseas versus those who are less hawkish, or supporters and opponents of a proposed local bill.

In strategic coverage, this focus on competing sides can activate cynicism or political mistrust (Cappella & Jamieson 1997). The literature on framing helps to shed light on how polls and horse race coverage in general shape political trust. First, because framing involves deciding which aspects to highlight over others and how to communicate those aspects (Entman 1993), specific frames can divert audience members from basic information about an issue (Valkenburg, Semetko & de Vreese 1999). Second, episodically framed stories, as shown by Iyengar (1987), tend to have two effects. These stories not only make particular characteristics of particular individuals more accessible but also have repercussions on how audience members assign blame and attribute responsibility to the solution of the problem (Iyengar 1987). Thus an individual exposed to strategy frames in poll-related stories will recall the parties' or candidates' strategic behaviors that in turn will activate cynical attributions. Indeed, Cappella and Jamieson (1997) found that exposure to a single strategically framed news story is sufficient to activate cynical attributions; sustained exposure consistently activates cynical responses.

The presence of polls in today's political landscape can exert an influence on citizens' levels of trust more subtly as well. The conflict embodied in a published poll typically is accompanied and often exacerbated by negative discourse, both in political circles and in the media. In their touchstone study of print coverage of democratic institutions,

Miller, Goldenberg and Erbring (1979) found that over half of all front-page articles related to confidence in government contained a critical reference. Of significance was the fact that criticisms were directed primarily at the president – not the presidency – and that criticisms directed at Congress that appeared were utterances by the president. The media negativity that appeared decades ago remains, leading Patterson (1993, p. 19) to conclude that 'the antipolitics bias of the press that came out of the closet two decades ago has stayed out'. Content analyses and surveys provide evidence of varying levels of media negativity towards democratic institutions and lowered trust as a consequence of exposure to that negativity (Moy & Pfau 2000).

Effects on political engagement

The pessimistic view espoused by those who believe that horse race coverage has trivialized the substance of politics can be offset by those who perceive polls to invigorate the electorate. Some scholars, like Patterson (1993, 2002), believe that horse race coverage is a primary reason for the decline in citizen engagement. Yet Bartels (1988) found that although nearly two-thirds of news media coverage went to the primary winner of the week, when prospective voters were asked to recall stories from a given week, four out of five stories dealt with horse race coverage – which, at a minimum, points to cognitive engagement on the part of the audience. Bartels attributed heightened recall and reported political knowledge to the dramatic unity that is represented in published polls. A slightly different view comes from Popkin (1991, p. 75), who describes people's tendency to avoid statistically oriented evaluations when it comes to generating judgments about candidates. That is, voters are predisposed to check whether candidates (or parties, for that matter) fit their mental models of what an agreeable office-holder looks like; they do so by drawing on vivid narrative information more than on dull statistics and figures.

The potential ramifications of sparking interest in an issue – such as that raised by a front-page story accompanied by an opinion poll – are great. Interest can spur discussion, motivate one to engage in information-seeking behaviors from a wide variety of media, and potentially gain knowledge of that issue (McLeod, Scheufele & Moy 1999) and perhaps make it easier for someone to become more politically engaged (Vedlitz & Veblen 1980).

The intervening variables that mediate the relationship between published polls and political engagement can also include political trust.

That is, if published polls depress levels of political trust, they ultimately may impact levels of political engagement. Indeed, there is some evidence that increased political cynicism can lead to political disengagement (Cappella & Jamieson 1997), though this empirical relationship has not always been replicated (de Vreese 2005).

Effects on opinion expression

The spiral of silence (Noelle-Neumann 1974, 1993) is a longstanding theory that treats opinion expression as a function of perceptions of opinion. Focusing less on public opinion as a democratic tool, Elisabeth Noelle-Neumann (1995) equated public opinion with social control, believing that public opinion fostered social integration and helped ensure a sufficient level of consensus such that actions could be taken and decisions made. If public opinion is reflected in agreement about values and goals, then public opinion is those 'opinions on controversial issues that one can express in public without isolating oneself' (Noelle-Neumann 1993, pp. 62–63).

Given this outlook, the spiral of silence theory is based on several key assumptions. Specifically, citizens are driven by a fear of isolation from society, and therefore are motivated to scan their environment to gauge the climate of opinion. Endowed with a 'quasi-statistical sense', they discern what public opinion is on an issue, and it is these perceptions that will determine their likelihood of expressing their views on that issue. In particular, if individuals perceive the prevailing climate of opinion to align with their own views, they will be more likely to share their opinions. However, in an opinion environment perceived to be hostile to their views, individuals will opt to remain silent.

These social-psychological processes engendered by the spiral of silence involve only the fears, thoughts and behaviors of disparate individuals. How then does the *spiral* of silence occur? If people's willingness to speak out on a controversial issue hinges on what they perceive to be the dominant view, 'the tendency of the one to speak up and the other to be silent starts off a spiraling process which increasingly establishes one opinion as the prevailing one' (Noelle-Neumann 1974, p. 44). This dynamic process relies on the mass media, which portray public opinion through various types of content, including published polls.

Intuitively appealing, the spiral of silence theory has found support in many discussion domains – for example, the Persian Gulf War (Eveland, McLeod & Signorielli 1995), biotechnology (Priest 2006; Scheufele, Shanahan & Lee 2001) and the O.J. Simpson trial (Jeffres, Neuendorf & Atkin 1999) – and in a broad array of countries including Israel (Shamir 1997), Singapore (Willnat, Lee & Detenber 2002) and Mexico (Neuwirth

2000). One commonality across these topics that has facilitated the processes outlined in the spiral of silence theory is the fact that the issues have a strong moral component, and these value-laden issues make it possible for one to isolate oneself in public (Noelle-Neumann 1993).

The spiral of silence theory, however, is not without its shortcomings (see Scheufele & Moy 2000 for a review). Most of the criticisms lodged against the theory have focused on how individuals may refrain from expressing minority views because of some force other than fear of isolation (or conversely, speak out because they share the majority view). As Neuwirth, Frederick and Mayo (2007) contend, fear of isolation 'is not limited to a unique situation or set of circumstances, but neither does it apply to all situations' (p. 452). After all, Noelle-Neumann (1993) identified hardcores and avant-gardes as individuals who do not fear isolation and would speak out in the face of majority opposition, and research has begun to identify factors explaining why one speaks out. Scholars have found that concern and strength of opinion (Salmon & Neuwirth 1990) and attitude certainty (Matthes, Morrison & Schemer 2010) predicted speaking out, as did personal interest (Kim et al. 2004) and perceived issue importance (Moy, Domke & Stamm 2001). Others have suggested that being on the 'winning side' can explain why individuals speak out (Glynn & McLeod 1985).

Also, is it really society *per se* from which individuals fear isolation? Grounding her theory in Asch's (1955) and Milgram's (1961) conformity experiments, Noelle-Neumann (1993) defined society as all those individuals participating in the study. Given how conformity rates dropped significantly when one other person dissented, Salmon and Kline (1985) raised the possibility that individuals would feel isolated from their reference groups, and not society at large. Indeed, Moy, Domke and Stamm (2001) found that opinion climates within one's reference groups, or 'micro-climates', held more sway than the perceived climate of opinion of the larger community.

It is clear that the spiral of silence theory inextricably links mediated portrayals of public opinion to the likelihood of individuals expressing their opinions. Despite the prevalence of public opinion polls in today's news media, scholars have begun to initiate research that has refined the explanatory power of the original spiral of silence theory. For example, research on the effects of exemplification indicates that in attempting to infer reality, audience members rely more on 'case-study' individuals than on base-rate information provided in polls (Daschmann 2000). This suggests that citizens are not processing published opinion poll data as much as they are attending to one or two individuals the journalist had sought to provide an interesting quote.

In addition, system-wide changes in media have meant that the mechanisms that elevated the spiral of silence to be a theory of powerful media effects no longer exist. The consonance that Noelle-Neumann (1974) found in the German media system of the 1960s has long disappeared. In its place (and in media systems around the world) is a plurality of outlets that run the ideological gamut and oftentimes frame the same controversy quite differently. The vast array of choices available to the media consumer of the twenty-first century means that selectivity processes may be at work, and that citizens are choosing content that aligns with their dispositions, rather than monitoring their behaviors so as to remain part of the group.

Impersonal influence: A general framework

By assuming an interplay between media content and one's social environment, in which the former shaped the latter, the spiral of silence theory differed greatly from early perspectives of public opinion and media effects, which juxtaposed the media against the influence of friends and family. Katz and Lazarsfeld's (1955) seminal study within this limited effects paradigm identified the presence of opinion leaders, individuals who exercised leadership within the smallest social systems – groups of friends, for example – and within the context of everyday, mundane settings. Termed 'personal influence', this type of power emanated from the direct social ties that one had.

Decades later, Diana Mutz (1992, 1998) coined the term 'impersonal influence' to denote an influence that stands in stark contrast to Katz and Lazarsfeld's notion of personal influence. Impersonal influence originates from representations of collective conditions, including collective opinions:

> This type of influence is deemed 'impersonal' because it is brought about by information about the attitudes, beliefs or experiences of collectives outside of an individual's personal life space. In other words, impersonal influence is not about the direct persuasive influence of media messages that attempt to promote one viewpoint over another; it is strictly concerned with the capacity for presentations of collective opinion or experience to trigger social influence processes.
>
> (Mutz 1998, p. 4)

While Mutz conceives of impersonal influence as a larger theoretical framework (and one that includes the spiral of silence), it stands to reason that effects of publicized polls are at the core of this theoretical enterprise given that they provide maybe the most straightforward representation of collective opinion possible. After all, polling information is part and parcel of a larger pseudo-environment created by the media – and one to which citizens need to react under conditions of a large-scale polity that extends beyond their immediate social environment. As such, the media play an important role in generating perceptions of the broader collective opinion climate (Mutz & Soss 1997). Indeed, there is evidence that opinion polls present information that is particularly capable of influencing such perceptions (Sonck & Loosveldt 2010). Still, impersonal influence exerted by polling information would be rather negligible if it was found that perceptions of collective conditions and opinion remained inconsequential for the most part. However, this does not seem to be the case in many contexts. One widely researched example of this is the phenomenon that people tend to base their 'economic vote' more on an assessment of how the economy as a whole is doing (sociotropic considerations) than of how they themselves are faring economically (pocketbook considerations) (Kinder & Kiewiet 1979; Markus 1988). Impersonal influence, Mutz (1998) argues, is a necessary condition for societal integration and democratic governance in the context of large-scale societies where much of people's larger social environment evades their immediate experience, which makes them reliant on representations of that environment in the media. This seems to be particularly true when it comes to information about others' opinions on political issues, candidates and parties provided by polls, the impact of which can be conceptualized as an instance of impersonal influence.

At first glance, the ideas behind impersonal influence suggest that polling information should contribute to a wider process of societal integration and thus generally lead to a convergence of public opinion towards political issues or actors by means of providing points of reference for social co-orientation. While this expectation ties in well with common accounts of polling effects as being based on conformity and social pressures (see, e.g., Marsh 1984, and the original spiral of silence literature cited above), the mechanisms through which published polls exercise impersonal influence have been shown to be more diverse and complex, thus prohibiting any sweeping generalizations of uniform effects across the citizenry. The most comprehensive account of the processes underlying the impersonal social influence of publicized opinion is presented by Mutz (1994, 1998), who focuses on three mechanisms.

First, polling information may exert impersonal influence to the extent that it informs citizens about the likelihood of success of different candidates, parties or policies (e.g. in referendum contexts) and leads them to rely on this information in a utility-maximizing manner once they are called to the ballot box. In this view, *strategic voting* is assumed to occur primarily among those that are highly involved with and informed about the issues at hand due to the cognitive demands of making the informed choices necessary to allot one's political support in a strategic fashion. Obviously, this type of impersonal influence of published polls is relevant mostly in electoral contexts of some sort.

Two points are particularly noteworthy about strategic voting. First, it is a possibility only in electoral contexts in which a person has more than two options available and is able to rank them by preference. Second, it suggests that the effects of published polls can be bidirectional: while strategic considerations may induce people to support their preferred candidate or party only as long as the polls indicate realistic chances of success (i.e. *viability*), thus leading to decreased support for trailing candidates or parties, they also may lead them to increase support for their favorite option on the ballot once polls indicate it is having trouble garnering sufficient public support. The obvious moderating factor regulating citizens' use of these strategic considerations is the strength with which they favor one option over the next best, so that a pronounced preference for a candidate or party should lead to increased support, rather than quick defection in the face of undesirable polling results. While Mutz (1998, p. 259) suggests that strategic voting does not occur for many people, this assumption has become increasingly tenuous with more recent research showing otherwise (Meffert & Gschwend forthcoming, see below).

The second mechanism through which polls can have an impersonal influence on people is the use of an *audience response* (Axsom, Yates & Chaiken 1987) or, more generally, a *consensus heuristic* (Giner-Sorolla & Chaiken 1997). A consensus heuristic is in use when information indicating the preferences of a collective of reference (e.g. polling data) cues people into assuming that the more popular option in the collective is the better option for no reason beyond its popularity. In a series of experiments, Mutz (1992, 1998) finds evidence of impersonal influence of popularity cues implicating the consensus heuristic, but only in cases where information about the candidates or issues in question is unnaturally low. These findings suggest that the effects of published polls based on this process are likely only in rare situations such as low-profile elections in which citizens have access to poll data but virtually no information on the candidates, parties or issues on the ballot.

Finally, the third mechanism through which polls might come to bear impersonal influence is what Mutz (1998) terms the *cognitive response mechanism*. The proposition here is that people who are exposed to information about levels of support for a candidate, party or policy are led to think about reasons for and against the position of the mass collective (Mutz 1997). In other words, exposure to a poll primes in people's minds reasons others could have for supporting or rejecting a candidate, a party or a policy. Rehearsing these arguments, in turn, influences their own opinion towards the respective voting option – in either possible direction. In this process, the effects of poll information are mediated by the cognitive responses of the audience which depend on personal characteristics (such as level of information and involvement) and characteristics of the wider information environment (such as the valence and quality of arguments circulating for and against any of the candidates, parties or policies at hand). Mutz observes this mechanism to be the most common among the three, since it is based on moderate levels of involvement and information that are typical for most people most of the time.

All in all, work on the impersonal influence of published opinion polls shows that polls generally are a far cry from leading citizens to low-information acquiescence into majority opinion. On the contrary, the corpus of literature suggests that one of its major 'impersonal influences' is to induce people to ponder reasons for adopting a certain political position. These reasons are typically derived from the media discourse surrounding the publication of any particular poll, making impersonal influences of polls contingent on their wider information environment. While in a diverse information environment polls might motivate people to reflect on a variety of aspects of a political issue or competition, a more narrow media diet characterized by partisan selectivity might thwart these deliberative benefits of published polls and instead lead them to promote political polarization in the electorate.

Final thoughts

The mechanisms underlying impersonal influence (Mutz 1998), similar to those outlined by Hardmeier (2008), outline various scenarios in which citizens may find themselves, some of which are more realistic than others. The processes by which published opinion polls can exert attitudinal or behavioral effects are grounded in the assumption that public opinion – whether in the form of voting or speaking out – involves a social system that somehow interacts with one's media content system. Both systems help shape citizens' definition of social reality and what constitutes acceptable, desirable or odious. Though some mechanisms like contagion, or the simple affective tendency to follow the crowd (Bartels 1988), do not demand much cognitive effort, the cognitive response mechanism allows for a more optimistic picture of the populace. This perspective recognizes that individuals are not merely lemmings in a political and social world, but they attend to, seek out and perhaps refute arguments for a particular side of an issue.

The effects of published polls ultimately are a function of how that information gets processed, and in a continuously shifting media landscape these effects are something of a moving target. If the Internet provides increased possibilities of exposing oneself to like-minded points of view (Bimber & Davis 2003; Stroud 2008), the conducive effects of the 'cognitive response' Mutz describes can become dubious. If citizens are aware, first and foremost, of arguments supporting their preferred political option and opposing the others, the internal deliberative processes initiated by polls may well be supplanted by 'enclave deliberation' (Sunstein 2007) in citizens, which consists of a rehearsal of these arguments, leading to increased anger with and alienation from segments of the population opposing one's own view as they are represented in the polls. In this scenario, the possibilities for partisan selectivity afforded by the new media landscape change the nature of the average poll effects we can expect. In such a scenario, they might turn out to promote political polarization rather than measured political judgment.

Consequently, a fuller understanding of the information environment is crucial for assessing the effects of polling information on citizens. It is important to note that poll effects are, by means of the mechanisms underlying them, particularly contingent on the political and media context in which the information has been conveyed. For instance, how do state–press relationships vary across countries and how do these relationships shape the publication of opinion polls? Are the media sufficiently autonomous to publish what editors and managers perceive to be newsworthy? How pluralistic is the set of media outlets to which a person turns for news? Understanding these contexts provides both challenges and opportunities for communication researchers. On the one hand, we are far from reaching any conclusive theory that can sufficiently explain the effects of the full information environment;

on the other hand, the effects of public opinion polls will be hard to pinpoint given macro-level changes, and therefore continue to present opportunities for theory-building and scholarly debate.

References

Abramowitz, A. I. (1987) 'Candidate Choice before the Convention: The Democrats in 1984', *Political Behavior*, 9(1), 49–61.

Andersson, P., T. Gschwend, M. F. Meffert and C. Schmidt (2006) 'Forecasting the Outcome of a National Election: The Influence of Expertise, Information, and Political Preferences', presented at the 2006, June 19–23 annual conference of the International Communication Association, Dresden.

Ansolabehere, S. and S. Iyengar (1994) 'Of Horseshoes and Horse Races: Experimental Studies of the Impact of Poll Results on Electoral Behavior', *Political Communication*, 11(4), 413–430.

Asch, S. (1955) 'Opinions and Social Pressure', *Scientific American*, 193(5), 31–35.

Asher, H. B. (2007) *Polling and the Public: What Every Citizen Should Know*, 7th edn (Washington, DC: CQ Press).

Axsom, D., S. Yates and S. Chaiken (1987) 'Audience Response as a Heuristic Cue in Persuasion', *Journal of Personality and Social Psychology*, 53(1), 30–40.

Babad, E. (1995) 'Can Accurate Knowledge Reduce Wishful Thinking in Voters' Predictions of Election Outcomes?', *Journal of Psychology*, 129(3), 285–300.

Babad, E. (1997) 'Wishful Thinking among Voters: Motivational and Cognitive Influences', *International Journal of Public Opinion Research*, 9(2), 105–125.

Bartels, L. M. (1988) *Presidential Primaries and the Dynamics of Public Choice* (Princeton, NJ: Princeton University Press).

Baumol, W. J. (1957) 'Interactions Between Successive Polling Results and Voting Intentions', *Public Opinion Quarterly*, 21(2), 318–323.

Bimber, B. and R. Davis (2003) *Campaigning Online: The Internet in U.S. Elections* (Oxford: Oxford University Press).

Blais, A., E. Gidengil and N. Nevitte (2006) 'Do Polls Influence the Vote?', in H. E. Brady and R. Johnston (eds), *Capturing Campaign Effects* (Ann Arbor, MI: University of Michigan Press).

Cappella, J. N. and K. H. Jamieson (1997) *Spiral of Cynicism: The Press and the Public Good* (New York: Oxford University Press).

Daschmann, G. (2000) 'Vox Pop and Polls: The Impact of Poll Results and Voter Statements in the Media on the Perception of a Climate of Opinion', *International Journal of Public Opinion Research*, 12(2), 160–179.

de Bock, H. (1976) 'Influence of In-State Election Poll Reports on Candidate Preference in 1972', *Journalism Quarterly*, 53(3), 457–462.

Delli Carpini, M. X. (1984) 'Scooping the Voters? The Consequences of the Networks' Early Call of the 1980 Presidential Race', *Journal of Politics*, 46(3), 866–885.

de Vreese, C. H. (2005) 'The Spiral of Cynicism Reconsidered', *European Journal of Communication*, 20(3), 283–301.

Downs, A. (1957) *An Economic Theory of Democracy* (New York: Harper).

Entman, R. M. (1993) 'Framing: Toward Clarification of a Fractured Paradigm', *Journal of Communication*, 43(4), 51–58.

Eveland, W. P., Jr., D. M. McLeod and N. Signorielli (1995) 'Actual and Perceived United States Public Opinion: The Spiral of Silence during the Persian Gulf War', *International Journal of Public Opinion Research*, 7(2), 91–109.

Faas, T., C. Mackenrodt and R. Schmitt-Beck (2008) 'Polls That Mattered: Effects of Media Polls on Voters' Coalition Expectations and Party Preferences in the 2005 German Parliamentary Election', *International Journal of Public Opinion Research*, 20(3), 299–325.

Flowers, J. F., A. A. Haynes and M. H. Crespin (2003) 'The Media, the Campaign, and the Message', *American Journal of Political Science*, 47(2), 259–273.

Forsythe, R., R. B. Myerson, T. A. Rietz and R. J. Weber (1993) 'An Experiment on Coordination in Multi-Candidate Elections: The Importance of Polls and Election Histories', *Social Choice and Welfare*, 10(3), 223–247.

Gallup, G. (1965) 'Polls and the Political Process – Past, Present, and Future', *Public Opinion Quarterly*, 29(4), 544–549.

Gallup, G. and S. F. Rae (1940) 'Is There a Bandwagon Vote?', *Public Opinion Quarterly*, 4(2), 244–249.

Gartner, M. (1976) 'Endogenous Bandwagon and Underdog Effects in a Rational Choice Model', *Public Choice*, 25(1), 83–89.

Geys, B. (2006) 'Explaining Voter Turnout: A Review of Aggregate-Level Research', *Electoral Studies*, 25(4), 637–663.

Gimpel, J. G. and D. H. Harvey (1997) 'Forecasts and Preferences in the 1992 General Election', *Political Behavior*, 19(2), 157–175.

Giner-Sorolla, R. and S. Chaiken (1997) 'Selective Use of Heuristic and Systematic Processing under Defense Motivation', *Personality and Social Psychology Bulletin*, 23(1), 84–97.

Glynn, C. J. and J. M. McLeod (1985) 'Implications of the Spiral of Silence Theory for Communication and Public Opinion Research', in K. R. Sanders, L. L. Kaid and D. Nimmo (eds), *Political Communication Yearbook 1984* (Carbondale, IL: Southern Illinois University Press).

Granberg, D. and E. Brent (1983) 'When Prophecy Bends: The Preference-Expectation Link in U.S. Presidential Elections, 1952–1980', *Journal of Personality and Social Psychology*, 45(3), 477–491.

Großer, J. and A. Schram (2010) 'Public Opinion Polls, Voter Turnout, and Welfare: An Experimental Study', *American Journal of Political Science*, 54(3), 700–717.

Hardmeier, S. (2008) 'The Effects of Published Polls on Citizens', in W. Donsbach and M. W. Traugott (eds), *The SAGE Handbook of Public Opinion Research* (Thousand Oaks, CA: Sage).

Hardmeier, S. and H. Roth (2003) 'Die Erforschung der Wirkung politischer Meinungsumfragen: Lehren vom ,Sonderfall' Schweiz', *Politische Vierteljahresschrift*, 44(2), 174–195.

Henshel, R. L. (1995) 'The Grünberg/Modigliani and Simon Possibility Theorem: A Social Psychological Critique', *Journal of Socio-Economics*, 24(3), 501–520.

Henshel, R. L. and W. Johnston (1987) 'The Emergence of Bandwagon Effects: A Theory', *Sociological Quarterly*, 28(4), 493–511.

Indridason, I. H. (2008) 'Competition and Turnout: The Majority Run-Off as a Natural Experiment', *Electoral Studies*, 27(4), 699–710.

Iyengar, S. (1987) 'Television News and Citizens' Explanations of National Affairs', *American Political Science Review*, 81(3), 815–831.

Jamieson, K. H. (1992) *Dirty Politics* (New York: Oxford University Press).

Jeffres, L.W., K. A. Neuendorf and D. Atkin (1999) 'Spirals of Silence: Expressing Opinions When the Climate of Opinion is Unambiguous', *Political Communication*, 16(2), 115–131.

Katz, E. and P. F. Lazarsfeld (1955) *Personal Influence* (New York: Free Press).

Kenney, P. J. and T. W. Rice (1994) 'The Psychology of Political Momentum', *Political Research Quarterly*, 47(4), 923–938.

Kim, S.-H., M. Han, J. Shanahan and V. Berdayes (2004) 'Talking on 'Sunshine in North Korea': A Test of the Spiral of Silence as a Theory of Powerful Mass Media', *International Journal of Public Opinion Research*, 16(1), 39–62.

Kinder, D. R. and D. R. Kiewiet (1979) 'Economic Discontent and Political Behavior: The Role of Personal Grievances and Collective Economic Judgments in Congressional Voting', *American Journal of Political Science*, 23(3), 495–527.

Kunce, M. (2001) 'Pre-Election Polling and the Rational Voter: Evidence from State Panel Data (1986–1998)', *Public Choice*, 107(1/2), 21–34.

Lavrakas, P. J., J. K. Holley and P. V. Miller (1991) 'Public Reactions to Polling News During the 1988 Presidential Election Campaign', in P. J. Lavrakas and J. K. Holley (eds), *Polling and Presidential Election Coverage* (Newbury Park, CA: Sage).

Markus, G. B. (1988) 'The Impact of Personal and National Economic Conditions on the Presidential Vote: A Pooled Cross-Sectional Analysis', *American Journal of Political Science*, 32(1), 137–154.

Marsh, C. (1984) 'Do Polls Affect What People Think?', in C. F. Turner and E. Martin (eds), *Surveying Subjective Phenomena*, 2nd vol. (New York: Russell Sage Foundation).

Matsusaka, J. G. (1993) 'Election Closeness and Voter Turnout: Evidence from California Ballot Propositions', *Public Choice*, 76(4), 313–334.

Matsusaka, J. G. and F. Palda (1999) 'Voter Turnout: How Much Can We Explain?', *Public Choice*, 98(3/4), 431–446.

Matthes, J., K. R. Morrison and C. Schemer (2010) 'A Spiral of Silence for Some: Attitude Certainty and the Expression of Political Minority Opinions', *Communication Research*, 37(6), 774–800.

McAllister, I. and D. T. Studlar (1991) 'Bandwagon, Underdog, or Projection? Opinion Polls and Electoral Choice in Britain, 1979–1987', *Journal of Politics*, 53(3), 720–741.

McKelvey, R. D. and P. C. Ordeshook (1985) 'Elections with Limited Information: A Fulfilled Expectations Model Using Contemporaneous Poll and Endorsement Data as Information Sources', *Journal of Economic Theory*, 36(1), 55–85.

McLeod, J. M., D. A. Scheufele and P. Moy (1999) 'Community, Communication, and Participation: The Role of Mass Media and Interpersonal Discussion in Local Political Participation', *Political Communication*, 16(3), 315–336.

Meffert, M. F. and T. Gschwend (2011) 'Polls, Coalition Signals, and Strategic Voting: An Experimental Investigation of Perceptions and Effects', *European Journal of Political Research*, 50(5), 636–667.

Mehrabian, A. (1998) 'Effects of Poll Reports on Voter Preferences', *Journal of Applied Social Psychology*, 28(23), 2119–2130.

Meirowitz, A. (2005) 'Polling Games and Information Revelation in the Downsian Framework', *Games and Economic Behavior*, 51(2), 464–489.

Milgram, S. (1961) 'Nationality and Conformity', *Scientific American* 205(6), 45–51.

Miller, A. H., E. N. Goldenberg and L. Erbring (1979) 'Type-Set Politics: Impact of Newspapers on Public Confidence', *American Political Science Review*, 73(1), 67–84.

Moy, P., D. Domke and K. Stamm (2001) 'The Spiral of Silence and Public Opinion on Affirmative Action', *Journalism & Mass Communication Quarterly*, 78(1), 7–25.

Moy, P. and M. Pfau (2000) *With Malice Toward All? The Media and Public Confidence in Democratic Institutions* (Westport, CT: Praeger).

Mutz, D. C. (1992) 'Impersonal Influence: Effects of Representations of Public Opinion on Political Attitudes', *Political Behavior*, 14(2), 89–122.

Mutz, D. C. (1994) 'The Political Effects of Perceptions of Mass Opinion', *Research in Micropolitics*, 4, 143–167.

Mutz, D. C. (1997) 'Mechanisms of Momentum: Does Thinking Make It So?', *Journal of Politics*, 59(1), 104–125.

Mutz, D. C. (1998) *Impersonal Influence: How Perceptions of Mass Collectives Affect Political Attitudes* (Cambridge and New York: Cambridge University Press).

Mutz, D. C. and J. Soss (1997) 'Reading Public Opinion: The Influence of News Coverage on Perceptions of Public Sentiment', *Public Opinion Quarterly*, 61(3), 431–451.

Nadeau, R., E. Cloutier and J. Guay (1993) 'New Evidence about the Existence of a Bandwagon Effect in the Opinion Formation Process', *International Political Science Review*, 14(2), 203–213.

Neuwirth, K. (2000) 'Testing the Spiral of Silence Model: The Case of Mexico', *International Journal of Public Opinion Research*, 12(2), 138–159.

Neuwirth, K., E. Frederick and C. Mayo (2007) 'The Spiral of Silence and Fear of Isolation', *Journal of Communication*, 57(3), 450–468.

Noelle-Neumann, E. (1974) 'The Spiral of Silence: A Theory of Public Opinion', *Journal of Communication*, 24(2), 43–51.

Noelle-Neumann, E. (1993) *The Spiral of Silence: Public Opinion – Our Social Skin*, 2nd edn (Chicago, IL: University of Chicago Press).

Noelle-Neumann, E. (1995) 'Public Opinion and Rationality', in T. L. Glasser and C. T. Salmon (eds), *Public Opinion and the Communication of Consent* (New York: Guilford Press).

Patterson, T. E. (1993) *Out of Order* (New York: Knopf).

Patterson, T. E. (2002) *The Vanishing Voter: Public Involvement in an Age of Uncertainty* (New York: Knopf).

Popkin, S. L. (1991) *The Reasoning Voter: Communication and Persuasion in Presidential Campaigns* (Chicago, IL: University of Chicago Press).

Priest, S. H. (2006) 'Public Discourse and Scientific Controversy – A Spiral-of-Silence Analysis of Biotechnology Opinion in the United States', *Science Communication*, 28(2), 195–215.

Robinson, C. E. (1937) 'Recent Developments in the Straw-Poll Field – Part 2', *Public Opinion Quarterly*, 1(4), 42–52.

Salmon, C. T. and F. G. Kline (1985) 'The Spiral of Silence Ten Years Later: An Examination and Evaluation', in K. R. Sanders, L. L. Kaid and D. Nimmo (eds), *Political Communication Yearbook 1984* (Carbondale, IL: Southern Illinois University Press).

Salmon, C. T. and K. Neuwirth (1990) 'Perceptions of Opinion 'Climates' and Willingness to Discuss the Issue of Abortion', *Journalism Quarterly*, 67(3), 567–577.

Scheufele, D. A. and P. Moy (2000) 'Twenty-five Years of the Spiral of Silence: A Conceptual Review and Empirical Outlook', *International Journal of Public Opinion Research*, 12(1), 3–28.

Scheufele, D. A., J. Shanahan and E. Lee (2001) 'Real Talk: Manipulating the Dependent Variable in Spiral of Silence Research', *Communication Research*, 28(3), 304–324.

Schmitt-Beck, R. (1996) 'Mass Media, the Electorate, and the Bandwagon: A Study of Communication Effects on Vote Choice in Germany', *International Journal of Public Opinion Research*, 8(3), 266–291.

Shamir, J. (1997) 'Speaking Up and Silencing Out in Face of a Changing Climate of Opinion', *Journalism & Mass Communication Quarterly*, 74(3), 602–614.

Shamir, J. and M. Shamir (1997) *The Anatomy of Public Opinion* (Ann Arbor, MI: University of Michigan Press).

Sigelman, L. and D. Bullock (1991) 'Candidates, Issues, Horse Races, and Hoopla: Presidential Campaign Coverage, 1888–1988', *American Politics Quarterly*, 19(1), 5–32.

Simon, H. A. (1954) 'Bandwagon and Underdog Effects and the Possibility of Election Predictions', *Public Opinion Quarterly*, 18(3), 245–253.

Simon, H. A. (1997) 'On the Possibility of Accurate Public Prediction', *Journal of Socio-Economics*, 26(2), 127–132.

Skalaban, A. (1988) 'Do the Polls Affect Elections? Some 1980 Evidence', *Political Behavior*, 10(2), 136–150.

Sonck, N. and G. Loosveldt (2010) 'Impact of Poll Results on Personal Opinions and Perceptions of Collective Opinion', *International Journal of Public Opinion Research*, 22(2), 230–255.

Spangenberg, F. (2003) *The Freedom to Publish Opinion Poll Results: Report on a Worldwide Update* (Amsterdam and Lincoln, NE: ESOMAR/WAPOR).

Straffin, P. D., Jr. (1977) 'The Bandwagon Curve', *American Journal of Political Science*, 21(4), 695–709.

Strömbäck, J. and L. L. Kaid (eds) (2008) *The Handbook of Election News Coverage around the World* (New York: Routledge).

Stroud, N. J. (2008) 'Media Use and Political Predispositions: Revisiting the Concept of Selective Exposure', *Political Behavior*, 30(3), 341–366.

Sudman, S. (1986) 'Do Exit Polls Influence Voting Behavior?', *Public Opinion Quarterly*, 50(3), 331–339.

Sunstein, C. (2007) *Republic.com 2.0* (Princeton, NJ: Princeton University Press).

Taylor, C. R. and H. Yildirim (2010) 'Public Information and Electoral Bias', *Games and Economic Behavior*, 68(1), 353–375.

Traugott, M. W. (2008) 'Polls and the Media', in W. Donsbach (ed.), *The International Encyclopedia of Communication* (Malden, MA: Blackwell).

Traugott, M. W. and P. J. Lavrakas (2007) *The Voter's Guide to Election Polls*, 3rd edn (Lanham, MD: Rowman & Littlefield).

Tyran, J. (2004) 'Voting when Money and Morals Conflict: An Experimental Test of Expressive Voting', *Journal of Public Economics*, 88(7–8), 1645–1664.

Valkenburg, P. M., H. A. Semetko and C. H. de Vreese (1999) 'The Effects of News Frames on Readers' Thoughts and Recall', *Communication Research*, 26(5), 550–569.

Vedlitz, A. and E. P. Veblen (1980) 'Voting and Contacting: Two Forms of Participation in a Suburban Community', *Urban Affairs Quarterly*, 50(1), 4–21.

Willnat, L., W.-P. Lee and B. H. Detenber (2002) 'Individual-Level Predictors of Public Outspokenness: A Test of the Spiral of Silence in Singapore', *International Journal of Public Opinion Research*, 14(4), 391–412.

Zech, C. E. (1975) 'Leibenstein's Bandwagon Effect as Applied to Voting', *Public Choice*, 21(1), 117–122.

12
Published Opinion Polls, Strategic Party Behavior and News Management

Jesper Strömbäck

Introduction

The relationship between opinion polls and political leadership is both complex and multifaceted. The same holds true for the relationship between published opinion polls, news management and political leadership. While having acknowledged support by public opinion is a great asset for any political party or politician, signs of weak or declining support are a great liability. The key term here is acknowledged support: it matters less if a political party or politician has actual support if nobody knows about it. In many respects, published opinion polls thus matter more than opinion polls in general.

Since the mass media – despite the increasing importance of digital media – constitute the most important source of information for most people, it becomes important for political parties and politicians to be seen both *by* and *in* the media as having support by public opinion. Assuming that political parties and politicians are strategic actors, this calls for pro-active news management using supportive opinion polls as a tactic to bolster one's case. At the same time, the media frequently commission their own opinion polls or publish the results of non-partisan or competitors' polls. This calls for reactive news management, either attempting to ride the wave when supportive polls are published or to question the validity, reliability or significance of findings when non-supportive polls are published. This also suggests a close linkage between strategic party behavior, published opinion polls, and proactive and reactive news management strategies.

While there is a significant body of research on how political parties and politicians use private opinion polls (Bowman 2000; Geer 1996; Genovese & Streb 2004), particularly as a tool when planning and running election campaigns (Burton & Shea 2010; Johnson 2007) but also when governing (Canes-Wrone 2006; Eisinger 2008; Jacobs & Shapiro 2000), there is however limited research on parties' use of opinion polls in news management processes. In addition, while there is a rich body of literature on the effects of published opinion polls on the electorate (see Moy & Rinke this volume; Hardmeier 2008; Mutz 1998), there is little research on how political parties and their leaders are affected by published opinion polls. The neglect of this kind of media effect is surprising, considering both the general scholarly interest in media effects and that the effects of published opinion polls on political parties and leaders may in fact be greater than on the electorate. This is not least because political parties and leaders have to take the results and the effects of published opinion polls into account to an extent that the electorate does not have to, and because politicians tend to believe that opinion polls influence people's political attitudes and behaviors (Aalberg 2010).

Against this background and building on theories of parties as strategic actors, the purpose of this chapter is to analyze and discuss how political parties are affected by published opinion polls, and how they strategically may use opinion polls in news management processes. Part research review, part theory-building, it is hoped that this chapter will contribute to further research on the relationship between political parties and leaders, published opinion polls, and news management strategies and tactics.

Political leadership and public opinion: A complex relationship

The basic premise of representative democracies is that political parties and leaders should represent the electorate. The concept of representation is however complex (see Chapter 1; Manin 1997; Pitkin 1967; Sartori 1987). On the one hand, politicians are supposed to be leaders, to act in the interest of the electorate but with freedom to go beyond the wishes of the electorate if the politician finds this to be in the public interest or to be more compatible with his or her own judgment and values. On the other hand, politicians are supposed to be followers, to act in the interest of the electorate by staying as close as possible to their wishes and with very little discretion to use his or her own judgment and values. And while not following public opinion may be considered democratically undesirable elitism and non-responsiveness, following public opinion too slavishly may be considered equally undesirable populism and pandering. Hence, Geer (1996, pp. 18–19) notes, 'a representative democracy must walk a tightrope between excessive leadership, which could lead to a less democratic regime, and the absence of leadership, which could allow a nation to pursue ill-conceived policies that might harm the interests of the citizenry'.

While most people or journalists may not be familiar with the nuances in the discussion about different concepts of representation and models of political leadership and followership in democracies, there is a general assumption that politicians' opinions, attitudes, actions and votes should at least roughly correspond to public opinion on the matters. Such policy representation is also at the heart of basically all theories of representative democracy (Canes-Wrone 2006; Esaiasson & Holmberg 1996; Jacobs & Shapiro 2000; Manin 1997; McDonald & Budge 2005; Miller et al. 1999; Sartori 1987; Soroka & Wlezien 2010; Wessels 2007; Wlezien & Soroka 2007). Since public opinion often is equated with the results from opinion polls (Splichal this volume), this means that deviations in politicians' opinions, attitudes, actions or votes from what opinion polls show is the majority or plurality view is likely to be perceived as non-responsiveness. It also means that is always a major strength being able to show support by public opinion for one's party, candidacy, leadership or policy positions.

Of course, this only holds true for opinion polls that are published in one form or another. Political parties (and other organizations) may conduct a range of opinion polls to guide their electoral strategies, their selection of issues or policies to push, or what language to use to frame their messages (Hillygus & Shields 2008; Jacobs & Shapiro 2000; Maltese 1994; Shaw 2006), but as long as the results of these polls remain private they do not pose any threat to the reputation or public standing of the party.

The situation changes significantly when there are publicly available results from opinion polls. Then political parties and politicians must decide how to respond, and then these results may have effects not only on voters' attitudes and behaviors, but also on the political parties, campaigns, candidates and leaders.

Strategic party behavior and published opinion polls

To understand the relationship between published opinion polls, political parties and news management, a key assumption is that political parties and politicians are strategic actors. They have certain goals that they want to accomplish, and these goals guide them in their behavior. The ultimate goal may be to 'maximize political support' (Downs 1957, p. 11) or that the 'party itself shall make the authoritative decisions in accordance with its evaluation system' (Sjöblom 1968, p. 73), but in either case, their approach to published opinion polls can be assumed to be instrumental and shaped by whatever goals they are attempting to accomplish. As a general observation, this should hold true for all parties, regardless of whether they may be office-seeking, policy-seeking or vote-seeking (Müller & Strøm 1999; Strøm 1990) or, to use a distinction from the political marketing literature, product-oriented, sales-oriented or market-oriented (Lees-Marshment 2001).

In this context, a useful starting point is Sjöblom's theory of strategic party behavior in multiparty systems (1968). According to this theory, political parties act on several different arenas, each accompanied by different members, decision types and strategic goals. On the *internal arena*, the strategic goal is to maximize internal cohesion; the members are party members and activists, and the most important decisions relate to 'whether or not they are to support the party's official standpoints and candidates' (Sjöblom 1968, p. 26). On the *parliamentary arena*, the strategic goal is to maximize parliamentary influence; the members are members of parliament of different parties, and the most important decisions relate to whether to collaborate or seek conflict with one another. On the *electoral arena*, the strategic goal is to maximize electoral support; the members are everyone entitled to vote, and the most important decision is whether to vote and which party to support.

On each of these arenas, the ability to accomplish the strategic goals may be affected by the support for particular policies or for the party or its leader in published opinion polls. Consequently, the publication of opinion polls may have effects not only on citizens but also on political parties with respect to each of these arenas. This holds particularly true since research suggests that politicians tend to believe that opinion polls have an influence on how people vote (Aalberg 2010). Following the theory of presumed media influence (Tal-Or, Tsfati & Gunther 2009), perceptions of influence may lead to actual influence (Cohen, Tsfati & Sheafer 2008).

The internal arena and support in published opinion polls

On the internal arena, the strategic goal is to maximize internal cohesion. The more cohesive the party is, and the stronger the internal support for official standpoints and candidates or the party leader, the better (Sjöblom 1968, pp. 183–184). In such situations, there are few doubts about what the party stands for, and the leadership does not have to use scarce resources in terms of attention and time to managing internal conflicts and avoiding that internal conflicts become public. It also becomes significantly easier to mobilize party members, which is crucial since they 'are the parties' foot-soldiers, they will run local offices, organise and coordinate campaign activities, deliver leaflets, canvass voters and knock-up their supporters on election day: as such they are the lifeblood of the party' (Lilleker 2005, p. 572).

If published opinion polls show that the party is increasing its vote share, this may help the party leadership in several different ways. First, it will decrease the risk that internal discontent gains a foothold or strength. As members of a political party want the party to succeed, they are generally supportive of the leadership as long as things are going well. When the party is perceived to be failing, many members will however start to question the leadership, the policies or how the party is run. This will not only increase the risk of internal discontent, it will also decrease the legitimacy and the degrees of operative freedom that the party leadership is granted. It may also open up disputes between different factions within the party. Second and consequently, published opinion polls that suggest that the party is increasing its vote share will grant the leadership increasing legitimacy and greater degrees of freedom, and keep factional disputes at bay. Both of these aspects mean that the party leadership does not have to use scarce resources to counteract internal problems, and that the party leadership instead can focus on more proactive measures to develop the party organization, its strategies and tactics, and its policies.

Third, perceived success in opinion polls will also help the party leadership to mobilize members when campaigning or for different volunteer activities. This effect may occur because success in opinion polls breeds enthusiasm within the party, or because members feel that it is socially more accepted to be a member of and campaign for the party, or because members presume that the party will make a successful election. The reasons may vary, but in either case success in the polls can be assumed to make it easier for the party leadership to mobilize its members both internally and for external activities.

If, on the contrary, published opinion polls show that the party is losing in the polls, this may likewise hurt the party and its leadership in corresponding ways. It will increase the risk that internal opposition gains a foothold or strength, that the party leadership loses legitimacy, which may curtail the leadership's degree of freedom, and it will make it more difficult for the party leadership to mobilize members.

All of this probably holds particularly true with respect to horse race polls, that is, opinion polls measuring party preferences or vote support, alternatively support for official candidates or party leaders. With respect to polls about different issues or policies, the impact may be less consequential, as long as perceived lack of support in general public opinion for different policies does not appear to affect the party's general support, and as long as the official policies are supported within the party.

The parliamentary arena and support in published opinion polls

On the parliamentary arena, the strategic goal is to maximize parliamentary influence. This arena includes both the government and those institutions that hold legislative power. While the most important factor shaping influence on the parliamentary arena is the share of seats, it is also a matter of negotiations, bargaining and coalition building (Edwards 2009; Kernell 2007; Sellers 2010). This holds true in multiparty as well as in majoritarian systems, although the rules and dynamics of decision making and policy making vary depending on the institutional setup and the configuration of the political system (unicameral, bicameral, presidential, the number of parties, degree of party fragmentation, etc.).

While the factors and strategic considerations guiding the behavior of parties or individual members of parliament in terms of conflict and cooperation are many, generally speaking, it can be assumed to be advantageous to be perceived as having the support of public opinion. This holds true both with respect to general support in public opinion and, perhaps in particular, in terms of support for different policies. First, being able to show or convincingly argue that a majority or plurality supports a particular policy functions as a strong rhetorical device, creating pressure on others to make a stronger case for why they may not support the policy. Second, even though other policy makers or parties may not agree with the policy, perceiving that the policy is supported by a majority or a plurality in public opinion increases the risks of opposing it, as this may be used against them in future election campaigns and this, regardless of whether it is actively used against them, may cost them votes when facing re-election. The prospects for legislative success may thus be at least partly a function of the strength of support different policies have in public opinion (Canes-Wrone 2006), particularly with respect to highly salient issues. Third, being able to convincingly argue that a majority or plurality supports a particular policy may help a party or individual policy makers to move the issue onto or higher on the policy agenda.

All of this follows from the 'law of anticipated reactions', which holds that politicians regularly pay close attention to their publics and public opinion when deciding what stance to take in negotiations and bargaining (Kernell 2007, p. 76), and from the notion that reputation and opinion strength functions as *political capital* that can be used to 'purchase' bargaining power (Kernell 2007, p. 40). It also helps explain why 'going public' has become a more prominent strategy to enlist public opinion for influencing not only campaigns but also policy-making processes (Kernell 2007).

The effects of support in published opinion polls may be particularly important with respect to polls showing support or opposition to particular policies. With respect to horse race polls, the impact may be less consequential, although opposing parties and leaders that are perceived as having strong or increasing support in public opinion may be perceived as more risky and potentially more costly, thus increasing the bargaining strength of parties or party leaders perceived as having strong or increasing public opinion support (Kernell 2007). Strong or increasing opinion support may also increase cohesion within the parliamentary party group. In general, opinion polls with respect to issues or policies can however be expected to be more important on the parliamentary arena than horse race polls, in contrast to the internal and the electoral arena.

The electoral arena and support in published opinion polls

On the electoral arena, the strategic goal is to maximize vote support. As such, this may be the arena most obviously linked to the importance and influence of published opinion polls. This is the arena where the battle for public opinion is waged, where success may breed success and where elections ultimately are decided. Although research suggests that both bandwagon and underdog effects may result from public perceptions of public opinion (see Moy & Rinke this volume; Hardmeier 2008; Mutz 1998), generally speaking, it is always advantageous for a party to be perceived as having strong public support either for itself or for its policies. This holds particularly true with respect to salient issues, or with respect to latent demands that can be made salient (Sjöblom 1968, p. 214). It is equally advantageous for a party to be perceived as winning increasing support, which is where bandwagon effects may be triggered. Also considering the spiral of silence theory (Noelle-Neumann 1993; Scheufele 2008), strong or increasing support may increase people's willingness to publicly support and speak out for the party or its policies, which may lead to further success in the battle for public opinion and votes. The fact that politicians believe that opinion polls have an influence on how people vote (Aalberg 2010) can also be expected to influence their strategies and tactics.

If published opinion polls show that the party is having strong or increasing support, this may consequently help the party in several ways. First, increasing or strong support in public opinion is a key indicator that the party will make a successful election. Second, it may trigger bandwagon effects, leading to further increases in opinion support. Third, it may make more people willing to publicly support the party, either offline or in different social media such as Facebook. Fourth, it may make more people willing to join and campaign for the party. Fifth, it may make more people consider the party, and although they may not vote for it on Election Day, it increases the future prospects of the party. Enjoying strong albeit perhaps not increasing support may also trigger these kinds of effects.

In terms of perceived public opinion support for specific policies, strong or increasing support may also have several positive effects. To begin with, it may trigger the consensus heuristic (Mutz 1998), leading more people to support a policy for no other substantial reason than the perception that others are supporting it. Furthermore, it may strengthen the perception that the party is responsive and is listening to the people. In addition, it may make more people willing to speak out and support the policy in interpersonal discussions on- or offline. Finally, it may make it more difficult for opponents to make their case heard.

In essence, enjoying strong or increasing support in public opinion not only makes it easier for a party to further make its case in public debates with opponents, it may also trigger spirals of increasing support, and it is instrumental when the parties act on the internal and parliamentary arenas. It thus has the character of being important both in itself, and as an instrument in the battle for votes, internal support or parliamentary influence.

Strong or increasing support in public opinion for the party, its leader, candidates or its policies may also have a significant impact on the media coverage, which in turn may lead to further effects on public support. This leads the discussion back to the role of the media.

The media arena and support in published opinion polls

In the original formulation of the theory of strategic party behavior (Sjöblom 1968), the media was hardly mentioned at all. To remedy this, subsequent theorizing has suggested the addition of a media arena (Nord 1997; Strömbäck 2007). On the media arena, the strategic goal is to maximize positive visibility; the members are journalists and editors, and the most important decision relates to whether to give positive or negative publicity.

The media arena is in many ways the most important in the context of published opinion polls, news management and political leadership. First, without the media publishing the results of opinion polls, they would not be publicly available, and there would be no potential for effects on either the electorate or political parties and actors. Second, the media constitute the most important source of information for most people, meaning that results from opinion polls published by the media will be widely disseminated. Third, the media themselves commission many of the polls from which the results are published (Brettschneider 1997, 2008; Frankovic 2005; Patterson 2005). Fourth, poll reporting constitutes an important and intrinsic part of election news coverage (Patterson 1993, 2005; Strömbäck & Kaid 2008; Chapters 5–10 in this volume), and contributes to shaping the overall news media coverage of elections, which means that the opinion polls both directly and indirectly shape the overall coverage of election campaigns.

From this perspective, if published opinion polls show that the party has strong or increasing support either with respect to the party or its candidate or leaders, or with respect to the party's policies, this will be advantageous in several ways. To begin with, news about polls showing strong or increasing support constitutes positive visibility in itself. Second, it may positively influence the tone towards the party in the overall coverage, which is particularly important since much of political reporting frames politics as a strategic game or a horse race (Cappella & Jamieson 1997; Lawrence 2000; Patterson 1993; Strömbäck & Kaid

2008). Thus, it may help create a momentum for the party. It may also increase the overall news value of the party and its proposals and actions, which may significantly help the party move other issues to or higher on the media agenda. All of this may contribute to subsequent media effects on the public that are beneficial for the party. Consequently, it may significantly help the party in its attempts to achieve its strategic goals on the internal, parliamentary and electoral arenas.

If, on the other hand, published opinion polls show that the party has weak or declining support with respect to the party or its candidates or leaders, or the party's policies, this may hurt in several different and corresponding ways. First, news about polls showing weak or declining support constitutes negative visibility. Second, it may negatively influence the tone towards the party in the overall news coverage, for example by triggering news stories focusing on why a party or candidate is failing in the polls. Third, it may decrease the general news value of the party. Fourth, it may hinder attempts to move issues to or higher on the media agenda. Fifth, it will hurt the party in its attempts to achieve its strategic goals on the internal, parliamentary and electoral arenas. For example, it may make it significantly more difficult to mobilize members and volunteers, create internal dissension and weaken the influence in negotiations with other parties. All this can, in turn, lead to subsequent decreases in opinion support, creating a downward spiral.

In essence, this suggests that success in influencing the media and the media coverage of polls may be not only important but also necessary for success on the internal, electoral and parliamentary arenas. This creates strong incentives for the parties to develop strategies for both proactive and reactive news management, particularly as contemporary media coverage of opinion polls is not only mediated but also mediatized.

The mediation and mediatization of opinion polls

While the concepts of mediation and mediatization are often used interchangeably and there is some disagreement on how these concepts should be understood, at heart, mediation refers to a rather neutral act of transmitting messages (Mazzoleni 2008). Mediatization, in contrast, refers to a process of increasing media independence and media influence (Hjarvard 2008; Mazzoleni 2008; Mazzoleni & Schulz 1999; Schulz 2004) where media logic becomes increasingly important both for the media in their coverage of politics and for political actors (Altheide

& Snow 1979; Strömbäck 2008, 2011; Strömbäck & Dimitrova 2011; Strömbäck & Esser 2009).

To the extent that the media just publish and neutrally report the results of opinion polls, without any active interference in the process, it represents a case of mediating opinion polls and their results. The media 'serve as mere conveyor belts' (Schoenbach & Becker 1995, p. 326) and the independent influence of the media is minimal beyond the mere act of publishing the results.

To the extent that the media are actively involved in the process of commissioning, reporting, interpreting and using the polls to guide their overall coverage, it rather represents a case of mediatization of opinion polls and their results. In such cases, the media function as 'molders' of public opinion (Schoenbach & Becker 1995, p. 327) and the independent influence of the media goes significantly beyond the act of just publishing the results.

With respect to the media's coverage of opinion polls, research clearly suggests that it is not only mediated (Frankovic 1998; Patterson 2005). It is also highly mediatized. Not only do the media devote extensive space to covering the results of different opinion polls (see Chapter 1, pp. 5–10; Brettschneider 2008; Strömbäck & Kaid 2008), oftentimes the polls are sponsored by media organizations or conducted in partnerships with polling organizations (Brettschneider 2008; Strömbäck 2009; Traugott 2009). Hence, the relationship between polling and media organizations has been described as symbiotic (Brettschneider 2008, p. 479; Traugott 2009).

As discussed in Chapter 1, there are many reasons why the media sponsor and cover opinion polls. Not least important is that opinion polls grant the media great freedom to select and emphasize those issues and views that they believe are most interesting or important from the perspective of the media, and in interpreting the results (Frankovic 1998).

Although it takes skill to analyze and accurately report the results from opinion polls, the results often appear objective, and by focusing on results from opinion polls, journalists appear to report objectively (Traugott & Powers 2000). The analysis may, however, be less objective than it appears. While research suggests that a majority of news stories on poll results use some kind of causal explanation (Bauman & Lavrakas 2000), in most cases, such attributions are unsupported by the polls or by other evidence. They constitute the result of journalists' or sources' analyses and interpretations, but are nevertheless often presented as facts. In this sense, opinion polls allow journalists to become more interpretive in their coverage while still being shielded from accusations of subjectivity (Lavrakas & Traugott 2000; Patterson 2005; Rosenstiel 2005). In the battle between the media and political actors for control over the news and how reality is socially constructed, this presents a major challenge for political parties and actors.

In addition, there is strong evidence suggesting not only that politicians think that opinion polls have an influence on how people vote (Aalberg 2010) but also that the media are powerful (Cohen, Tsfati & Sheafer 2008; van Aelst et al. 2008). This makes the media arena crucially important and creates strong incentives for proactive and reactive management of news related to opinion polls.

Since the media often base their coverage and confront political parties and leaders with questions referring to results from published opinion polls, and since political parties and leaders believe opinion polls as well as the media in general are influential, they simply cannot avoid some kind of management of news related to opinion polls. The question then is not whether political parties and leaders try to manage news related to opinion polls. The question is rather: what proactive and reactive news management strategies do political parties and leaders have at their disposal, and how do political parties and politicians use opinion polls in news management processes?

The use of opinion polls in news management

Often referred to as spinning (Franklin 2004; McNair 2004; Palmer 2000), media relations or news management is ultimately about strategies and tactics designed to increase the likelihood that a party or other organization receives as extensive and positive publicity as possible while minimizing the risk or impact of negative publicity. It forms an important part of public relations, although public relations is a broader concept and should *not* be equated with media relations (Grunig 1992; Strömbäck & Kiousis 2011; Zoch & Molleda 2006).

A key part of successful news management is to understand the media's needs and standards of newsworthiness, that is, media logic, and the extent to which political actors adapt to the media and their logic constitute a key part of the mediatization of politics (Meyer 2002; Strömbäck 2011). Although news making can be understood as a coproduction between journalists and political actors, 'this coproduction pushes political actors to anticipate the needs of the news in designing what they will say and do' (Cook 2005, p. 114). In the words of McNair (2003, p. 136), news management 'requires giving the media organization what it wants, in terms of news or entertainment, while exerting some influence over how that something is mediated and presented to the audience'. Palmer (2000, pp. 125–126) similarly concludes that the extent to which political or other organizations manage to influence the news 'derives from the capacity to produce events that conform to news values'.

If the purpose of news management is to promote the organization and increase the likelihood that the organization receives as extensive and positive publicity as possible, the most important means towards this end is to adapt to the media and their logic by providing them with information that appeals to the media's standards of newsworthiness. Proactively, news management is consequently about serving the organization's needs for positive visibility by serving the media's need for stories that have high news value, while reactively it is about minimizing the risk that the organization offers information that also has high news value but that reflects negatively on the organization.

The media's standards of newsworthiness help explain why they find opinion polls appealing. New opinion polls constitute new and potentially surprising information; there is an embedded conflict between different parties or points of view; the results can be used to inform the framing of politics as a dramatic strategic game or a horse race; they deal with issues and actors that have societal impact and are considered important; negativity is often embedded as opinion polls suggest both winners and losers; and opinion polls are relatively easy to cover (Frankovic 1998; Traugott & Powers 2000).

In the context of proactive news management, the concept of news subsidies is central (Lieber & Golan 2011; Tedesco 2011; Zoch & Molleda 2006). As defined by Gandy (1982, p. 8), news subsidies include all 'efforts to reduce the process faced by others for certain information, in order to increase its consumption'. News subsidies thus include making spokespersons available, producing press releases or staging pseudo-events designed to suit the media's production needs and attract the media's attention (Boorstin 1964), producing reports including new statistics or results from more or less scientific research in a format that makes it easy for journalists to process and report the information, making statements that fit the media's standards of newsworthiness, and to prepare and format information as journalistically as possible.

Conducting and presenting the results of opinion polls constitute a typical news subsidy tailored to manage and influence the news. Not only do opinion polls hold great news value; by covering the costs associated with conducting the opinion poll and presenting the results in an easy-to-cover format, political parties make the results both cheap and easy to cover. An added benefit is that the results from opinion polls appear factual, which is important since 'the value of an information subsidy is increased to the extent that the source can disguise the promotional, partisan, self-interested quality of the information' (Gandy 1982, p. 14). Although most journalists realize that political parties (and other organizations) would not present an opinion poll if the results reflected badly on them, the results have a 'matter-of-fact' appearance that, in combination with the strong interest the media have in opinion polls, increases the likelihood that the opinion poll will be turned into news (Traugott & Powers 2000).

Political parties (and other organizations) may thus attempt to manage the news proactively by conducting and presenting the results of opinion polls. By doing opinion polls on some but not other issues, they can attempt to influence the media agenda. By carefully framing the question wordings or the response alternatives, they may also influence the actual results of the opinion poll (Bishop 2005; Moore 2008). In such cases, the main interest is not to find out what public opinion is, but to produce results that are favorable for the party and its positions (Traugott 2008; Traugott & Powers 2000). Regardless of whether the opinion poll is more or less manipulated, the political party may release only those results that reflect positively on the party or negatively on its competitors. In conjunction with or after the poll has been released, the party can also attempt to frame the interpretation of the results in a way intended to strengthen the preferred framing of the party or weaken that of its competitors. Finally, by having the results released through collateral organizations (Poguntke 2006), the political party may attempt to be perceived as disinterested, while at the same time being ready to provide comments on and to spin the results.

To sum up, proactively political parties can use opinion polls in news management by (1) conducting opinion polls; (2) doing opinion polls on strategically important issues they want to move (higher) on the media agenda; (3) manipulating the opinion poll to increase the likelihood that the results reflect positively on the party and its policies; (4) presenting the results in a format that is as journalistically appealing as possible; and (5) framing and spinning the results. The ideal is having the media report extensively on opinion polls that focus on issues of strategic importance and whose results support the political party or its policies or frames, allowing the party to position itself as aligned with public opinion and speaking for the people, to position competitors as out of touch with and unresponsive to public opinion, and to frame the terms of and the alternatives in the debate.

Most published opinion polls are, however, conducted by the media themselves. This means that political parties need to have strategies and tactics to reactively manage the news when opinion polls are presented, particularly when the results reflect negatively on the party. In such cases, there are several strategies that political parties can apply. If unfavorable poll results come from non-partisan organizations or the media, one response may be to downplay the importance of the results by, if possible, pointing towards results from other polls. Another response may be to question the reliability or validity of the findings, for example by questioning the number of respondents, how questions or response alternatives were phrased, or zero in, if possible, on whether findings were significant and outside of the margin of error. An additional, and related, response may be to question whether people have enough knowledge or information, or have had enough time to think about, the issue at hand, although such a strategy may backfire and create the impression that the party is non-responsive. Another response may be attempts to re-frame the interpretations of the results, by highlighting those results from the same or other polls that are more or most favorable. All these responses are also applicable if or when the results come from a poll done and presented by partisan organizations and competitors. In such cases, an additional response may be to question the reliability of the poll by highlighting the self-interest of the organization that sponsored the poll.

The reactive strategies for managing the news when unfavorable poll results are presented all serve to make the unfavorable poll results appear either less credible or significant, thus decreasing the news value and trustworthiness of the poll results in the perceptions of the media. If successful, unfavorable poll results will gain no or only minimal media attention. If unsuccessful, the political party may however appear as unresponsive, and as if it is only trying to spin the news. Which, of course, it is trying to, but successful news management should never be perceived as spinning.

Thus, political parties do not only use private opinion polls to 'assemble information on public opinion to design government policy' – suggesting responsiveness – or to 'pinpoint the most alluring words, symbols, and arguments in an attempt to move public opinion to support their desired policies – suggesting "crafted talk" ' (Jacobs & Shapiro 2000, pp. xiv–xv). They also conduct and release opinion polls as a news subsidy intended to influence the news, and to enlist the media in their attempts to shape perceptions of political reality and to frame the political issues and processes at stake.

Conclusion

Generally speaking, political parties and politicians have two goals: to influence policy and to win re-election. While it can be debated whether the overriding goal is vote maximization or to influence policy, and there may be differences across both party types and individual politicians, having support by public opinion is always advantageous.

Equally, or at times even more, important may however be whether a political party politician is *perceived* to have support. This holds particularly true with respect to support for different policies, since on most issues people do not hold strong or even consistent opinions (Bishop 2005; Moore 2008; Moy 2008; Zaller 1992).

The role of the mass media thus becomes crucial. Not only do the media often have substantial effects on public opinion (Kepplinger 2008; Nabi & Oliver 2009). The media also influence perceptions of public opinion, and politicians tend to believe that both opinion polls and the media in general are highly influential (Aalberg 2010; Tal-Or, Tsfati & Gunther 2009; van Aelst et al. 2008). These perceptions may, in turn, have effects on public opinion (Mutz 1998; Noelle-Neumann 1993) as well as on political parties and leaders (Cohen, Tsfati & Sheafer, 2008). In addition, the media themselves sponsor many of the opinion polls that are published, alongside those that have been sponsored by outside actors but are published by the media. As the effects of opinion polls can only occur when the results are publicly available, the media not only reflect public opinion. They also shape or mold public opinion, both directly and indirectly.

Although most research on the effects of published opinion polls has focused on their effects on public opinion, the effects on political parties and politicians may be equally or even more important. Assuming that political parties are rational and strategic actors, and knowing that they tend to believe that opinion polls have an influence on how people think and vote, they have to take published opinion polls into account to an extent that ordinary citizens do not have to. Hence, the likelihood that political parties are affected by published opinion polls is greater than the likelihood that ordinary citizens are affected. The true power of mediated and mediatized public opinion polls may be exerted over political parties and other political actors, rather than over the public.

Considering this, the deficit of research on how political parties are affected by published opinion polls and on how they use opinion polls in news management processes is both surprising and troubling. From this perspective, it is hoped that this chapter will provide a springboard for further research in this area. Admittedly, this is just a first attempt to suggest a framework for understanding how political parties are affected by published opinion polls and how they use opinion polls in news management processes. Much more theorizing and empirical research is hence warranted and needed if we are to fully understand the impact of the media and published opinion polls both in and for contemporary democracies.

References

Aalberg, T. (2010) 'Mektige meningsmålinger? Journalisters og politikeres oppfatning av meningsmålingers troverdighet og innflytelse', *Tidsskrift for sammfunnsforskning*, 50(3), 445–463.

Altheide, D. L. and R. P. Snow (1979) *Media Logic* (Beverly Hills, CA: Sage).

Bauman, S. L. and P. J. Lavrakas (2000) 'Reporter's Use of Causal Explanation in Interpreting Election Polls', in P. J. Lavrakas and M. W. Traugott (eds), *Election Polls, the News Media, and Democracy* (New York: Chatham House).

Bishop, G. F. (2005) *The Illusion of Public Opinion: Fact and Artifact in American Public Opinion Polls* (Lanham: Rowman & Littlefield).

Boorstin, D. J. (1964) *The Image: A Guide to Pseudo-Events in America* (New York: Harper Colophon).

Bowman, K. (2000) 'Polling to Campaign and to Govern', in N. Ornstein and T. Mann (eds), *The Permanent Campaign and Its Future* (Washington, DC: AEI/Brookings Institution).

Brettschneider, F. (1997) 'The Press and the Polls in Germany, 1980–1994', *International Journal of Public Opinion Research*, 9(3), 248–264.

Brettschneider, F. (2008) 'The News Media's Use of Opinion Polls', in W. Donsbach and M. W. Traugott (eds), *The SAGE Handbook of Public Opinion Research* (London: Sage).

Burton, M. J. and D. M. Shea (2010) *Campaign Craft: The Strategies, Tactics, and Art of Political Campaign Management*, 4th edn (Santa Barbara, CA: Praeger).

Canes-Wrone, B. (2006) *Who Leads Whom? Presidents, Policy, and the Public* (Chicago, IL: University of Chicago Press).

Cappella, J. N. and K. H. Jamieson (1997) *Spiral of Cynicism. The Press and the Public Good* (New York: Oxford University Press).

Cohen, J., Y. Tsfati and T. Sheafer (2008) 'The Influence of Presumed Media Influence in Politics. Do Politicians' Perceptions of Media Power Matter?', *Public Opinion Quarterly*, 72(2), 331–344.

Cook, T. E. (2005) *Governing With the News. The News Media as a Political Institution*, 2nd edn (Chicago, IL: University of Chicago Press).

Downs, A. (1957) *An Economic Theory of Democracy* (Boston, MA: Addison Wesley).

Edwards, C. C. (2009) *The Strategic President. Persuasion & Opportunity in Presidential Leadership* (New Haven, CT: Princeton University Press).

Eisinger, R. M. (2008) 'The Use of Surveys by Governments and Politicians', in W. Donsbach and M. W. Traugott (eds), *The SAGE Handbook of Public Opinion Research* (London: Sage).

Esaiasson, P. and Holmberg, S. (1996) *Representation from Above: Members of Parliament and Representative Democracy in Sweden* (Aldershot: Dartmouth).

Franklin, B. (2004) *Packaging Politics: Political Communications in Britain's Media Democracy*, 2nd edn (London: Arnold).

Frankovic, K. A. (1998) 'Public opinion and polling', in D. Graber, D. McQuail and P. Norris (eds) *The Politics of News: The News of Politics* (Washington, DC: Congressional Quarterly).

Frankovic, K. A. (2005) 'Reporting "the Polls" in 2004', *Public Opinion Quarterly*, 69(5), 682–697.

Gandy, O. H., Jr. (1982) *Beyond Agenda Setting: Information Subsidies and Public Policy* (Norwood, MA: Ablex Publishing).

Geer, J. G. (1996) *From Tea Leaves to Opinion Polls: A Theory of Democratic Leadership* (New York: Columbia University Press).

Genovese, M. A. and M. J. Streb (eds) (2004) *Polls and Politics: The Dilemmas of Democracy* (Albany, NY: State University of New York Press).

Grunig, J. E. (ed.) (1992) *Excellence in Public Relations and Communication Management* (Mahwah, NJ: Lawrence Erlbaum).

Hardmeier, S. (2008) 'The Effects of Published Polls on Citizens', in W. Donsbach and M. W. Traugott (eds), *The SAGE Handbook of Public Opinion Research* (London: Sage).

Hillygus, D. S. and T. G. Shields (2008) *The Persuadable Voter: Wedge Issues in Presidential Campaigns* (Princeton, NJ: Princeton University Press).

Hjarvard, S. (2008) 'The Mediatization of Society: A Theory of the Media as Agents of Social and Cultural Change', *Nordicom Review*, 29(2), 105–134.

Jacobs, L. R. and R. Y. Shapiro (2000) *Politicians Don't Pander: Political Manipulation and the Loss of Democratic Responsiveness* (Chicago, IL: University of Chicago Press).

Johnson, D. W. (2007) *No Place for Amateurs. How Political Consultants are Reshaping American Democracy*, 2nd edn (New York: Routledge).

Kepplinger, H. M. (2008) 'Effects of the News Media on Public Opinion', in W. Donsbach and M. W. Traugott (eds), *The SAGE Handbook of Public Opinion Research* (London: Sage).

Kernell, S. (2007) *Going Public: New Strategies of Presidential Leadership*, 4th edn (Washington, DC: CQ Press).

Lavrakas, P. J. and M. W. Traugott (2000) 'Why Election Polls are Important to a Democracy: An American Perspective', in P. J. Lavrakas and M. W. Traugott (eds), *Election Polls, the News Media, and Democracy* (New York: Chatham House).

Lawrence, R. (2000) 'Game-Framing the Issues: Tracking the Strategy Frame in Public Policy News', *Political Communication*, 17(2), 93–114.

Lees-Marshment, J. (2001) *Political Marketing and British Political Parties: The Party's JustBegun* (Manchester: Manchester University Press).

Lieber, P. S. and G. J. Golan (2011) 'Political Public Relations, News Management, and Agenda Indexing', in J. Strömbäck and S. Kiousis (eds), *Political Public Relations: Principles and Applications* (New York: Routledge).

Lilleker, D. G. (2005) 'The Impact of Political Marketing on Internal Party Democracy', *Parliamentary Affairs*, 58(3), 570–584.

Maltese, J. A. (1994) *Spin Control: The White House Office of Communications and the Management of Presidential News*, 2nd edn (Chapel Hill, NC: University of North Carolina Press).

Manin, B. (1997) *The Principles of Representative Government* (New York: Cambridge University Press).

Mazzoleni, G. (2008) 'Mediatization of Politics', in W. Donsbach (ed.), *The International Encyclopedia of Communication* (Malden, MA: Blackwell).

Mazzoleni, G. and W. Schulz (1999) 'Mediatization of Politics: A Challenge for Democracy?', *Political Communication* 16(3), 247–261.

McDonald, M. D. and I. Budge (2005) *Elections, Parties, Democracy: Conferring the Median Mandate* (Oxford: Oxford University Press).

McNair, B. (2003) *An Introduction to Political Communication*, 3rd edn (London: Routledge).

McNair, B. (2004) 'PR Must Die: Spin, Anti-Spin and Political Public Relations in the UK, 1997–2004', *Journalism Studies*, 5(3), 325–338.

Meyer, T. (2002) *Media Democracy: How the Media Colonize Politics* (Cambridge, UK: Polity).

Miller, W. E., R. Pierce, J. Thomassen, R. Herrera, S. Holmberg, P. Esaiasson and B. Wessels (1999) *Policy Representation in Western Democracies* (Oxford: Oxford University Press).

Moore, D. W. (2008) *The Opinion Makers: An Insider Exposes the Truth Behind the Polls* (Boston, MA: Beacon Press).

Moy, P. (2008) 'Pluralistic Ignorance and Nonattitudes', in W. Donsbach and M. W. Traugott (eds), *The SAGE Handbook of Public Opinion Research* (London: Sage).

Mutz, D. C. (1998) *Impersonal Influence. How Perceptions of Mass Collectives Affect Political Attitudes* (New York: Cambridge University Press).

Müller, W. C. and K. Strøm (eds) (1999) *Policy, Office, or Votes? How Political Parties in Western Europe Make Hard Decisions* (New York: Cambridge University Press).

Nabi, R. L. and M. B. Oliver (eds) (2009) *The SAGE Handbook of Media Processes and Effects* (London: Sage).

Noelle-Neumann, E. (1993) *The Spiral of Silence. Public Opinion – Our Social Skin*, 2nd edn (Chicago, IL: University of Chicago Press).

Nord, L. (1997) *Spelet om opinionen* (Lund: Studentlitteratur).

Palmer, J. (2000) *Spinning Into Control: News Values and Source Strategies* (London: Leicester University Press).

Patterson, T. E. (1993) *Out of Order* (New York: Vintage).

Patterson, T. E. (2005) 'Of Polls, Mountains', *Public Opinion Quarterly*, 69(5), 716–724.

Pitkin, H. A. (1967) *The Concept of Representation* (Berkeley, CA: University of California Press).

Poguntke, T. (2006) 'Political Parties and Other Organizations', in R. S. Katz and W. Crotty (eds), *Handbook of Party Politics* (London: Sage).

Rosenstiel, T. (2005) 'Political Polling and the New Media Culture: A Case of More Being Less', *Public Opinion Quarterly*, 69(5), 698–715.

Sartori, G. (1987) *The Theory of Democracy Revisited. Part One: The Contemporary Debate* (Chatham: Chatham House).

Scheufele, D. A. (2008) 'Spiral of Silence Theory', in W. Donsbach and M. W. Traugott (eds), *The SAGE Handbook of Public Opinion Research* (London: Sage).

Schoenbach, K. and L. B. Becker (1995) 'Origins and Consequences of Mediated Public Opinion', in T. L. Glasser and C. T. Salmon (eds), *Public Opinion and the Communication of Consent* (New York: Guilford Press).

Schulz, W. (2004) 'Reconstructing Mediatization as an Analytical Concept', *European Journal of Communication*, 19(1), 87–101.

Sellers, P. (2010) *Cycles of Spin. Strategic Communication in the U.S. Congress* (New York: Cambridge University Press).

Shaw, D. R. (2006) *The Race to 270: The Electoral College and the Campaign Strategies of 2000 and 2004* (Chicago, IL: University of Chicago Press).

Sjöblom, G. (1968) *Party Strategies in a Multiparty System* (Lund: Studentlitteratur).

Soroka, S. N. and C. Wlezien (2010). *Degrees of Democracy: Politics, Public Opinion, and Policy* (New York: Cambridge University Press).

Strøm, K. (1990) 'A Behavioral Theory of Competitive Political Parties", *American Journal of Political Science*, 34(2), 565–598.

Strömbäck, J. (2007) 'Antecedents of Political Market Orientation in Britain and Sweden: Analysis and Future Research Propositions', *Journal of Public Affairs*, 7(1), 79–89.

Strömbäck, J. (2011) 'Mediatization of Politics: Toward a Conceptual Framework for Comparative Research', in E. P. Bucy and R. L. Holbert (eds), *Sourcebook for Political Communication Research. Methods, Measures, and Analytical Techniques* (New York: Routledge).

Strömbäck, J. and D. V. Dimitrova (2011) 'Mediatization and Media Interventionism: A Comparative Analysis of Sweden and the United States', *International Journal of Press/Politics*, 16(1), 30–49.

Strömbäck, J. and F. Esser (2009) 'Shaping Politics: Mediatization and Media Interventionism', in K. Lundby (ed.), *Mediatization: Concept, Changes, Consequences* (New York: Peter Lang).

Strömbäck, J. and L. L. Kaid (eds) (2008) *The Handbook of Election News Coverage Around the World* (New York: Routledge).

Strömbäck, J. and S. Kiousis (2011) 'Political Public Relations: Defining and Mapping an Emergent Field', in J. Strömbäck and S. Kiousis (eds), *Political Public Relations: Principles and Applications* (New York: Routledge).

Tal-Or, N., Y. Tsfati and A. C. Gunther (2009) 'The Influence of Presumed Media Influence: Origins and Implications of the Third-Person Perception', in R. L. Nabi and M. B. Oliver (eds), *The SAGE Handbook of Media Processes and Effects* (London: Sage).

Tedesco, J. C. (2011) 'Political Public Relations and Agenda Building', in J. Strömbäck and S. Kiousis (eds), *Political Public Relations: Principles and Applications* (New York: Routledge).

Traugott, M. W. (2008) 'The Uses and Misuses of Polls', in W. Donsbach and M. W. Traugott (eds), *The SAGE Handbook of Public Opinion Research* (London: Sage).

Traugott, M. W. (2009) *Changes in Media Polling in Recent Presidential Campaigns: Moving from Good to 'Average' at CNN*, Discussion paper #R-33 (Cambridge, MA: Joan Shorenstein Center on the Press, Politics and Public Policy).

Traugott, M. W. and M.-E. Kang (2000) 'Public Attention to Polls in an Election Year', in P. J. Lavrakas and M. W. Traugott (eds), *Election Polls, the News Media, and Democracy* (New York: Chatham House).

Traugott, M. W. and E. C. Powers (2000) 'Did Public Opinion Support the Contract with America?', in P. J. Lavrakas and M. W. Traugott (eds), *Election Polls, the News Media, and Democracy* (New York: Chatham House).

Van Aelst, P., K. Brants, P. van Praag, C. de Vreese, M. Nuytemans and A. van Dalen (2008) 'The Fourth Estate as Superpower? An Empirical Study of Perceptions of Media Power in Belgium and the Netherlands', *Journalism Studies*, 9(4), 494–511.

Wessels, B. (2007) 'Political Representation and Democracy', in R. J. Dalton and H.-D. Klingemann (eds), *The Oxford Handbook of Political Behavior* (Oxford: Oxford University Press).

Wlezien, C. and S. N. Soroka (2007) 'The Relationship between Public Opinion and Policy', in R. J. Dalton and H.-D. Klingemann (eds), *The Oxford Handbook of Political Behavior* (Oxford: Oxford University Press), 799–817.

Zaller, J. R. (1992) *The Nature and Origins of Mass Opinion* (New York: Cambridge University Press).

Zoch, L. M. and J.-C. Molleda (2006) 'Building a Theoretical Model of Media Relations Using Framing, Information Subsidies, and Agenda-Building', in C. H. Botan and V. Hazleton (eds), *Public Relations Theory II* (New York: Lawrence Erlbaum).

13
Polls, Media and the Political System

Christina Holtz-Bacha

Across the world, polls have long become a major staple of media reporting. Since the media commission polls themselves, they not only produce their own news but also – intentionally or not – intervene in the political process through the publication of poll results. The political actors – politicians, parties and their advisers – on the other hand, commission polls to help and bolster their decision making and to assess the approval of their policies and their personal popularity. They also use polls to conceive their communication strategies, either for election campaigns or for day-to-day politics. The findings of political polling are often kept secret because they primarily serve strategic purposes. They may nevertheless be passed on to the media in the interest of strategic targeting of the press and the citizens.

The proliferation of polls – in the media as well as in politics – and their use have been widely discussed and not been greeted unanimously. All in all, there is a certain consensus today about polls enabling the 'self-observation of societies' (Kaase and Pfetsch 2001, p. 126). Polls allow individuals to observe their environment, get an impression about what others think and compare their own stands on issues with the opinions of their fellow citizens. This assessment serves as a basis for individual behavior and may lead to an adjustment to the assumed majority opinion, either in order to not isolate oneself with a divergent opinion (according to the spiral of silence theory) or simply in search of the good feeling of being on the side of the winners (bandwagon effect). Under specific circumstances or in certain environments, there may be other effects, which, however, have received less confirmation than the bandwagon effect (cf. Moy and Rinke in this volume).

Polls are also supposed to give a voice to the people and strengthen their position in the political process *vis-à-vis* their representatives. Polls enable political actors to learn about the expectations of citizens and thus challenge the responsiveness of decision makers. It is this role as an intermediary between citizens and the political system that particularly underlines the democratic function of polling, but it is also where polls compete with the media. By establishing close links to pollsters and by setting up their own polls, the media also try to defend their role in order not to relinquish the field to the polling industry.

However, doubts have been raised as to the extent to which polls are indeed an adequate instrument to mirror public opinion. George Gallup, the founder of modern survey research, has often been cited with his conviction that 'polls are a tool for deciphering public sentiment and enabling policy makers to respond to what their constituents want' (Jacobs and Shapiro 1995, p. 519). First of all, this statement reflects Gallup's trust in the methodology and its careful employment. Second, Gallup saw survey research as an instrument that politicians could use to assess the attitudes of the people they represent and consider them in their decisions. Both arguments refer to the role of polls as mirrors of public opinion, implying that they deliver a true picture of reality. From an early stage of the newly developing business, Gallup's view has been contested, both theoretically and in practice. Among the first to take a critical stand on polls were the journalist Walter Lippmann (1922, 1925) and the sociologist Herbert Blumer (1948), both contemporaries of Gallup (cf. also Splichal in this volume).

In addition to the reflective function, polls have taken on an active role as molders of public opinion: 'They not only sample public opinion, they define it' (Frankovic 1998, p. 150). The collection of data through surveys and their analysis is a process, which is characterized by selectivity on each step. What is asked and the way it is asked influences the way respondents think about an issue and how they react to the questions. Therefore, polls construct their own reality and this, once it is in the media, again influences the public: 'When polls are publicized, the same opinion-shaping forces that affect the answers given by poll respondents ripple out to the public, possibly with enhanced force when certain views seem to be widely shared and therefore legitimized' (Graber 1998, p. 217). Thus, the reality constructed by the polls and further shaped by the reporting of the polls provides a reference for those who commission polls and those who see their results.

Because people learn about poll findings mostly through the media, the quality of poll reporting has been a permanent issue for research and professional standards. Therefore, many studies have been devoted to the analysis of poll reporting. Studies from different countries again and again revealed deficiencies in the presentation of public opinion polls by the media (e.g. Biroli, Miguel and Ferreira Mota in this volume; Holtz-Bacha in this volume; Strömbäck 2009; Szwed 2011; Willnat, Lo and Aw in this volume). Even though the professional associations of pollsters or the media's ethical codes recommend the disclosure of certain methodological details that allow the audience to assess the context of poll findings and their credibility, they are often insufficient or even left out completely. What is more, the media often do not even cite specific polls and findings, but rather 'refer to findings of "the polls" which are usually unspecified and unsourced' (Frankovic 1998, p. 162; cf. also Holtz-Bacha in this volume). Reference to quasi anonymous polls, which are not in any way identified and contextualized, accords them an apparent authority without accountability. The polls thus become a pawn in the hands of the media, who use them in their own strategic interest.

In addition, the selection of the topics addressed in the polls, the reporting of results and their interpretation are subject to the media's own logic (cf. also Strömbäck Chapters 1 and 12, in this volume), which is influenced by the professional criteria that guide the work of journalists and by the mechanisms of the media market. With a view on the increased importance of poll-driven reporting in the media, Frankovic concluded already in 1998 that the polls' 'significance sometimes overwhelms the phenomena they are supposed to be measuring or supplementing' (1998, p. 156). In particular, polls are part and parcel of so-called horse race coverage and the framing of politics as a strategic game – not only during election campaigns, but also in the coverage of day-to-day politics. By commissioning surveys and reporting about the outcome according to their own production criteria (news value), the media thus contribute to the construction of the image of the political world. Due to the fact that most citizens do not have direct contact with the political world and only get second-hand experience, the image conveyed by the media is highly influential.

Since the media stepped in as independent players by commissioning polls themselves, the critique of polls in general has been extended to the media as well. Beyond the frequently discussed question of to what extent the findings from a survey, even among a representative sample, stand for the opinions of a mass public (see, e.g., Splichal in this volume; Althaus 2003, pp. 245–252), the selectivity of survey topics and questions has been addressed as a crucial point. Those who commission surveys determine the topics or even the specific questions they want to be asked in an interview. Mostly, these topics serve short-term interests and emerge from current discussions or events. Since telephone and more recently online surveys have accelerated the survey business and lowered the costs, it has become particularly tempting to conduct polls spontaneously and at short notice.

Moreover, polls have been criticized for selectively serving the interests of the political and the media elite. The topics that get their attention and their perspectives on matters are not necessarily those of the general public. As Herbst noted with reference to Bourdieu's critique of public opinion polls: '[S]urvey questions reveal and reinforce the agendas of political elites' (1992, p. 222), and pollsters belong to the same circles as journalists and politicians.

This kind of social selectivity also contributes to the often lamented and well-documented fact that surveys ask questions and make people react upon issues that they have not yet thought about or that do not have any relevance for them. In his book on 'The Opinion Makers', Moore (2008) puts together numerous examples demonstrating that many respondents answer survey questions without much knowledge of the problems at hand and give their opinion on topics that do not mean much to them and that they do not really care about. Therefore, Moore contends, the outcome of polls is highly misleading and does not account for what the public really thinks. Instead it is a 'manufactured opinion' (Moore 2008, p. 26) in the interest of those in power and the legitimization of their activities. Decisions taken on the basis of what allegedly is public opinion do not consider these limitations and pitfalls of surveys, thus acting on an artificially constructed picture of the public's opinion. At the same time, the contorted picture of the public's opinion serves the media and their interest in clearcut and controversial information and therefore, as Moore ascertains, 'the polls simply avoid measuring what the media don't want to report' (2008, p. 27).

When they commission surveys, political actors direct their interests either at the opinions and attitudes towards past decisions, parties or individual politicians, or at problems to be dealt with in the future. These polls are used for strategic purposes and the political sponsors often choose to keep the findings to themselves. Findings may be leaked to the media if the publication also serves the strategic end (cf. Strömbäck, Chapter 12 in this volume).

The media instead conduct polls to make them public and thus challenge the political system. By assessing the citizens' attitudes towards policies and leaders they submit the political actors to constant evaluation. The publication of approval ratings in ever shorter time intervals may put decision makers under pressure to discuss their activities in the public arena or seduce them to give in to fleeting or superficial public moods. The media may also bring up their own issues and, as a consequence, impose them upon the political agenda. By presenting poll findings about what citizens supposedly regard as the most important problems or indicating new problems that have not yet been on the public agenda, the media exert an agenda-setting function and compel decision makers to deal with those issues. In a study on the role of polls in Finland, Suhonen therefore concludes: 'Public opinion polls have strengthened the position of media in the political process' (1997, p. 235).

When it comes to polls, the media, however, play a somewhat ambiguous role. On the one hand, the media rely on polling to an increasing extent and use polls to set the agenda for public debate and thus to buttress their position *vis-à-vis* the political system. Polls provide the media with a useful tool to control the activities and claims of the political actors and to remind them of the public's expectations. On the other hand, the media criticize the decisions makers for using the same tool because they suspect manipulation and populism, and they complain if they fall victim to the pollsters and are 'hijacked by campaign strategists' (Jacobs and Shapiro 2005, p. 638). However, politicians themselves often do not like to admit their dependence on polls and popularity rankings, and rather demonstrate strong leadership unaffected by public moods. That is what George W. Bush had in mind when he emphasized: 'We believe in principles, not polls or focus groups' (cited in Greenberg 2009, p. 1). Finally, pollsters – aware of their controversial reputation – also flirt with their negative image. Greenberg writes in the introduction to his book: 'Yes, I'm a "pollster", even if the word catches in my throat when people ask me what I do. I never write "pollster" on the immigration form lest I be refused admittance to the country' (2009, p. 1).

Responsiveness or pandering to public opinion?

Just like the media, the political system has become dependent on polls. Political actors and their advisers rely on polls for monitoring public opinion. As Gallup envisioned, the results can serve decision makers to take into account the opinions of the people they represent and respond to their expectations. At the same time, during election campaigns and beyond, polls are used as an instrument to support the political actors' strategic communication and to check its effectiveness. The extent to which pollsters are part of campaign management and surveys are employed for the planning has become an indicator of the professionalization of political communication (cf. Holtz-Bacha 2007, 2010). However, as the country chapters (Chapters 5–10) in this volume demonstrate, the role polls play in the political process varies according to national specifics, for instance the electoral system or the degree of competition among parties.

Whereas the responsiveness of the representatives to the expectations and demands of the represented is regarded as being desirable and commensurate to democracy theory, the temptation for politicians to use polling results in order to increase their personal popularity seems to be great, and the borderline to giving in to 'pandering' (Jacobs and Shapiro 2000) and cheap populism to be porous. Similarly, the disposition to carry campaign mode and the use of survey research for strategic purposes into governing mode has grown and brought up the term 'permanent campaign' to describe the phenomenon of governing just like campaigning.

In the USA Franklin D. Roosevelt was the first president who used private polling (cf. Bowman 2000, p. 64), and John F. Kennedy is mentioned as the first presidential candidate to employ a pollster for private surveys during his election campaign (cf. Bowman 2000, p. 56). This is one factor why 1960 has been regarded as 'the first modern campaign' (Donaldson 2007). Since Kennedy, 'the White House's sensitivity to public opinion became an enduring institutional characteristic of the modern presidency' (Jacobs and Shapiro 1995, p. 164). Nevertheless, as Jacobs and Shapiro still noted in the mid-1990s, 'there has been relatively little investigation of how politicians actually use polls and interact with pollsters' (1995–96, p. 519). The two terms of President Clinton revived the interest in the presidents' use of polls because he was known for his strong reliance on polling, and was soon cited as a prime example for leading a permanent campaign and blurring the lines between campaigning and governing (e.g. Bowman 2000; Jacobs and Shapiro 1997).

Based upon agenda-setting theory, many studies have demonstrated a good amount of responsiveness on the part of decision makers. This was indicated by the congruencies of the public agenda and the policy agenda (e.g. Brettschneider 1996; Page and Shapiro 1994). Following the model of Miller and Stokes (1963), other studies compared citizens' expectations with the roll-call voting behavior of their representatives (e.g. Erikson 1978; Kuklinski 1978, 1979). However, more recent studies point to a decline in responsiveness, and see that in connection with the increasing political malaise (cf. Shernisky 2007, p. 5). While the equality aspect that guides representative sampling suggests that polls provide a basis for the responsiveness of the political actors to the expectations of all citizens, some studies have shown that responsiveness oftentimes is a highly selective matter, which favors the interests of high-income citizens and not necessarily the preferences of the general public (e.g. Bartels 2005; Gilens 2005; Jacobs and Page 2005). In addition, Canes-Wrone and Shotts (2004) found that presidents are more responsive to issues that have relevance in citizens' daily lives, and that presidential responsiveness is higher with the proximity of an election. In its extreme form, responsiveness degenerates into pandering 'defined as an instance in which a president takes a policy position due to its public popularity despite knowledge that said policy might not be in the long term interest of the country' (Shernisky 2007, p. 3; cf. also Canes-Wrone, Herron and Shotts 2001; Jacobs and Shapiro 1997, 2000). Critics denounce poll-driven decisions in the interest of the personal image as a weakness of politicians. As Sudman writes in 1982: 'A really serious concern arises when a president or any elected official is so concerned about what the polls are saying that he advocates or opposes programs on the basis of the polls, rather than attempting, as Roosevelt did, to lead the public in the direction he thinks is right. This use of the polls usually comes from presidents who cannot exert effective leadership' (p. 307).

Several researchers have pointed to the risk of politicians employing polls for pushing their policies and for their private use to enhance their popularity rather than for responding to the issues and the demands of the people they represent. The 'manipulation theory' (Shernisky 2007, p. 2), as brought up primarily by Jacobs and Shapiro (2000), ascertains that decision makers use polls to support the implementation of their policies and with an eye on their re-election. It plays for presidents that public opinion is 'susceptible to manipulation' due to its 'unsettled nature' (Shernisky 2007, p. 11) and because 'presidents have an unparalleled ability to circulate their political messages widely and visibly via the bully pulpit' (Shernisky 2007, p. 11). The proponents of the manipulation theory counter the idea of politicians pandering to public opinion, and instead opine that 'Polls can be used as a tool to enhance substantive responsiveness [...] or to manipulate public debate and move public opinion [...]' (Jacobs and Burns 2004, p. 553). In this sense, poll data are collected as a basis for designing strategies on how to present policies even, or particularly, when they are not popular with the citizens: 'What presidents say, how they say it, and where they make their comments is a function of what the White House learns from the public' (Jacobs and Burns 2004, p. 537).

Another argument brought up against the notion of pandering to public opinion is the fact that while polling intensified over the years the polling on policy issues declined. Comparing the use of polls by Kennedy, Johnson, Nixon and Reagan, Jacobs and Burns (2004) found that polling on personality attributes and other non-policy issues increased under the latter two presidents. The authors interpret the move away from policy polling as an attempt 'to identify non-policy grounds for appealing to voters' (p. 553), which nevertheless serves the pursuit of their policies.

Polling for the permanent campaign?

The professionalization of political communication went hand in hand with the adoption of the marketing arsenal including the whole methodological range of the social sciences. While professionalization is a process that seizes the communication activities in and of the political system in general, its features and consequences become visible particularly during election campaigns when the retention and the conquest of power is at stake. Surveys and focus groups are at the core of modern campaigning. Political actors rely on surveys of any sort to decide their campaign strategies. The relevance of surveys is also reflected in the increasing importance of pollsters in the candidates' 'war rooms', and the book-length accounts of campaign advisers, for instance Bill Clinton's strategist Dick Morris (1997) or Stanley Greenberg (2009), who worked for Clinton and other prominent candidates abroad.

Surveys are used as a strategic instrument to help decisions on policies and for the work on the candidates' image. Since John F. Kennedy, polling on non-policy issues, particularly during election campaigns, increased. Kennedy's campaign focused on image as no other campaign before. He had to deal with 'the catholic issue' (Donaldson 2007, p. 193), which was subjected to polling in order to prepare Kennedy's campaign appearances in critical states. An outcome of the 1960 campaign was 'the manufactured candidate' (Donaldson 2007, p. viii), and polling made a major contribution to it. Polls conducted by Dick Morris helped President Clinton to get through his diverse scandals. Legendary by now is Morris' claim that he even polled on where Clinton and his family should spend their summer vacation (1997, p. 235). Stanley Greenberg was credited for 'stage-managing Al Gore's passionate kiss with his wife at the Democratic convention' (Greenberg 2009, p. 3) during the 2000 election campaign, which brought the candidate a bounce in the polls afterwards.

Another indicator of the increased importance of polls for the planning of communication activities is the integration of the pollsters and other strategists into the leaders' staff. By now, the political marketing experts, who advise and organize the campaigns, often move into the administration after the election. Clinton's adviser since his campaigns in Arkansas, Dick Morris, stayed '[b]ehind the oval office' when Clinton moved into the White House. Karl Rove, who ran two Texas gubernatorial campaigns as well as the presidential campaigns for George W. Bush, became the senior adviser to the president and headed the White House Office of Political Affairs. The most recent example is David Axelrod, who managed Barack Obama's 2008 campaign and was also made the president's senior adviser afterwards.

The integration of pollsters and other strategists into the leaders' staff that makes the former 'outsiders' to 'insiders' (Tenpas 2000) is regarded as a feature of the presumptive trend to the permanent campaign. The creation of the term is usually attributed to Sidney Blumenthal, who published a book on *The Permanent Campaign* (1980), but Patrick Caddell, who was Jimmy Carter's pollster, also takes credit for coining the term (cf. Bowman 2000, p. 62). In a memo written by Caddell to Carter after his election in 1976, he expressed his 'thesis that governing with public approval requires a continuing political campaign' (cited in Bowman 2000, pp. 62–63). The constant preoccupation with public approval, and campaign mode thus being taken over to governing, characterizes the permanent campaign that does no longer 'successfully separate politics and government' (Caddell cited in Bowman 2000, p. 62). The distinction 'between the use of polls to get elected and the use of polls to govern wisely' (Sudman 1982, p. 306) disappears. Governing with public approval puts an end to polls being used FDR-style to listen to the people and as a support of leadership. Instead, polls serve as an instrument to constantly track and possibly influence approval ratings. Bill Clinton and the former British premier Tony Blair have been cited as examples of poll-driven leaders who 'both engaged in activities which were specifically designed to raise their approval scores' (Needham 2005, p. 346).

From Kennedy to Reagan, the number of polls conducted for the White House, the number of questions asked in the surveys and the number of reportings increased from one president to the other, thus indicating the use of polls beyond electoral purposes (Jacobs and Burns 2004, p. 541). Tenpas and McCann (2007) analyzed polling expenditures from Carter to George W. Bush and show that all presidents increased their spending for polls the longer they were in office and closer to an election. The shift from polling on policy issues to personality polling at the same time further underlines the continuous concern of presidents with their popularity. In particular, it is the job-approval question that 'cements the notion of a permanent campaign' (Bowman 2000, p. 64). Over the years, leaders have become more and more obsessed with their approval ratings, which is reflected in the increase of the number and frequency of the job-approval questions being asked during a president's first hundred days in office: whereas the question was asked only once for Harry Truman in 1945, 37 job-approval questions were asked during Clinton's first hundred days in 1993 (Bowman 2000, p. 65).

The creation of the Office of Political Affairs in the White House by Ronald Reagan soon after the 1980 election has been considered another step to the permanent campaign. It was established for keeping contact with the parties and supporters, and its staff also engage in the re-election campaign (cf. Tenpas 2000, p. 111). There has often been an exchange of staff from a candidate's campaign headquarters into the Office and back again. After the integration of polling and pollsters, the establishment of the Office of Political Affairs was another institutional component indicating the trend towards the permanent campaign in support of the president's popularity.

Conclusion

Although it is still controversial if at all and to what extent polls represent public opinion, polls have become a vital factor in the political process, from campaigning to governing. Decision makers rely on the data delivered to them and seek advice by pollsters. Since the 1960s, the White House built up its own 'public opinion apparatus' (Jacobs and Shapiro 1995). The polls commissioned by political actors are private and only made public for strategic purposes.

Similarly, the media have come to rely on polls to such an extent that – as Beniger writes in 1992 – 'most polls exist only to be reported in the news media' (Beniger 1992, S. 216). However, the media do not function as a 'neutral transmission belt' (Jacobs and Shapiro 2005, p. 638). Polls serve the media 'as information source, as attention-getters, as a source of journalistic power' (Frankovic 1998, p. 162). By integrating polls in their reporting, the media reinforce trends that characterize the use of polls in the political system. The shift from policy polling to personality polling and the increased concern with approval ratings on the part of the political system is reflected in the media's focus on horse race aspects. At the same time, the publication of poll findings can put pressure on leaders by bringing up issues that have not been on the political agenda or drive certain positions or solutions to problems. The latter has become even more of a problem with the rise of polling on the Internet, because Internet polls cannot reach any representativeness, can easily be manipulated and their questions are often slanted. Therefore, instead of giving people a voice, these polls denigrate to 'on-line demagoguery' (Wu and Weaver 1997).

The pervasiveness of polls in political life and in the media has found many critics – among scholars of various disciplines, politicians and journalists. Beyond methodological questions, including the ongoing debate about whether polls reflect public opinion, the use of polls by political actors and the media is the subject of discussion. In particular, there have been warnings of all kinds of manipulation through polls, and these have often been connected with concerns about the consequences for the democratic political process (cf. also Klein 2006). These may affect the relationship between the political system and the media, or between the political system and the citizens, or the media and the citizens. As the journalist Bill Kovach wrote with a tone of self-criticism after the 1988 US presidential election: 'The tools of persuasion and manipulation are awesome and they are cynically used. [...] The political system adjusts its messages to appeal to these measured emotions in order to move the opinion in one direction or another suppress or increase its intensity. [...] I am afraid the press is unwittingly a part of the process of manipulating opinion devised by the political campaigns' (1999–2000).

The research done on the use of polls by decision makers and the politics-pollsters complex has mostly been done in the USA and often focused on the presidency. The findings thus refer to a candidate-oriented political and electoral system and to a media system that has always been characterized by commercial media and competition. Less research is available on the use of polls in parliamentary systems (cf. e.g. Mills and Tiffen in this volume) and on media systems with public service and commercial media. Comparative research is missing completely. The chapters on Australia, Brazil, Germany, South Africa, Taiwan and the USA stand for different geographical regions and represent a variety of political, electoral and media systems. The differences provide for specific constellations of the relationship between the political system and the media, which have implications for the role of the polling industry. At the same time, the country chapters (Chapters 5–10) demonstrate the necessity to draw up systematic comparisons in order to assess the influence of the individual factors in the triadic relationship.

Studies on effects have primarily focused on the individual leaving many questions open that refer to effects at the aggregate level even though the implications for democracy have frequently been addressed in the literature. Therefore, about 80 years after the introduction of scientific polling, about 60 years since the start of poll-based campaigning and an almost equally long interest of the media in polling, there are still several black holes that research will have to tackle.

The chapters of this book have opened up new perspectives on the diverse and interdependent relationships among the media, polls, public opinion and politics, and on their democratic implications. They have provided some answers to the questions in this multifaceted field, but at the same time they have also pointed to lingering problems. By this combination of both answering some and raising new questions, they will hopefully serve to inspire further research.

References

Andersen, R. (2000) 'Reporting public opinion polls: The media and the 1997 Canadian election', *International Journal of Public Opinion Research*, 12, 285–98.

Althaus, S. L. (2003) *Collective Preferences in Democratic Politics: Opinion Surveys and the Will of the People* (Cambridge: Cambridge University Press).

Blumenthal, S. (1980) *The Permanent Campaign: Inside the World of Elite Political Operatives* (Boston: Beacon Press).

Bartels, L. M. (2005) *Economic Inequality and Political Representation* (revised), http://citeseerx.ist.psu.edu/viewdoc/download?doi=10.1.1.172.7597&rep=rep1&type=pdf date accessed 30 March 2011.

Beniger, J. R. (1992) 'The impact of polling on public opinion: Reconciling Foucault, Habermas, and Bourdieu', *International Journal of Public Opinion Research*, 4, 204–19.

Blumer, H. (1948) 'Public opinion and public opinion polling', *American Sociological Review*, 13, 542–54.

Bowman, K. (2000) 'Polling to campaign and to govern', in N. Ornstein and T. Mann (eds) *The Permanent Campaign and its Future* (Washington, DC: American Enterprise Institute and The Brookings Institution).

Brettschneider, F. (1996) 'Public opinion and parliamentary action: Responsiveness of the German Bundestag in comparative perspective', *International Journal of Public Opinion Research*, 8, 292–311.

Canes-Wrone, B. and Shotts, K. W. (2004) 'The conditional nature of presidential responsiveness to public opinion', *American Journal of Political Science*, 48, 690–706.

Canes-Wrone, B., Herron, M. C. and Shotts, K. W. (2001) 'Leadership and pandering: A theory of executive policymaking', *American Journal of Political Science*, 45, 532–50.

Donaldson, G. A. (2007) *The First Modern Campaign* (Boston: Rowman & Littlefield).

Erikson, R. S. (1978) 'Constituency opinion and congressional behavior: A reexamination of the Miller-Stokes representation data', *American Journal of Political Science*, 22, 511–35.

Frankovic, K. A. (1998) 'Public opinion and polling', in D. Graber, D. McQuail and P. Norris (eds) *The Politics of News: The News of Politics* (Washington, DC: Congressional Quarterly).

Gallup, G. H. and Rae, S. F. (1940) *The Pulse of Democracy. The Public Opinion Poll and how it Works* (New York: Simon and Schuster).

Gilens, M. (2005) 'Inequality and democratic responsiveness', *Public Opinion Quarterly*, 69, 778–96.

Graber, D. (1998) 'Whither research on the psychology of political communication?', in A. N. Crigler (ed.) *The Psychology of Political Communication* (Ann Arbor: The University of Michigan Press).

Greenberg, S. B. (2009) *Dispatches from the War Room: In the Trenches with Five Extraordinary Leaders* (New York: Thomas Dunne Books).

Herbst, S. (1992) 'Surveys in the public sphere: Applying Bourdieu's critique of opinion polls', *International Journal of Public Opinion Research*, 4, 220–29.

Holtz-Bacha, C. (2007) 'Professionalisation of politics in Germany', in R. Negrine, P. Mancini, C. Holtz Bacha and S. Papathanassopoulos (eds), *The Professionalisation of Political Communication* (Bristol: Intellect).

Holtz-Bacha, C. (2010) 'Wahljahr 2009 – Professionalisierung verzögert?', in C. Holtz-Bacha (ed.), *Die Massenmedien im Wahlkampf. Das Wahljahr 2009* (Wiesbaden: VS Verlag für Sozialwissenschaften).

Jacobs, L. R. and Burns, M. (2004) 'The second face of the public presidency: Presidential polling and the shift from policy to personality polling', *Presidential Studies Quarterly*, 34, 536–56.

Jacobs, L. R. and Page, B. I. (2005) 'Who influences U.S. foreign policy?', *American Political Science Review*, 99, 107–24.

Jacobs, L. R. and Shapiro, R. Y. (1995) 'The rise of presidential polling: The Nixon White House in historical perspective', *Public Opinion Quarterly*, 59, 163–95.

Jacobs, L. R. and Shapiro, R. Y. (1995–96) 'Presidential manipulation of polls and public opinion: The Nixon administration and the pollsters', *Political Science Quarterly*, 110, 519–38.

Jacobs, L. R. and Shapiro, R. Y. (1997, April–May) 'Debunking the pandering politician myth', *The Public Perspective*, 3–5.

Jacobs, L. R. and Shapiro, R. Y. (2000) *Politicians don't Pander: Political Manipulation and the Loss of Democratic Responsiveness* (Chicago: University of Chicago Press).

Kaase, M. and Pfetsch, B. (2001) 'Polling and the democratic process in Germany– Analyses of a difficult relationship', *International Review of Sociology*, 11(2), 125–47.

Klein, J. (2006) *Politics Lost: How American Democracy was Trivialized by People who Think you're Stupid* (New York: Doubleday).

Kovach, B. (1999–2000; first 1990) '1990: The impact of public opinion polls. Do they shape or measure opinions?' Nieman Reports (Winter/Spring), http://www.nieman.harvard.edu/reportsitem.aspx?id=100546, date accessed 5 March 2011.

Kuklinski, J. H. (1978) 'Representativeness and elections: A policy analysis', *American Political Science Review*, 72, 165–77.

Kuklinski, J. H. (1979) 'Representative-constituency linkages: A review article', *Legislative Studies Quarterly*, 4, 121–40.

Lippmann, W. (1922) *Public Opinion* (London: G. Allen & Unwin).

Lippmann, W. (1925) *The Phantom Public* (New York: Harcourt, Brace and Co.).

Miller, W. E. and Stokes, D. E. (1963) 'Constituency influence in congress', *American Political Science Review*, 57, 45–56.

Moore, D. W. (2008) *The Opinion Makers: An Insider Exposes the Truth behind the Polls* (Boston: Beacon Press).

Morris, D. (1997) *Behind the Oval Office: Winning the Presidency in the Nineties* (New York: Random House).

Needham, C. (2005) 'Brand leaders: Clinton, Blair and the limitations of the permanent campaign', *Political Studies*, 53, 343–61.

Page, B. I. and Shapiro, R. Y. (1994) *The Rational Public: Fifty Years of Trends in Americans' Policy preferences* (Chicago: University of Chicago Press).

Shernisky, L. T. (2007) Public opinion polling and presidential responsiveness: Effects on policy making and democracy. *Center for the Study of the Presidency*. http://www.thepresidency.org/storage/documents/Vater/Shernisky.pdf, date accessed 3 April 2011.

Strömbäck, J. (2008) 'Four phases of mediatization: An analysis of the mediatization of politics', *International Journal of Press/Politics*, 13, 228–46.

Strömbäck, J. (2009) 'Vox populi or vox media? Opinion polls and the Swedish media, 1998–2006', *Javnost*, 16(3), 55–70.

Sudman, S. (1982) 'The president and the polls', *Public Opinion Quarterly*, 46, 301–10.

Suhonen, P. (1997) 'The media, polls and political process: The case of Finland', *European Journal of Communication*, 12, 219–38.

Szwed, R. (2011) 'Printmedia poll reporting in Poland: Poll as news in Polish parliamentary campaigns, 1991–2007', *Communist and Post-Communist Studies*, 44, 63–72.

Tenpas, K. D. (2000) 'The American presidency: Surviving and thriving amidst the permanent campaign', in N. Ornstein and T. Mann (eds) *The Permanent Campaign and its Future* (Washington, DC: American Enterprise Institute and The Brookings Institution).

Tenpas, K. D. and McCann, J. A. (2000) 'Testing the permanence of the permanent campaign: An analysis of presidential polling expenditures, 1977–2002', *Public Opinion Quarterly*, 71, 349–66.

Wu, W. and Weaver, D. (1997) 'On-line democracy or on-line demagoguery? Public opinion "polls" on the Internet', *The Harvard International Journal of Press/Politics*, 2(4), 71–86.

Index